FIVE PLAYS

by Goran Stefanovski

The Black Hole

—ᴧᴧ—

Shades of Babel

—ᴧᴧ—

Sarajevo

—ᴧᴧ—

Odysseus

—ᴧᴧ—

Figurae Veneris Historiae

—ᴧᴧ—

Five Plays by Goran Stefanovski

Published by The Conrad Press in the United Kingdom 2019

Tel: +44(0)1227 472 874
www.theconradpress.com
info@theconradpress.com

ISBN 978-1-911546-62-7

Typesetting and cover design by: Charlotte Mouncey, www.bookstyle.co.uk

The Conrad Press logo was designed by Maria Priestley.

Printed and bound in Great Britain
by Clays Ltd, Elcograf S.p.A.

Contents

Some biographical notes on Goran Stefanovski

G oran Stefanovski was a truly international figure, whose work deals with issues of war, history, migration, post-communist transition and identity, as well as what it means to be human. He was born on 27th April 1952 in Bitola, a town then in Yugoslavia, near the border with Greece on the Balkan Peninsula in Eastern Europe. His father, Mirko, was a theatre director and his mother, Nada, a leading actress. Much of Goran's childhood was spent in theatres.

Having fallen in love with all things English during his teenage years through the influence of the Beatles and Rolling Stones, Goran went on to study English Language and Literature at the University of Skopje. However, he couldn't get the theatre out of his system and spent his third year of studies at the Faculty of Dramatic Arts (FDU) in Belgrade. He graduated as the best student of his generation in Skopje and took a job in the Drama Department of Skopje TV, although he was soon to return to the University to teach English Literature, with a particular focus on Shakespeare.

In October 1974 he met Pat Marsh, an English linguist who came to teach English at Skopje University. They married in March 1976. When they met, he was writing a play based on Macedonian folklore for Slobodan Unkovski, one of the directors of a theatre group he had become involved with as a student; Unkovski was to become a lifetime collaborator and friend. *Yané Zadrogaz* achieved great success and went on to be presented at the prestigious Belgrade International Theatre Festival (BITEF), then in Paris and finally at the Caracas Theatre Festival in Venezuela.

A radio play about Shakespeare, two TV plays with a contemporary setting and a six-part TV series set in the 1940s followed Goran Stefanovski's early success in the second half of the 70s. In 1979 he wrote his best-known play, *Wild Flesh*, which has had fifteen productions to date all over Europe, including London, and is on the secondary school curriculum in his homeland. The play is based on the experiences of his father and uncles during World War II. It brought him the October Prize of the Republic of Macedonia for exceptional artistic achievement, the highest award of the Republic, as well as the 1980 Award for Best Yugoslav Play of the Year at the Yugoslav National Theatre Festival.

Two years later, *Flying on the Spot* had its first production, a play which dealt with the fraught Macedonian Question of the late nineteenth century and the identity of the nation; it was to endear Stefanovski to his compatriots worldwide.

Almost every year for the next thirty-three years was to see a new and successful play by Goran Stefanovski, many of them award-winners. In the 1980s he continually pushed the boundaries of Yugoslav theatre, both in an artistic and political sense. *The False Bottom* (1983) was particularly bold in its challenge to state censors. In 1988 *The Black Hole* received its first productions; with its unique structure and stunning theatricality, it is generally considered to be his greatest contribution to European theatre.

1985 marked a departure for the dramatist into a TV serial for children, each episode teaching one of the 31 letters of the Macedonian alphabet through a combination of animation and sketches. Stefanovski's son, Igor, had been born in 1980 and his daughter, Jana, was to be born in 1986. That year he founded the playwriting department at the Faculty of Dramatic Arts in Skopje, where he was a full professor until 1998.

In 1987 Stefanovski wrote the first version of a screenplay for film director, Stolé Popov, dealing with the aftermath of the catastrophic 1903 Ilinden Uprising against Ottoman rule. This film, *To the Hilt*, was not to be made until 2014, after it had been through two revisions, but it was the first of six screenplays Stefanovski was to write and began his involvement with film.

In 1990 he took his family to Providence, Rhode Island, USA, where he spent six months as Outstanding Artist Fulbright Scholar at Brown University and began a lifelong friendship with Prof. John Emigh.

In 1991 Yugoslavia began to fall apart and descended into civil war. The constantly deteriorating situation led his wife Pat to decide to make a new life for the family in Canterbury, England, from September 1992. For the next six years, Stefanovski was to commute between Macedonia and the UK, continuing his teaching in Skopje.

In 1992, Dragan Klaić, one of Goran's former teachers at the Belgrade Faculty of Dramatic Arts and a close friend, put him in touch with Chris Torch of the Jordcirkus theatre group in Stockholm, who commissioned a play, in cooperation with the Antwerp European Capital of Culture, about Sarajevo, the Bosnian city then undergoing a brutal siege. *Sarajevo, an oratorio for the theatre*, went on an extensive tour across Europe in the summer of 1993, including the London International Theatre Festival and the Hamburg International Summer Festival. *Sarajevo* was published in London, New York and Illinois. This successful venture was followed by performance scripts for the festivals of European Capitals of Culture in Copenhagen, Stockholm, Avignon and Bologna, all in collaboration with Chris Torch.

Through this connection, Stefanovski had become known in Sweden and between 1998 and 2000 he was a visiting professor at the Dramatic Institute in Stockholm. The Institute published his *A Little Book of Traps (a scriptwriting tool)* in 2002. It has been translated and published in five languages, including Chinese. By this time, Stefanovski had become used to writing in English and only later translating his work into his mother tongue.

In September 2000 he settled in Canterbury and taught classes in screenwriting and playwriting at the University of Kent before taking up his post at Canterbury Christ Church University in 2002, teaching screenwriting there until his death in 2018. He was an extraordinarily popular teacher and a well-loved colleague.

Stefanovski continued writing successful plays which were translated and produced all over the world throughout the rest of his life, perhaps the most notable being his two adaptations of Ancient Greek texts, *Bacchanalia* after Euripides' *The Bacchae* and *Odysseus* after Homer's *Odyssey*. Both had clear and moving references to the Yugoslav wars and their aftermath.

A highly regarded essayist, public intellectual and lecturer, Stefanovski contributed papers to a large number of conferences and held workshops all over Europe. In 2006 he was elected member of the European Cultural Parliament, a forum for outstanding artists, thinkers and cultural personalities from Europe. In 2009 he was elected member of the European Council for Foreign Relations, a distinguished think-tank consisting of former prime ministers, presidents, European commissioners, current and former parliamentarians and ministers, public intellectuals, business leaders, activists and cultural figures from the EU member states and candidate countries.

Stefanovski's last public lecture was as keynote speaker at the International Federation for Theatre Research World Congress in Belgrade in July 2018. His last public appearance was to receive an honorary doctorate from the Bulgarian National Academy for Theatre and Film Arts in Sofia.

Goran Stefanovski died of an inoperable brain tumour in 2018 at the age of 66. His death brought scores of tributes to his brilliance as a writer and teacher, as well as outpourings of admiration and love for him as a human being of great wisdom, modesty and kindness.

Foreword

Goran Stefanovski's plays have been divided into three phases[1]. The first two plays in this collection (*The Black Hole* and *Shades of Babel*) belong to the first one, characterised as absurdist and experimental, blending folklore and modernism. The third play (*Sarajevo*) is from the middle phase, where the years of the horror and chaos of the Yugoslav wars are reflected in a new austerity and restraint. The last two plays published here (*Odysseus* and *Figurae Veneris Historiae*) are from Stefanovski's final stage of writing, in which he returned to a certain playfulness and inventiveness, but always with dark undertones.

The Black Hole (1987)

There is a saying in the Balkans that you will never die in the same country in which you were born. Anyone born in Bitola in 1952, like Stefanovski, would have grown up in Tito's Yugoslavia, but that state disappeared from the map after the internecine wars of the 1990s and, from September 1991, he or she would have been in the Republic of Macedonia until February 2019. Dying now in that same town would put you in a country called the Republic of North Macedonia. The political instability of the Balkans is

---

1   Nikola Vangeli (2012) "Goran Stefanovski and the "Curse" of the Balkans, The Portrait of a Playwright from the "Wild East"", Summary of the Doctoral Thesis in Theatre Studies, Faculty of Theatre, George Enescu University of the Arts, Iasi, Romania http://goranstefanovski. co.uk/wp-content/uploads/2012/11/n.vangeli_phd-thesis_summary.pdf Vangeli calls the phases 'acts'.

reflected in *The Black Hole* in the Father's obsessive revisiting of the three occasions during his life as a lorry driver when he was tasked with removing the statues which symbolised the successive different regimes under which he had lived: two kings and an unknown hero.

The wars which followed the break-up of Yugoslavia were brutal and bloody with many atrocities, the perpetrators of which were later tried for war crimes[2]. Part Two of *The Black Hole* thus turned out to be prophetic, depicting, as it does, a state of barbaric war into which the characters from Part One have all been plunged.

The Black Hole is based on the Macedonian folk tale of *Silyan, The Stork*, reminiscent of the Bible's parable of The Prodigal Son, although its origins are thought to be in the Far East[3]. Silyan is an irresponsible young man, unwilling to work in the fields or care for his family, a good-for-nothing spending his time in town drinking and feasting. His family curse him and he leaves home, eventually persuading a holy man to take him on a pilgrimage. Their ship is wrecked and Silyan is washed up on the shores of an unknown land, the sole survivor. To his amazement, he meets people who speak his language and know him. It turns out that their ancestors were cursed for their bad behaviour and disrespect for their elders. They were transformed into storks which migrate to his village every year to make their nests, lay their eggs and

---

2   The International War Crimes Tribunal for the Former Yugoslavia was established at The Hague in the Netherlands by Resolution 827 of the United Nations Security Council, which was passed on 25th May 1993. A total of 161 persons were indicted.

3   Goran Stefanovski cited one of his professors, probably Svetozar Brkić, Professor of English Literature at the University of Skopje, as having stated the likelihood of a Far Eastern origin to the tale in an interview during rehearsals for the play at the Yugoslav National Theatre in Belgrade.

hatch their young before flying back in the autumn. They bathe in a brook which turns them into people again and, when they are to fly back to Silyan's land in the spring, they bathe in another brook to turn back into storks. They explain that, if he bathes in that brook, he can be changed into a stork and fly back home with them. This Silyan does, carrying a bottle filled with the magic water to bathe in on his return, to change back into a man. But his joy at seeing his home again makes him drop the bottle and he has to spend the summer as a stork on the roof of his house, watching his family but unable to communicate with them. It is only after further troubles and wanderings that he is finally able to turn back into a man and return to his family, much chastened.

Stefanovski spoke in an interview[4] about his fascination with this tale from childhood, having read it at primary school. He found particularly harrowing Silyan's inability as a stork to talk to his family and the suffering this entailed. In his teenage years he was to read Kafka's *Metamorphosis* and empathise with the same anguish experienced by Gregor Samsa. Kafka became Stefanovski's favourite author and *The Black Hole* is his most Kafkaesque play.

Samuel Beckett is another clear influence. Stefanovski's MA thesis was on the importance of the stage directions in the Irish dramatist's plays[5] and he admired the Theatre of the Absurd. There are echoes of *Waiting for Godot* here, not only in the structure but also in the setting, with no specific time or place established, "freed from the usual determiners

---

4   ibid.
5   eg *Waiting for Godot*: Vladimir: Well? Shall we go?   Estragon: Yes, let's go.   [*They do not move.*]

of theatre"[6]. Black humour, nonsense rhymes and songs are other features Stefanovski shares with Beckett, as well as the spare dialogue also reminiscent of another playwright he held in high regard – Harold Pinter.

Paolo Magelli, the Italian director of the first production of the play at the Macedonian National Theatre in 1988, was lavish in his praise of *The Black Hole*. He said it marked a departure for the author, a work very different from its predecessors, ushering in Stefanovski's mature phase and his outgrowing of national borders; he declared it to be "the best text in Europe in the last decade"[7]. What sets the play apart from other absurdist works is its unique structure and its excursions into the supernatural and the fantastic, where a man can be cursed to be metamorphosed into two birds, forever seeking each other, never to be reunited:

> "*Let me tell you a tale, my son, of Seevey and Chooley. You've seen them and heard them in the fields, those two birds, perching in the blackthorn and the haw and chirruping. One of them sings "seevey, seevey" and the other one "chooley, chooley". Now I've heard tell, son, that those two birds were once upon a time one man. He was a bad 'un. Running wild…*"   (Scene Eight)

The play's protagonist, named Silyan after the folk tale, is driven by an "aspiration to escape from the mundane to another world with a higher level of consciousness"[8]. He

6   Eurokaz programme, Zagreb, 1988
7   Programme for the Macedonian National Theatre production 1988.
8   This phrase is contained in a letter to Goran Stefanovski from Paul Atkins, who directed *The Black Hole* at the University of Leeds Workshop Theatre in Leeds, UK. Performances ran from 19th February to 24th February 1990.

seeks this escape through the ultimate orgasm, a permanent form of ecstasy:

> "*There are no stars. Those are tiny openings in the black sky, through which some amazing light from the other side is seeping through. I look at my seed, through which some amazing force from the other side is seeping through. I want to be there. This isn't enough. This is nothing. This is all fixed. Imagine being there all the time!*" (SceneSix)

He yearns for there to be something left of the bliss achieved in orgasm:

> "**Silyan** *...Nothing will be left of this. Just a blur. Like the slime left by a snail.*
>
> **Svetlé** *What d'you want to be left?*
>
> **Silyan** *Marks. Proof that what is happening is real.*"
> (Scene One)

The orgiastic, immoral nature of Silyan's quest shocked audiences and strained the boundaries of good taste[9], but Stefanovski was determined to explore the relationship between Eros and Thanatos, the Life and Death Instincts identified by Freud. Silyan consciously risks death in order to experience the ultimate pleasure.

> "**Silyan** *Ether... Lets you come for hours. Makes you worn out for days afterwards. It can suffocate you if you overdo it.*" (Scene One)

In a hotel room he meets his death after experimenting with ether, but his life doesn't end. He enters a kind of purgatory where he is present in the world but unseen and unheard by the same characters from Part One, who

---

9   Vladimir Stamenković, *Nin*, 21.02.1988

appear again in Part Two of the play. The repetition of scenes and dialogue from Part One, the "dramatic fugue"[10] with characters swapped around and living out a very different experience in a vicious war, gives a new and haunting resonance to the repeated action. Silyan now looks at the world from a metaphorical black hole:

> *"Is this bare land the underworld? Ah, woe is me, for I shall see no deliverance, no homecoming."* (Scene Fifteen)

It is only at the end of the play, when Silyan recognises the selfishness and futility of his search and seeks forgiveness, that he can come into the light, and find the bliss which evaded him in life. Here Stefanovski again explores the supernatural, specifically the Christian notion of purgatory combined with the Ancient Greek vision of the underworld, from which a man might return. At the end of the play, Silyan uses language from the folk tale, promising to serve the Mother of God in a monastery for three years if he can become a man again. Addressing the Christian God, he says:

> *"I beseech Thee, do not take my soul 'ere I become a man again!"*

Stefanovski was as steeped in ancient pagan folklore as in the awareness that Macedonia had been part of the Christian Byzantine Empire for a thousand years of its history. Here he merges the two traditions into a unique vision.

Shades of Babel (1989)

This play ('The Tower of Babel' in the original) has at its heart the Biblical tale from Genesis. A united people build a tower to reach to heaven but are stopped by God, who considers this an act of hubris. He makes them all speak

---

10   Dalibor Foretić, *Danas*, 22.03.1988

different languages so they can no longer understand each other and are scattered across the face of the Earth. Stefanovski was interested in the implications of the story, particularly the idea that "language has a rebellious and wayward vitality compared to which the foundations of the pyramids are as dust"[11]. The play is dedicated to his wife Pat, a linguist with a strong interest in history and archaeology, in what may lie beneath our feet[12].

The play's parallels are clear between the Tower of Babel and the unfinished seven-storey car park planned by corrupt local politicians in a small provincial town with no main roads leading to it or cars to fill even a quarter of the parking spaces. The project is fraught with accidents and insoluble construction problems, becoming a white elephant for which a use is found as a secret warehouse for toxic waste imported from abroad, with a large bribe for the town council leader. During the construction, Petar, the Head of Urban Planning, has lost the power of speech:

> "*His speech got all garbled. He mixed up the names of things. Said 'potato' when he meant 'meat'. Nobody could understand a word he said. His favourite expression was "Hunderd dievils inteered". Soon he stopped talking altogether. It's pretty commonplace around here. Ask them anything and they'll start to stutter, go red and roll their eyes.*" (Scene Ten)

In another echo of the Biblical story, the chief statistician for the car park project has lost his mind, seeing conspiracy theories everywhere and making confused allusions to folk

11 Chatwin, Bruce, (1987) *The Songlines*, Viking, New York, pp 210-11
12 Pat Marsh is the author of *The Enigma of the Margate Shell Grotto*, Martyrs Field Publications, Canterbury, an examination of the theories on this shell grotto's unknown origins, soon to go into its third edition.

tales. The locals associate the building with the descent into deprivation which has affected the town, where there is no decent employment to be found and they feel cursed. One critic called *Shades of Babel* "a requiem to communist times", a tale of "failed lives and lost legends"[13], another saw it as located in "a place forsaken by God and man … a nightmare world"[14].

As in *The Black Hole*, Stefanovski introduces a supernatural element into the play. The car park 'tower' is the site of apparitions from the past. Damian, the unemployed young protagonist, who drags out his pointless days learning chess moves, is witness on the top floor to three scenes evoking the traumatic history of the area. The first is from the time of rival liberation groups in Ottoman times who turn on each other; the second from the Balkan Wars and First World War in the early twentieth century when Macedonia was a battlefield for opposing sides; the final scene is from the time of mass migration to America in search of a better life.

> "*This place is cursed. All kinds of weird things build up here. One on top of another, another on top of yet another.*" (Scene Six)

The multi-storey car park and its foundations are a symbol of the palimpsest of history underlying the town's existence, which has been disturbed. The ghosts of the past have come back to haunt the living.

> "*Under that theatre there was another theatre, and under that – a church, and under that a pagan temple.*" (Scene Fifteen)

---

13 *Književna reč*, details lost
14 Dalibor Foretić, *Danas*, 12.06.90

There may also be the implication that those who forget, or in this case bury their past, are doomed to repeat it. *Shades of Babel* was written only two years before the break-up of Yugoslavia. There were already cracks appearing in the surface unity of the Yugoslav republics. The small town of the play could be interpreted as a microcosm of the country, its 'tower' a grand project to unite its peoples in fact tempting Providence and causing their separation. According to Slobodan Unkovski, the first director of the play, *Shades of Babel* expressed "the harshness and uncertainty of the time we live in"[15] and Stefanovski himself said it spoke of a life "which was once music with a strong, solid rhythm, now turned into a tortured and painful improvisation."[16]

But theatre is seen as a possible way of regenerating the community, of bringing a better understanding of the world.

"**Rina** *...What do you want?*

Damian *The rules of the game.*

Rina *You only get that in the theatre... In the theatre there is order, connection and logic. A move once played cannot be played again. Speech is full-blooded and precise. One person speaks, the others listen. There's a beginning, a middle and an end."* (Scene Eight)

The character of Rina in the play has grown up in the theatre, like the author himself. Stefanovski's mother, Nada, was an actress and his father, Mirko, an actor-director. The theatre was his world from birth. As a baby, he would wait backstage to be breast-fed by his mother. At the age of five, the young Goran sat in the audience for the first time for a performance of *The Macedonian Blood Wedding* by

15   Nova Makedonija, 09.01.1990
16   ibid.

18

Voydan Chernodrinski. He was never to forget the trauma of witnessing his mother "killed" on the stage at the end of the play. The shock was overwhelming and he never quite believed that it had been an illusion.

Rina shares this background and Stefanovski's childhood experiences, except that her mother works backstage as a prompter. Rina becomes an actress but, when the theatre is demolished to make way for the multi-storey car park, she leaves town. At the beginning of the play Rina returns from a life spent abroad in order to revive theatre in her birthplace. Not only does she bring new hope to the ageing actress who was her childhood idol, she is also seen as the saviour of the town, someone with supernatural powers who can right all their wrongs. The depressed Damian falls in love with her and finds a new purpose in life. But Rina is too much of a threat to the corrupt local officials and she meets with an "accident". She falls, or is pushed, from the top of the car park. The town reverts to its mood of hopelessness.

It is easy to see why Unkovski called this play Chekhovian[17], though less clear, perhaps, why Ducy Knežević called it "a homage to Edward Bond"[18]. However, Bond did write that "only the mad know how to live with so much despair"[19]. After Rina's death, Damian loses his mind like the chief statistician, repeating his father's phrase

---

17 ibid.
18 The provenance of her article has been lost. Stefanovski spent a year at The University of Manchester in 1979-80 with a grant from The British Council doing research for a PhD on Edward Bond's plays, during which he met and interviewed the English playwright. He also worked as dramaturg on a production of Bond's *Lear* at the Dubrovnik Summer Festival in 1981. The PhD never materialised; the 1980s were to prove as prolific a period for his creative work as the rest of his life.
19 Introduction to *Bingo*, (1974), Eyre Methuen, London, p.viii

"Hunderd dievils inteered", suggesting the evil underground which has resurfaced.

Shades of Babel again follows a Beckettian, expressionist model, with the logic of a dream rather than that of reality. Stefanovski called it "the story of life from which structure has been drained"[20]. The play ends with meaningless rhymes, the confused babble of the modern Babel.

Sarajevo (1993)

Sarajevo, the capital of Bosnia, part of Yugoslavia until 1991, was for centuries the epitome of multiculturalism, a city of different religions, ethnic groups, languages and cultures. Mutual understanding and tolerance were nurtured and preserved for many generations until the spring of 1992, when the city was subjected to artillery fire from the surrounding hills and ordinary people became target practice for snipers.

Stefanovski had lived a contented life in Yugoslavia with his family but the country had fallen apart and war was spreading further and further south. That summer Stefanovski's wife Pat decided the family should make a new life in Canterbury, UK. This marked the start of the dramatist living between two homes, two languages and two cultures.

He was contacted by Dragan Klaić, his friend and former teacher at the Faculty of Dramatic Arts in Belgrade, and asked to work with a leading theatre director from Sarajevo, Haris Pašović, on his concept for a theatre project about the besieged city. Klaić linked them up with Chris Torch of Jordcirkus in Stockholm, who was to produce the project. Goran and Haris spent months together in the dark, wintry

---

20   *Nova Makedonija*, 09.01.1990

Swedish capital trying to come up with a text which would strike the right note and express the anguish they felt for what was happening in the Balkans. Stefanovski wrote: "How does one write a play about Sarajevo today? How does one dare touch an open wound? How does one shoot at a moving target?"[21]

One thing he knew for certain was that he had no wish to write about what people were seeing every night on the television news. He was interested in the *soul* of the city. "What does it do as it hovers over the ruins?"[22] Haris Pašović managed to get back into Sarajevo for his sister's birthday in mid-winter, but then he found it impossible to get out again. The producers turned to Slobodan Unkovski, Stefanovski's friend and long-term collaborator, to direct the play ready for the Antwerp 93 Cultural City of Europe Festival in the spring. It received its dedication: "The play is intended to be a candle lit for the health of the soul of the city of Sarajevo. It is dedicated to the heroic struggle of the people of the city in their tragedy and to one Haris Pasović."

The momentous nature of the project which had finally come to fruition was noted by Michael Kustow in The Independent newspaper: "...it is unsentimental, pitiless and, in its understated condemnation of Europe's betrayal of Sarajevo, devastating. It is already a theatrical and civic milestone, created in the harshest conditions."[23]

Sara, the protagonist of the play, has come to Sarajevo from the future, one which doesn't now seem so far away:

21 Goran Stefanovski, "Sara in Murderland", programme for the Antwerp 93 Cultural Capital of Europe Festival

22 ibid.

23 Michael Kustow, "Pinning down a moving target", *The Independent*, Wednesday 31 March 1993.

"I come from the gloom of Europe,
from what once had dreams of being united,
but is now only a series of lonely, uneasy and small
tyrannical city states.
Our life is uncomfortable, our future shaky,
our cities grey, violent and dirty,
the people unhappy and in fear,
the ozone hole larger, the toxic waste worse,
the acid rains regular." (Scene 1)

Stefanovski returns to this lyrical form at frequent intervals throughout the play. He is evoking the poetry of W.B.Yeats in *The Second Coming*, one of his favourite poems. In the second scene Sara recognises Rudi, the City Eater, "a shape with lion body and the head of a man, a gaze blank and pitiless as the sun", who has "slouched from here towards Bethlehem to be born"[24]. The City Eater is the reincarnation of God as monster, as in Yeats's poem.

Sara comes to know the soul of Sarajevo through a parade of characters and objects from its past, present and future. All things typically Bosnian cross the stage from the simple-minded Muyo and Sulyo, the butt of jokes, through the crafty Nasreddin Hodza, the Winter Olympics held in the city in 1984, the assassin of the Austro-Hungarian Crown Prince Ferdinand seventy years earlier (leading to World War I), the cuisine, the fountains, courtyards, trees and bridges, culminating in sevdah, an ineffable feeling which includes love, joy, nostalgia and heartache.

---

24 The shape of the beast is a direct quote from W.B.Yeats's *The Second Coming* and the last two lines are:
"And what rough beast, its hour come round at last,
Slouches towards Bethlehem to be born?"

Stefanovski's special brand of ironic humour does emerge in the play, although it is far less pronounced than in most of his plays. The small-time smuggler wants to go back to dealing in foreign currency in small denominations, leather goods from Turkey and jeans from Italy. He isn't a war profiteer:

Could we go back to the small times please? And watch the match on Sundays like all normal people?   (Scene 16)

Interspersed with the scenes Sara passes through are the moving songs of the common people, of migrant birds, of roofs from where snipers targeted people going about their everyday lives, of the tram which just wants to get moving again, of the waters in the drinking fountains, of the skyscrapers where people just want to live an ordinary life with tea and toast for breakfast. The stork staying in Sarajevo during the winter out of solidarity with the birds which can't migrate makes a telling point:

"So here we are
Brother helps brother
I hope it's a lesson
of some kind or other."   (Scene 24)

Sara reflects the feelings of the vast majority, including Stefanovski:

"Please tell me more. Why is this happening? I have never read more papers in my life, or watched more television or listened more to the news, and I have never understood less. Why so much hatred? Where does this evil come from? What does it mean? What purpose does it serve?"
                                                        (Scene 14)

At the end it turns out that Sara's strange meetings in the city have taken place inside her head. She is wounded and dying. But it is no coincidence that she is called Sara in Sarajevo. As she dies, a rainbow grows out of her body, a miracle in the bleak landscape. "Was she just another casualty or was she, perhaps, the soul of Sarajevo itself, rising from the ashes like a phoenix?"[25]

The Woman at the Window expresses the eternal hope:

"But we shall overcome. Love will overcome. It always has. It always will."   (Scene 31)

Odysseus (2012)

Odysseus is typical of the final phase of the author's work and it is written in his favourite genre, tragi-comedy, which often descends into farce. The play is a reworking of Homer's epic poem, *The Odyssey*. The main character is Odysseus, King of Ithaca, one of the Greek generals who took part in the ten-year siege of Troy after the Trojan prince Paris had abducted Helen, wife of Menelaus, King of Sparta. It was Odysseus who had the idea of building the huge wooden horse which the Trojans found on the beach after the Greeks had supposedly left in their ships. The horse was thought to be an offering for the god Poseidon and was taken into the city with great festivities. At night the Greek warriors hidden inside came out and opened the city gates for the rest of their army to enter and sack Troy.

On his way home Odysseus is faced with numerous obstacles and dangers caused by the vengeful Poseidon; it is ten years before he reaches Ithaca. In the meantime, his wife Penelope has to cope with more than a hundred suitors who want to marry her and become king, thinking Odysseus dead.

---

25   Goran Stefanovski, "Sara in Murderland", programme for the Antwerp 93 Cultural Capital of Europe Festival

Stefanovski's play is a burlesque subversion of Homer's melodramatic and heroic epic. Odysseus is an anti-hero. He lives in a world of gangsters, the accountant to the mafia-like gods, where no one can be trusted and anyone might be out to get him. Helen, "the face that launch'd a thousand ships And burnt the topless towers of Ilium"[26], is an ageing, over-made-up strumpet, the distinguished general Nestor an insane arms and drugs dealer, while Athene, the mighty goddess of wisdom herself, is a pathetic middle-aged virgin love-sick for Odysseus, anxious to know which shade of lipstick he likes. His wife Penelope, the archetype of the faithful wife, is dying for a drink, scheming with her maid about how to string along the suitors clamouring to marry her at the same time as running the kingdom. Did she love Odysseus?

> "*I was a girl. He was already thirty. Arranged marriage. Love? Yes. And no. And maybe. I didn't have time to decide before he went off to war.*" (Scene 9)

This lack of any romanticising of the characters is particularly stark in the portrayal of Odysseus. He is an Everyman, "a manic depressive"[27]. The first time we see him, he is preoccupied with one of his teeth falling out, his heartburn and arthritis, reflecting one of Stefanovski's notes for the programme accompanying the first production: "What happens to action heroes when they grow old? Imagine a grey-haired James Bond looking at himself in a hotel mirror one morning and asking himself for the first time: "Who exactly am I, and what do I actually do?"[28]

The question of identity is key to the play. The author

---

26 Christopher Marlowe, *Doctor Faustus*, Scene XIII, lines 87-88

27 Tomislav Čadež, Nedjeljni Jutarnji, 22 July 2012, p.10

28 Ulysses Theatre Zagreb-Brijuni, Season 12, premiere 20 July 2012, Mali Brijuni, p.6

noted: "Perhaps the whole story happens in the head of someone going through an intense identity crisis, trying to process the forces of family, history, politics and ageing."

The Bard provides a running commentary on Odysseus's plight and its universal implications:

> "*People wander in search of their identity, the story of who they are and what they are. They invent various tricks while they're doing that. They present being lost as being found. They think up new maps and pretend they're exactly where they should be. They look for an alibi for their actions, think up excuses for their mistakes, try to give sense to their lives at any cost. So it comes about that adventuring is presented as principled travel, selfishness as aspiration towards higher goals, robbery as a fight for freedom, attack as self-defence, genocide as a sacred quest.*" (Scene 8)

This last phrase raises the spectre of the Yugoslav wars again, which were never far from Stefanovski's work after 1991. Odysseus recognises that the cycle of war and peace is never-ending, that war and hatred get "*brushed under the carpet, replaced by peace and unity*" (Scene 19), but, a few years later, peace and unity will be cut short and there will be war and hatred again. Stefanovski doesn't shrink from revealing the terrible truth of how this affects the combatants:

> "**Odysseus**   *The war haunts me.*
>
> **Circe**   *It doesn't haunt you, but you haunt it. You miss it. You don't know what to do with yourself when you're not warmongering.*" (Scene 11)

We gradually become aware that Odysseus is a war criminal, guilty of almost casual atrocities at Troy and in his wandering since conquering the city. His soldiers follow his example and have made a way of life out of plundering cities, maiming and murdering the men, raping the women:

"*First Soldier   We all followed your example, Master. I never did care much for tilling the soil and running a household. I only really liked ships, oars, battles, sharp spears and death-dealing arrows. What others found terrible and repulsive, I was rather fond of.*"   (Scene 8)

Telemachus, Odysseus's son, who has grown up with the idealised image of his father fed to him by his mother, slowly discovers the reality behind the legend and is left desperately trying to scratch off the tattoo of his father's name on his arm.

"*Daddy came home from the war a psychopath.*"
(Scene 17)

Stefanovski also points up the difficulty of ever knowing the truth when everyone has their own story of what happened:

"*Telemachus   But didn't Odysseus build the Trojan horse? And wasn't that the turning-point in winning the war?*

Nestor   There you are, there's your war propaganda. It turns out that those who've never seen Troy even in a picture book know all about it, while we, who left our youth there, we don't know anything.

Menelaus   The Trojan horse was my idea. Odysseus had nothing to do with it."   (Scene 3)

The Bard reflects the justification given by tabloid journalists for how they report the news, and brings the play right up-to-date with its reference to the power of social media:

> "*I sing what the audience likes. Once there was a fashion for songs about how the Trojan veterans were heroes. Now it's the opposite. Now it's democracy. Freedom. Earlier it was just the gods and the muses who sang, and now everyone tweets away. Universal din and competition. Calypso's a goddess for some, for others a high-class whore. It's all spin.*"　　　　　　　　　　　　(Scene 7)

The name of Odysseus is, of course, inseparable from the notion of Ithaca, his island kingdom, to which he desires above all to return. Stefanovski's programme note[29] shows what Ithaca means in a universal sense and for the author himself:

"Each in our own way, we all yearn for an ideal refuge, the right place to find ourselves and be ourselves, at peace and fulfilled. We believe we once had that place but have lost it, so we persist in trying to find it again, convinced that it is promised us and that we possess a natural right to it. For some it is the refuge of childhood, for others first young love, and for yet others the old country. For Odysseus it was Ithaca. As we get older, this restless search for the ultimate place becomes deeper and deeper and more and more uncertain. Everything seems to be unstable except for that illusion of stability, which, like hope, never leaves us. The human need for stories is the constant yearning to capture those illusions. It is particularly strong for those whose Ithaca is the theatre."

---

29 ibid.

The play begins and ends with a troupe of actors, much like those in Shakespeare's *Hamlet*, wandering around and putting on plays when they find an audience. As already noted, Stefanovski's world from childhood was the theatre and he felt most at home writing plays. It was indeed his Ithaca.

Nevertheless, Ithaca is also home for Odysseus and it is this concept which haunted Stefanovski in exile from his homeland in the last two decades of his life. As Vangeli notes, "Like Odysseus, Stefanovski is consumed by nostalgia: apparently born under the sign of ambivalence, he seems destined to wander the world, striving to conquer it, in its entirety, but to always bear in mind his *nostos*, the ideal image of his beloved home."[30] But the flip side of this longing for home is the pain it causes:

> "*I'm coming, home, you poison, you bone in my throat, you thorn in my soul!*"　　　　　　　　　　(Scene 5)

The play begins and ends with a song about home where this dual nature of the notion is expressed in a paradox:

> "*I can never go back home*
> *For now I've lost my way,*
> *I can never leave my home*
> *No, never go away.*"

30　Nikola Vangeli (2012) "Goran Stefanovski and the "Curse" of the Balkans, The Portrait of a Playwright from the "Wild East"", Summary of the Doctoral Thesis in Theatre Studies, Faculty of Theatre, George Enescu University of the Arts, Iasi, Romania http://goranstefanovski.co.uk/wp-content/uploads/2012/11/n.vangeli_phd-thesis_summary.pdf p.13

Vangeli writes that Odysseus is "a self-ironic, fictional projection of the author"[31]. The protagonist's last words in his role are "*Home is where it hurts!*".

Odysseus reflects the universal experience of going back home to discover it is no longer how we remember it, because, of course, we are no longer who we were:

Odysseus *... This doesn't look like Ithaca to me.*

Athene *You don't look like Odysseus either.*

Odysseus *Where's that Ithaca of mine?*

Athene *Gone with that Odysseus.* (Scene 15)

This discovery is particularly poignant when one's homeland has changed out of all recognition, as in Stefanovski's case, where the name of his country, its political system and stated beliefs are all different from those of his childhood:

"You've ruined Ithaca! You've destroyed my homeland! ... You've spat on the vows that were made. You've put up monuments to foreign gods. You've burnt the flags, banned the songs, changed the locks on the doors." (Scene 19)

As Athene says, "*Ithaca is where you set out from but can't go back to*" (Scene 19).

Odysseus takes a legend and uses it to illustrate unpleasant or unwelcome truths about the human condition through a tragi-comic treatment. In a third programme note for the first production, Stefanovski wrote: "It is sad and funny to look at us human beings floundering around and trying to wake up from what Joyce called the nightmare of history"[32].

---

31   ibid. p.12
32   Programme of Ulysses Theatre Zagreb-Brijuni, Season 12, premiere 20 July 2012, Mali Brijuni, p.6

Figurae Veneris Historiae (2014)

Joyce's nightmare of history underlies Stefanovski's last finished and performed play, *Figurae Veneris Historiae*. He described the title as deliberately ironic and pompous. In Latin it sounds extremely erudite but its meaning is 'History's Sexual Positions': the play concerns the way History 'screws' human beings in a variety of ways.

This work was commissioned by the Slovenian National Theatre in Ljubljana to mark the one-hundredth anniversary of the beginning of the First World War in 2014. It gave Stefanovski another opportunity to approach from a new angle one of the obsessive themes of tragedies from Homer to Shakespeare: the impossibility of love in the world of politics[33].

He had been fascinated from early puberty by two volumes he found on the shelves of his father's library: *Sittengeschichte des Weltkrieges* (The Sexual History of the First World War) by Magnus Hirschfeld, originally published in Berlin in 1931. It was full of expressionist drawings by Georg Grosz and Otto Dix, erotic pictures, posters and soldiers' postcards, photos from the time of the War, disturbing sketches of war invalids and prostitutes – a lot of blood, human flesh and horror.

Stefanovski discovered that Magnus Hirschfeld (1858-1935) was a writer and a scientist who published more than 500 titles on various topics of sexuality, health, politics, morality and the history of racism. In 1919, in the liberal atmosphere of Berlin during the Weimar Republic, Hirschfeld founded the Institut für Sexualwissenschaft

---

33   From Goran Stefanovski's presentation *From First Idea to First Night* for Canterbury Christ Church University's Centre for Practice-Based Research in the Arts https://www.youtube.com/watch?v=7C2SDPD9KTk

(Institute for Sexual Science). The Institute had a vast library and archive, as well as organising lectures and medical consultations. As a Jew who advocated progressive ideas, Hirschfeld became a frequent target of the Nazis. He was often attacked and severely injured. In 1928 he participated in the founding of the World League for Gender Reform. In 1930 Hirschfeld went on a long tour of the USA and around the world. In his absence in 1933, the Nazis destroyed the Institute for Sexual Science and the library. Hirschfeld was stripped of his German citizenship. He died in Nice in 1935.

Hirschfeld's book was an inspiration for Stefanovski's play. The scene titles reflect its chapters, showing "war as human mass orgy, a bacchanalia. War is pornography. It is a case of grand copulation and historical rape."[34] As in *The Black Hole*, the playwright is re-examining the relationship between Eros and Thanatos, where Eros is the creative instinct of love, peace, creativity and cooperation, while Thanatos represents the instinct of hatred, war, evil and destruction. "War is a negative sublimation of the erotic. Love and hate, eroticism and perversion, construction and destruction, war and peace are constantly overlapping in a dialectal embrace, like a snake pit."[35]

Each of the fourteen scenes is split up into sub-scenes and gives the staccato impression of a silent film, conveying the same sense of tragic farce told in stilted language. The Young Lady imagines herself saying goodbye to her fiancé at the station as he goes off to war as if writing the scene for the movie:

---

34 Programme for the first production at the Slovenian National Theatre, Ljubljana
35 From Stefanovski's original *Treatment for a theatrical project* submitted to the Slovenian National Theatre

"You'll be boarding a train and I'll cry on the platform. It'll be embarrassing. The train doesn't move and we've already said our goodbyes many times over. Then you disappear and I drown in my own tears." (Scene 2)

The Young Lady is one of the ten stereotypical characters who have no names, only titles: Baron, Baroness, Student, Convict, Maid, Widow, Ploughman, Land Woman, Handyman. As the eleventh character in the play, Magnus Hirschfeld recounts how he observed many people for his book:

"It was a study of war as sexual hypnosis, pornographic trance, mass orgy. (He looks at the characters around him.) Millions were raped. Some in their bodies, some in their minds, some in both. I was one of them." (Scene 1)

Each scene in the play illustrates how easily human beings allow themselves to be taken over by the hypnosis of war. Magnus knows all the characters and has some kind of control of them. He seems to be shadowing them in different guises. Each character is given a moment when they stand back from their role and sum up what happened to them during the War. This is probably part of the group therapy session we see them having at the end of Act 1:

*"**Baron** Everyone has their wars and I've had mine... I followed its development, like a photograph, in the dark room of my soul. My capitalist greed exploded! My great empires went for each other's throats. I'd been piling up armaments for decades. My bourgeois morality fell apart. I descended into a spiritual cave. My base urges were unleashed and I turned into a – beast!"* (Scene 5)

Stefanovski said "When wine turns sour, it becomes

vinegar; when love turns sour, war begins."[36] Throughout the play, this absence of love in war is symbolised by the characters pausing to listen. Magnus explains they want to hear "the silence behind… the silence of love".

Although all the characters strain to hear this "silence of love", they find it impossible during the war.

> **Handyman**   *Sex was urgent and it couldn't wait. Love could wait. Love had time and patience. And it would appear one fine day, in the future, hand in hand with peace.*   (Scene 6)

Songs again play a part in this play but they reflect the cruel lasciviousness of the soldiers:

> **Maid**   *… And all the time I could hear the Muses. They were singing lewd songs. It's not true that in war the Muses are silent. They are obscene!*

There is, however, one song which is very different. It is sung twice, at the end of each act. It is about love and seems intended to provide a small ray of hope for humanity. At the end of the play, Magnus speaks of the universal human music, of our "*unique hum, resonances, an ocean of harmony. Musica humana universalis. But we hardly hear it, we're so busy doing other things. And love just sits there, silent and abandoned, drowned in the noise of shrieks and explosions. But we are strongest where we hurt. We will pan the bloodshed of war to search for the gold dust of love.*" (Scene 14)

The play's characters are stereotypes, as their titles imply. Stefanovski called them "a human gallery going through the pressure cooker of war and blender of history. They all undergo violent, tectonic changes which turn them upside

---

36   Article in the newspaper *Vest*, Saturday 22/Sunday 23 August 2015

down and inside out. With farcical speed they become tragicomic caricatures. Metaphorically speaking the main character is War."[37] The author paid special attention to giving equal weight to each character; they each take the lead in a scene and all undergo the same number of changes. These can be so traumatic that at the end of the play, for example, the Convict and the Widow don't recognise each other although they were a married couple before the War.

The play is full of irony in Stefanovski's inimitable style:

Convict *I'm going to war. I will kill again, but this time they will give me a medal.*

Student *I went and protested. I told them that war is legalised mass murder, that it leads to cruelty and sadism.*

Baroness *What did they say?*

Student *They said that it also offers infinite erotic possibilities.*

The need to believe dehumanising fictions about the enemy is highlighted with black humour in the discussions about all the inhuman things the enemy do, although no one had ever heard about them before the war. Two of the women talk about how the enemy tie nuns to the clappers of church bells; they speculate on how long it takes for a nun to die when the bell is rung. Neither of them even entertains the possibility that this is not a common practice among the enemy.

---

37 From Goran Stefanovski's presentation *From First Idea to First Night* for Canterbury Christ Church University's Centre for Practice-Based Research in the Arts https://www.youtube.com/watch?v=7C2SDPD9KTk

All the characters are under the spell of War. The question Stefanovski poses is: "...if we managed to dispel this shameful hypnosis, would we be ashamed?"[38] The Widow gives one answer:

Widow *And then the war ended. And I felt caught like a cockroach in the light. In the war every activity was directed towards a definite end. Life had meaning. But peace didn't seem to lead to anything. It was an anti-climax. I had worked myself up to an unnatural pitch of excitement and daring. And then I collapsed. I felt soiled and spent. It was time for despair.*   (Scene 13)

Stefanovski wrote that the tone of the play was one of "hanging on in quiet desperation"[39] and also of merciless social satire. "This approach befits the twentieth century, the cruellest in human history, when the sky was empty and there was no hope of easy redemption."[40]

The play ends with all the characters emerging from their hypnosis. They are holding a séance and have summoned Magnus Hirschfeld back from the dead. He implies that the action of the play has been a reliving of the characters' experiences of the First World War to prepare them to prevent the Second World War. They have been through a counselling session. He gives them a word of warning:

---

38 A Note on the play Figurae Veneris Historiae http://www.drama.si/repertoar/delo?id=1777
39 A line from Pink Floyd's song 'Time' on The Dark Side of the Moon album
40 Programme for the first production at the Slovenian National Theatre, Ljubljana

How come love is constantly annihilated and yet always survives? Against all the odds! How come? Answer me that. We hurt, we wander blindly. History has abused us, many times and in various positions. Figurae Veneris Historiae. Don't let it do it again.   (Scene 19)

Pat Marsh, Canterbury, March 2019

THE BLACK HOLE

a play by Goran Stefanovski (1987)
Translated from the Macedonian by
Patricia Marsh Stefanovska

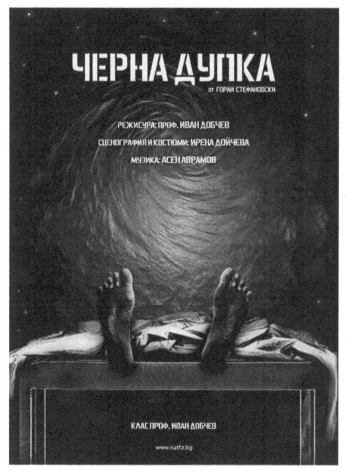

Poster for the 2017 production of *The Black Hole*
at the National Academy of Theatre and Film Studies,
Sofia, directed by Ivan Dobčev

Characters

Silyan, 35

Svetlé, 18

Sania, 40

Tsveta, Silyan's wife, 30

The Father, his father, 65

The Mother, his mother, 60

Pero, 35

Anna, Pero's wife, 30

Magda, 35

Makso, 33

The Children, a boy and a girl

PART ONE

Scene One

A room. **Silyan** *and* **Svetlé** *are lying naked, covered by a sheet.* **Silyan** *gives* **Svetlé** *a cigarette. They smoke.*

Silyan (*Singing*)

> Love me not, my dear,
> Don't lose your heart,
> For I come from far away, my dear,
> Tomorrow I'll depart
> For foreign lands, my dear,
> For foreign parts.

Pause.

Svetlé   D'you always shout out like that? (*Pause.*) I've never heard anyone make such a noise. I thought you'd died.

Silyan   I *did* die.

Svetlé   You must really get off on it. You're old. I'll have learnt to shout like that at your age. I live in a small flat. My Mum and Dad don't make a sound when they do it. I watched you while you were shouting. You looked like an animal. A wild animal. Your mouth all twisted. Your face all distorted. Like you were in terrible pain. Like you were having a tooth out.

Silyan   Show me what I looked like.

Svetlé *opens her mouth, contorts her face and closes her eyes.*

Silyan   I watched myself in the mirror once. But I missed the vital moment. When the best part came, I had to shut my eyes.

Svetlé You went cross-eyed first, and then you shut them.

Silyan That's when they look inside.

Svetlé I'm afraid to let go. I think I might come apart. Burst like a pumpkin.

Silyan Don't hold it back. It comes from God.

Svetlé Pity it doesn't last long.

Silyan It can last much longer. With ether.

Svetlé Ether?

Silyan It's a liquid. Lets you come for hours. Makes you worn out for days afterwards. It can suffocate you if you overdo it.

Svetlé You tried it?

Silyan Not yet.

Svetlé You're so experienced.

Silyan I learn something new every time. Just now with you, too. You've got sharp hair. I thought I knew all the different kinds.

He touches her.

Svetlé What is it?

Silyan You have a body. (*Pause.*) So have I. (*Pause.*) Heavenly bodies. For carving up. How do you feel when you come?

Svetlé I don't know. Like warmth, like some force flowing up through me from my toes. Something like that. I've never really thought about it.

Silyan Well, think now.

Svetlé That's all you think about.

Silyan It's all that's left.

Svetlé You don't take enough care of yourself. You need a bath, and a haircut.

Silyan I'm happy.

Svetlé Statement of the year.

Silyan Really.

Svetlé You must be the only person in this country who is!

Silyan I have a lump here in my throat from pure joy. Waves of warm blood come up my body.

Svetlé Congratulations.

Silyan Thank you.

Svetlé I'm on the edge all the time. Haven't got enough money. I only feel happy when I go and buy something new – and then only for a little while. I wish there was someone to take me away from all this. The Good Life. Wine and Roses. There's nowhere to run to.

Silyan Here. Where we've run to.

Svetlé Aren't you married?

Silyan No.

Svetlé Time you were. What d'you do?

Silyan I'm a butcher.

Svetlé   In a shop?

Silyan   In a slaughter-house.

Svetlé   You're lying.

Silyan   I'm lying.

Svetlé   What *do* you do?

Silyan   I'm a butcher. (*Pause.*)

Svetlé   Whose flat is this?

Silyan   My friend's. His wife's in the country. He works at the ironworks. This is their marriage bed. There are traces of their movements and bodies here. Their spirits are floating in the air.

Svetlé   Where?

Silyan   Here somewhere. Ssssshhhhh!

Svetlé   What's the matter?

Silyan   Hear that?

Svetlé   What?

Silyan   Thought I heard something. I've been hearing voices lately.

Svetlé   What kind of voices?

Silyan   Human ones. Like an echo. Like something that was said once before and now comes back again.

Svetlé   Stop trying to scare me.

Silyan   It's beautiful.

Svetlé   It's terrifying.

Silyan   That's why it's beautiful. We're huddling together here. Of all the billions of people in the world, just you and me.

Svetlé You do talk a lot. Other men either fall asleep straightaway or get me to go home.

Silyan D'you know what it's like in the ironworks? Working up there by the furnaces? Impossible. You wouldn't think any normal person'd want to work there. They lose ten pounds a day in sweat. It's incredibly hot. You know why they do it? Want me to tell you why they do it? 'Cos they have orgasms all the time, that's why. Keep on and on coming all the time. It's not funny. They're close to the source. Thousands of degrees of heat. Lava. It's a state of grace. Remember when they said someone had fallen into the molten iron? They were lying. He threw himself in. The ecstasy of it was too much for him.

Svetlé *That's* why they're all smiles when they have their pictures taken for the front page on Labour Day.

Silyan What did his body look like when it hit the lava? When all those sinews and veins and bloody flesh exploded?

Svetlé Don't shout so much. You're spitting on me.

Silyan It'll be dawn soon. The buses'll start and the workers'll be swarming like ants all over the place. The misery will begin, known in the parlance as our waking hours. Nothing will be left of this. Just a blur. Like the slime left by a snail.

Svetlé What d'you want to be left?

Silyan Marks. Proof that what is happening is real.

He touches her.

Svetlé   You're a bit weird.

Silyan   D'you want to be my girlfriend?

Svetlé   I've got a boyfriend.

Silyan   We can go on dates – fixed time and place, hand in hand, through the park, along the river, listening to the nightingales.

Svetlé   I've got to go.

Silyan   Stay 'till morning.

Svetlé   My father'll kill me. He thinks I'm doing a typing course. (*Pause.*) You scare me when you look at me like that. You're scary, you know. You were scary when you came up to me. You had some deadly lust in your eyes. That's why I came here with you. Other men talk rubbish, take me out to dinner, give me presents, promises, and I turn them down. I love turning them down. But you're a live wire. Will you give me the money for a taxi?

Silyan   Won't I be seeing you again?

Svetlé   No.

Silyan   What's your name?

Svetlé   What's yours?

Scene Two

A tastefully and expensively furnished two-room flat. **Silyan** *unlocks the door from the outside and enters. He is wearing a winter overcoat and hat. He sits down on the sofa. Pause.* **Sania** *enters from the bedroom, wearing a silk kimono.*

Sania   Where've you been?

Silyan   At work.

Sania   'Till this hour? (*Pause.*) You said you'd be here for dinner. I opened some caviar. Waited for you. What were you doing at work?

Silyan   Butchering.

Sania   'Till this hour?

Silyan   Jealous?

Sania   Yes.

Silyan   How beautifully contrived this all is.

Sania   You fly by night, like a bat.

Silyan (*Picking up a newspaper*)   You read the papers?

Sania   I like to know what's going on.

Silyan   Oh, do *please* tell me what's going on!

Sania   The Titanic's going down.

Silyan   You need papers to know that? (*Throws down the paper*) There. No more foreign affairs, home affairs, culture, sport, or weather forecasts. Nothing. Just you and me. (*Pause.*) Got any whisky?

Sania   You finished it this morning. Want some coffee, tea?

Silyan *suddenly turns to look behind him.*

Sania   What's the matter?

Silyan   I thought there was someone behind me.

Sania   Someone?

Silyan   Or something.

Sania   Something?

Silyan   Someone or something alive.

Sania   Nonsense.

Silyan   Nonsense, Silyan. You're too tense. Overdoing things. Imagining things. It's not really like that. You're always so negative. Be realistic. Be realistic.

Sania   Be realistic.

Silyan (*Lifting Sania's kimono to reveal black stockings and suspender belt*)   You're wearing what I asked. Chinese silk, French underwear, Balkan breast and leg.

Sania   Leave me alone.

Silyan   No?

Sania   No. When I wait for you, you don't come. This isn't a brothel.

Silyan   How's your doctorate coming along?

Sania (*Taking a piece of paper from the table and reading*)   "In the next few years the artist's serene melancholy gave way to a fretful, dramatic restlessness. Feverish animation borders on the bizarre, although the precision of the drawing is maintained. The intentional, melodramatic lack of harmony has an obvious connection with the crisis provoked by

Savonarola, which called into question the legitimacy of the painter's world. He reacted to this with contorted forms and the neurotic style of that period, which fits in with the wave of NeoGothic expressionism then enveloping Ferrara and Venice". (*She puts the piece of paper down.*)

Silyan Which happy man is all that about?

Sania Botticelli. (*Pause.*) They seem to have known about restlessness before you appeared on the scene.

Silyan I'm an animal in your intellectual laboratory.

Sania I'm an intellectual in your animalistic laboratory.

Silyan Get your clothes off.

Sania We should go off for a weekend somewhere. Our nerves are all frayed. You lie to me, then I feel guilty for not having any feelings. How am I supposed to feel anything? You're cold and sterile, not me. I made this into a nest for you. Warmth and security. A bomb shelter in a minefield.

Silyan You know the next item on the agenda?

Sania What?

Silyan We vanish. Cease to exist. This sofa, this room, this town, this language we speak, the square, the people, their habits and customs, all the files, newspapers, dishes and drinks. All swept away. Vanished. Into thin air.

Sania Well put. You taking those pills I gave you?

Silyan I took them this morning with tripe soup and white wine.

Sania And?

Silyan Tasted nice. Got any more?

Sania I'll make you some mint tea. There's an explanation for all this. The mid-life crisis. They've done research on it. I'll buy you a new suit. You can't go on wearing those rags. You need something new. Need to shape up. I'm going on a study trip to Italy. The Renaissance – Siena, Florence, Padua, Ferrara, Venice. Come with me. Get the hell out of this place.

Silyan I wasn't at work.

Sania You were with some girl. I knew it. No doubt illiterate. No doubt young enough to be your daughter. It didn't hurt her like it hurts me, did it? Did she scream? Did she?

Silyan *stands up suddenly and goes to the window. He draws the curtains and looks out into the darkness.*

Sania What's the matter?

Silyan Look !

Sania What?

Silyan Night.

Sania Silyan!

Silyan Ssssshhhhh.

They listen tensely and look into the darkness.

Scene Three

A small flat. **The Father** *is sitting watching television. The programmes are over. Pause. Enter* **Tsveta** *from the other room in a nightdress.*

Tsveta   What're you doing?

The Father   Watching TV.

Tsveta   There's nothing on.

The Father   I'm watching the snow. Ever seen snow like that? That's how the world's going to end. A snow like that's going to fall. Heavy, hissing.

Tsveta   What time is it?

The Father   Some unearthly hour.

Tsveta   Isn't Silyan back yet? (*She pours herself a drink.*) I'll smear pitch all over him and set him on fire.

The Father   Having a drink, are you?

Tsveta   Me? (*Drinks*) He's hardly set foot in this house since they gave him the sack. These men all leave some slave at home and prance around drinking with the boys. In three years he's only taken me out once – for fish and chips. I hope to God he gets some nasty disease and his piss comes out green.

The Father   (*Calmly rolling a cigarette*) You're like ostriches. Fat arses and heads in the sand.

Tsveta   Heads in the shit you lot left.

The Father   Things'll get better.

Tsveta They can't get worse. We're breathing lead and eating horns and hooves.

The Father When I was your age, there was a big statue of the King in the square. On horseback, sword in hand.

Tsveta I've heard this one before.

The Father We used to cross ourselves in front of that statue and that was where we had all our celebrations. Actors gave performances, actresses strolled about with the officers, and boys and girls would set doves free into the air. Times changed. The government fell. We got a new one. The statue of the ex-King had to be pulled down. I was a lorry driver. I got the order. Pull down the statue and throw it in the river. Late one night I put the tow-rope round the King's neck and set off in the lorry. I look out through the back window and there's the ex-King on his horse, his sabre in his hand, being dragged through the dust.

Tsveta I've heard this one before.

The Father The new government built a new statue, of the new King. We learnt a new way of crossing ourselves and of celebrating events. Actors gave performances, actresses strolled about with new officers, and boys and girls set doves free into the air. It wasn't long before the times changed and the government fell. Now it was us in power. I was still a lorry driver. I got the order again. I was the one with the tow-rope again. I look out through the back window and there's the ex-King, on his horse, his sabre in his hand, being dragged through the dust.

Tsveta And ?

The Father We built a new statue in the square. A young man with a gun. The unknown hero. Sometimes I give the children history lessons. I evoke memories. They give me flowers.

Tsveta   You know how many times you've told that story?

The Father   Well, we've eaten bread plenty of times, but we still go on eating it, don't we?

The front door opens. Enter **Silyan**. *Pause. They look at each other.*

The Father   You look about as fresh as a spring onion in December.

Tsveta   Why've you come? Why d'you bother to come at all?

The Father   If you don't come home now and then, there's no fun in staying out.

Tsveta   Aren't you going to say anything? (*Pause.*) Haven't you got anything to say?

The Father   He could give us a song maybe.

Tsveta   Eat your supper and go to bed. I've got to get up at five.

Silyan   Don't shout. You'll wake the children.

Tsveta   Where've you been all this time?

Silyan   Don't ask.

Tsveta   I'm asking. (*Pause.*) I'm listening.

The Father   But be honest, now.

Silyan   First I was with a girl who's doing a typing course and then I was with a divorcee who's got a two-room flat.

Tsveta And?

The Father Interesting story, uh?

Tsveta The beginning's good, I wonder how it'll end.

The Father Like a white mouse in mayonnaise. That's how it'll end.

Tsveta What were you doing with them?

Silyan What d'you think I was doing?

The Father What d'you think he was doing?

Tsveta You're lying !

Silyan If I'd lied you'd've believed me. Not a mark on me. You'd never have known.

The Father If I'm in the way...

Silyan Don't get me wrong. I have real regard for you. I love you and respect you. You've given me two beautiful kids. We've been married so many years. We haven't said a bad word to each other.

Tsveta You're a fucking male whore.

The Father You should give blood.

Silyan There's a voice inside me keeps saying "Don't, Silyan, don't be a fool, don't tell her", but I'm managing to overcome it.

The Father If only I had a big stick, I'd give you sixty of the best, not six.

Silyan You should know about our neighbour Elizabeta, too. Her husband, Makso, was off somewhere in the jeep. You were at work. Elizabeta came to borrow some cooking oil.

Tsveta And?

Silyan It happened.

Tsveta Where?

Silyan Here.

Tsveta On my bed?

Silyan She said that, too. Not on her bed. We started off on the table, but it didn't work.

The Father You should give blood.

Silyan Everybody does it. If you could hear all the squeaking and creaking of all the beds, it'd drive you crazy. (*Pause.*)

Tsveta What else?

Silyan What?

Tsveta You seem to have made up your mind to tell us everything. So what else?

The Father Did you give her the cooking oil?

Silyan Listen. (*Pause.*) Can you hear something?

Tsveta What? You think you can hear and see and feel things nobody else can hear or see or feel. You're suffering so much and we don't understand a thing about it! Shit! I've got eyes and ears and a heart, too, you know! You come home from your wanderings at five o'clock in the morning and you're suffering terribly, and I go off to work at five o'clock in the morning and I'm not suffering, of course. Who *isn't* suffering? We all hear things, but we still live a normal human life. Work, struggle to make ends meet, freeze things for the winter. I want us to have our meals together, take the children to the amusement park, go to the pictures. Go out for meals. Have birthday parties and celebrate national holidays. Sunday mornings you wash the car and I make the lunch. You'd ask, what's so special about that, but there *is* nothing else. I want to know where you stand. Either come or go. Get out of this house and come back when you're another man, a new man. Either do that or I never want to see you again. Never! Never!

The Children *appear at the door to the other room.* **Silyan** *looks at them.*

Silyan Finery. Frippery. Frumpery. Trumpery. Chivalry. Gallantry. Pleasantry. Dysentery.

The Children *run into his arms and sit in his lap, snuggling up to him. Pause.*

The Father You should give blood. I gave blood thirty-five times. It purges your body, gets all the poison out. You become one with others. (*He takes a newspaper cutting out of his pocket.*) "Bozhin Silyanovski, who works as a lorry driver for the Cigarette Factory, has given life thirty-five times. Thirty-five times he has donated that most precious of liquids – blood, and so has fulfilled his obligations to mankind on many occasions. "Giving blood has become a habit with me. I can't imagine my life without it", said modest Bozhin, a father, grandfather, and exemplary husband. "I regularly give this noble liquid, every three months, and there are never any bad side-effects. On the contrary. It helps me to feel bright and healthy." Silyanovski is not the only one to set such an example. There are many like him in the company. "I am the president of the Blood

Donors' Society and we have attended several gatherings of blood donors both in the Republic and in the Federation as a whole."

He folds up the cutting and puts it back in his pocket. Pause. **Tsveta** *leads* **The Children** *back into the other room and closes the door behind her.* **The Father** *starts rolling a cigarette.* **Silyan** *watches him.*

The Father   We've eaten all the stew. Now there's only the pan to lick.

Silyan   Is this it?

The Father   There's nothing else.

Silyan   There must be.

The Father   You'll get used to it. People get used to having ulcers. Hunchbacks to having humps. (*Pause. He smokes.*) You want to live forever or something?

Silyan   Yes.

The Father *makes an obscene gesture.*

Scene Four

The street. **Silyan** *and* **Makso**. **Makso** *is wearing loud fashionable clothes.*

Makso Hey, neighbour!

Silyan Makso.

Makso Want a lift in my jeep?

Silyan I'll walk, thanks.

Makso You leaving? We heard you having a row last night. Thin walls, modern flats. Cheating on the wife, uh? What a scandal. Why go and admit it? If you've had some on the side, keep quiet about it. What're women anyway? Consumer goods. Can't keep count of all the ones I've had. They don't mean a thing to me, though. When I'm angry, I kick Elizabeta all the way up the stairs from the ground floor to the ninth. Where you going to now?

Silyan On an outing.

Makso You're so naive, Silyan. They shout at you, you believe them. You think everything's up to you, you're to blame for everything. Like 'cos there's no money, exports declining, a bridge collapsed somewhere, babies dying because of the unhygienic conditions in the maternity ward, price of bread's gone up – they point the finger at you from the radio, the TV, the papers, and you believe it all. Look at yourself. Got no money, you just don't *count*, mate. No economic crisis for *me*. This is my street, my territory. I'm sure of myself. Casually dressed. Fresh. Now's the moment. Get a loan. Steal. Take dollars to Russia, buy roubles, go to Helsinki, sell the roubles, get dollars, and come back here.

Open up a pizza place. A photocopying place. Sell candy floss. Sell fog. Sell shit. They'll buy anything. What're you waiting for? The market's open. Shillings, francs, drachmas, lira, marks, crowns, dollars, American, Canadian, Australian. Smuggle, deal, con. Left hand, right pocket. I can't reach my full potential here. I'm going to Germany. Spreading out. I'll hunt kangaroos.

Silyan Kangaroos?

Makso Kangaroos.

Silyan In Germany?

Makso What d'you mean, Germany?

Silyan You said Germany.

Makso Australia. I said Australia. Toronto, Quebec, Montreal.

Silyan They're in Canada.

Makso It's Canada I'm talking about. Whenever you and your wife were doing it, we could hear you. The bed creaking and that. I listen every time. I love it. I'm sure Elizabeta listens too. She just pretends to be asleep. Have a good trip.

Silyan Where am I going?

Makso Wherever it is you're going.

Silyan Look!

Makso What?

Silyan It's passing by.

Makso What?

Silyan Life.

Makso I'll catch it up in my jeep. What'll *you* do?

Scene Five

A flat. Night-time. **Pero**, **Anna** *and* **Silyan** *are sitting round a table. They've finished dinner.* **Pero** *is wearing a suit and bow-tie.*

Pero   Have some more. It'll only get thrown away. We throw piles of food away.

Silyan   It's late. I'd better go.

Pero   Where? You've been thrown out of your home. I won't let you go to a hotel. We've been friends for donkey's years. Stay here. I've got ten rooms. He can sleep here, can't he, Anna?

Anna   Of course.

Pero (*Raising his wine glass*)   Which doesn't mean we can't go on drinking. (*They clink glasses and drink.*) I want to tell you again, I've got nothing against you personally. It was just an unfortunate set of circumstances. I was chairman of the commission. I had no choice.

Anna   What's all this about?

Pero   You say you like the wine?

Silyan   It's excellent.

Pero   My own label.

Anna   What commission?

Pero   Our friend here did an incredibly silly thing. (*Pause.*) He took out a heart.

Anna   What?

61

Pero   Ask him. We on the commission, we asked him, too. All the local and urban forums have been discussing it for days. And it'll go higher, believe you me.

Anna   What's happened?

Pero   A friend's a friend, but there're limits, you know. They'll lock you up, for God's sake. They'll put you in a straightjacket.

Anna   Why, Silyan?

Pero   We were having an important meeting, discussing principles. Things have tightened up. No time for playing games. And then old Silyan here gets up. Shocks everyone. Holds out this heart on his hand. Can you imagine the reaction? Everyone immediately thought it was some kind of subversive act. An insult to the patriotic feelings of those present.

Anna   Why, Silyan?

Pero   *Why*, of course. That's what *we* asked him. He started blathering. Something about stars, bodies, erections. How he doesn't believe he's alive. A breakdown, metal fatigue, general overhaul. How there are no marks left. I remember that bit. How terrible it is that when you make love there are no marks left. And how in olden days the man would slit the woman open with a knife at the really passionate moment and take out her heart, and then kill himself with the same knife.

Anna   Wonderful.

Pero   She thinks that's wonderful.

Anna   And?

Pero   And now it's being misinterpreted in certain quarters. I know Silyan, but the others don't. I can't go and explain to each one in person. And bring discredit on myself, too.

Anna   And?

Pero   And he's been suspended. I chaired the commission. I had no choice. We are all masters of our own fate.

Silyan   The animals were roaring.

Pero   What?

Silyan   In the zoo. The animals were roaring. It's a danger signal.

Pero (*To* Anna)   Listen to him.

Silyan   I wanted to comb my hair yesterday.

Pero   Yes?

Silyan   I went into the bathroom.

Pero   Yes?

Silyan   And then I see the comb's got no teeth.

Pero   How d'you mean?

Silyan   No space between the teeth. Just one solid piece of useless tortoiseshell.

Pero   Plastic. They don't make combs out of tortoiseshell any more. It's all plastic.

Silyan   Combs don't comb anymore. Knives don't cut. Wheels don't turn. Things refusing to work.

Pero   You should go somewhere for a rest.

Silyan   All we need now is for gravity to stop operating.

Pero Somewhere with lots of fresh air. The mountains, for instance. You're obsessed with trivialities, my dear Silyan. You're married, you've got two kids, it's all over. Stars, bodies, erections! Flick it down with your thumb and forefinger. Deaden it.

Silyan What d'you want me to think about, then?

Pero Productive forces. Relations of production. There are more important things than your individual destiny. Our individuality is a tiny drop in the great sea of the universal. There is a real world of production out there. The world of history. With one move you can be eliminated.

Silyan Me?

Pero You.

Silyan What about you lot?

Pero I'm engaged in a selfless struggle to avoid that eventuality. While you're out fornicating, I'm here to ensure you can do that in peace, security and plenty. You think things are in chaos, but I can assure you there is still order.

Anna Depending on your point of view.

Pero You can mock, but it's true. Incredible, but true. You ought to curb your desires a bit. You don't think there're things *I* long for? You don't think I feel like going out and roving around every night? I know how to control myself. I say to myself, stay at home, Pero. Get ready for the meeting tomorrow. Write something in your diary. Read. Listen to a symphony. Go into public life, Silyan. Local council. Be useful. You'll stop feeling cut off from the world. You've taken your plug out and now you wonder why you haven't got any electricity. You're not really here, Silyan. Absent.

After all these years with your wife, it's not like it was at the beginning. It isn't. It can't be. It's perfectly normal. Natural. Anna and I are relatively happy as far as that's concerned. Aren't we, Anna? I say "relatively" so as not to tempt Providence. We're very happy. (*He kisses Anna on the cheek.*) I'll go and get some more wine from the cellar. (*To Silyan*) You think about what I've been saying.

Exit. Pause. **Silyan** *and* **Anna** *look at each other.* **Anna** *goes up to him, parts her legs and sits on his lap. She kisses him. They look at each other.*

Silyan   And are you relatively happy, my dear Anna?

Pause. Anna gets up and goes to the window.

Anna   D'you really like the wine?

Silyan   It's disgusting.

Anna   What d'you think you're doing ? Burning your bridges behind you.

Silyan   I work with an electric saw. One of those circular ones. Not much skill in it. You learn by just watching. I have the corpse lying there naked on the table in front of me. First I chop off the top of the skull. It falls on the floor-tiles and goes bonk, bonk, bonk! Then all the way down the backbone, to the waist, along the human vertical. The experts come along and do their bit. Then I come in at the end again. With a big needle and thread. Then I go and drink. I sit there boozing and wondering where the passion was in those bodies and where it went.

Anna   That morbid imagination of yours will be the death of you.

Silyan   I know.

Anna   My husband doesn't know anything. He hasn't the faintest idea what you and I were up to the night before the wedding.

Silyan   All cattle think they're sacred cows.

Anna   Where does he get all that self-satisfaction from? That terrible presence. You know what he wears under his shirt? A bulletproof jacket. He's afraid they might assassinate him.

Silyan   Poor man.

Anna   He gets me to punish him.

Silyan   How?

Anna   Golden showers, silver showers, whips, enemas, needles under his nails. I have to tie him to the bed with barbed wire.

Silyan   Why?

Anna   He thinks up all kinds of reasons. The last one was it's his fault Czechoslovakia's got no sea.

Silyan   It is, too! (*Pause.*) Who mentioned 'morbid'?

Enter **Pero** *with a bottle of wine in his hand.*

Pero   Have a look at this. Red as blood. (*Opening the bottle*) Where were we?

Silyan   Subjective and objective.

Pero   What about subjective and objective?

Silyan   I thought *you* were going to explain.

Pero   What is there left for me to explain? It's all been explained a long time ago by the classics of Marxism.

Anna   Which doesn't mean we can't go on drinking.

They all raise their glasses.

Scene Six

A hill above the town. **Magda** *and* **Silyan**. **Magda** *is dressed in white and looks clean and tidy, like a bride.*

Magda Why did you bring me up here?

Silyan It's high up. Above the excrement.

Magda Look at the town. White and beautiful. My husband 'd kill me if he could see me now.

Silyan What does he do?

Magda He's in the army. A captain.

Silyan Children?

Magda Two. Daddy's boys. How long is it since we last saw each other? Ten years? Fifteen? I hope you're not still in love with me.

Silyan It wasn't love...

Magda It was an illness. I remember what you said. Puppy love. You asked me if I wanted to be your girlfriend.

Silyan And you said "No, thank you".

Magda And after that you kept looking at me for years. Whenever I'd turn round, wherever I was, there you'd be, looking at me.

Silyan I loved you.

Magda Oh, yes.

Silyan I fell at your feet and you stuck your nose in the air.

Magda Life.

Silyan   You had any teeth out? Your breath smell? I thought your husband would have turned you into a mop. I expected to find you with folds around your middle. You still look good. Your perfection is unbearable. D'you want to run away with me?

Magda   Run away?

Silyan   I'll take all the money from work. This month's wages plus the extra for the pay rise dating back to January, plus the overtime, bonuses and special allowances for living away.

Magda   Where would we go?

Silyan   Bangkok. Malaysia, Indonesia.

Magda   What would we do there?

Silyan   What do we do here? Don't you walk around on tiptoe so as not to wake the captain? You wear a chastity belt.

Magda   You're boring me.

Silyan   There'll be no me there any more. No name, no past, no future. No tradition. No morality. I won't owe anybody anything. I won't expect anything. I'll just *be*.

Magda   Why did you ask me up here? What did you want to tell me?

Silyan   What I've been telling you.

Magda   If you didn't want me to understand anything, you succeeded.

Silyan (*Pointing upwards*)   Look!

Magda (*Looking up*)   Stars.

Silyan   There are no stars. Those are tiny openings in the black sky, through which some amazing light from the other side is seeping through. I look at my seed, through which some amazing force from the other side is seeping through. I want to be there. This isn't enough. This is nothing. This is all fixed. Imagine being there all the time! What are your orgasms like?

Magda   I beg your pardon?

Silyan   Your spasmic muscular contractions lasting from two to four seconds, three to fifteen rhythmic contractions of the muscles around the outer third at eighth of a second intervals, with contractions of the uterus and rectum. (*Pause.*) Don't shake your head. You know what I'm talking about.

Magda   I'd like to love you, Silyan, but I can't. I simply don't fancy you. Try to understand. To me you're ugly. I realise you have deep thoughts and feelings and they impress me, but I don't like you physically. It's just not on, you and me. If you've said what you wanted to say, then it was nice seeing you again.

Silyan (*Taking a toothbrush out of his pocket*)   This is all I have left of my past life. (*Throwing it away*) Now I have nothing. (*He opens up his coat. He is naked to the waist.*) Touch me.

Magda (*Embarrassed*)   Touch yourself.

Magda *walks away.* **Silyan** *looks after her. Then he looks at the sky. He lets out a long, loud shout, his face contorted, his mouth wide open and his eyes closed.*

Scene Seven

Silyan's *flat. A Christmas tree in the middle of the room.* **The Children** *are decorating it.* **The Father** *and* **Tsveta**.

The Father   What's it like outside?

Tsveta   Go and look out of the window.

The Father   I like it when someone describes it to me. I imagine it looking nicer than it really does.

Tsveta (*Goes to the window and looks out*)   The square. Cars. People shopping, waiting at traffic lights. Lots of colours, smiling faces. Getting ready for New Year's Eve. The trees are all decked out. The shop windows are all lit up. Christmas decorations. Stars made of neon lights. Christmas trees. Mothers and fathers and children on sledges. Red cheeks, scarves, warm gloves. High boots leaving prints in the fresh snow. Like a Christmas card.

The Father   Can you see Silyan anywhere?

Tsveta   No.

The Father   Not hurrying along with his arms full of presents? Not hurrying home to us?

Tsveta   No.

The Father   He'll come, wherever he is. Before I've finished this sentence, there he'll be, bursting through the door. Talk of the devil. He'll come. He's nearly here. Here he comes.

The Children *suddenly turn to look behind them, as if something had happened.*

Scene Eight

A hotel room. **Silyan** *is lying on the bed in a deep sleep. There is a long, hard knocking on the door.* **Silyan** *wakes up. He is puzzled about where he is. He gets up and sleepily opens the door.* **The Mother** *is standing there, dressed in a grey cloak.*

Silyan Mother.

The Mother Silyan.

Silyan What're you doing here?

The Mother What about you?

Silyan Who told you I was here? Come in.

The Mother (*Entering*) How long have you been in this hotel?

Silyan I fell asleep. Good thing you woke me up. Who knows how long I've been asleep. I've been terribly tired lately.

The Mother It's stuffy in here. (*She opens the window. It is night time.*) You've left home. (*Looking at the bottles on the bedside table*) What are these bottles?

Silyan Oh, nothing.

The Mother (*Opening a chemist's shop bottle and sniffing at it*) What's this?

Silyan Nothing. Take your coat off.

The Mother What've you been doing with this?

Silyan Why've you come?

The Mother To give you a good talking to.

Silyan Why?

The Mother [41]O Silyan, my boy, my own dear heart! Leave the life of idleness you're leading. Leave those bad companions – they're not home-loving lads. They're deceiving you, my boy. They want to have you earning money in a desert and becoming a poor man like them. Don't listen to them, my boy, pay no mind to them and their ways. Listen to me, my boy, do as I say, else a curse will fall on you on account of us, Silyan. Boys and girls who pay no heed to their fathers and mothers are sorely punished by the Lord, believe you me. Let me tell you a tale, my son, of Seevey and Chooley. You've seen them and heard them in the fields, those two birds, perching in the blackthorn and the haw and chirruping. One of them sings "seevey, seevey" and the other one "chooley, chooley". Now I've heard tell, son, that those two birds were once upon a time one man. He was a bad 'un. Running wild. He paid no mind to his father or his mother and they got all riled up, both of them, and they cursed him roundly many a time. And it came about that the Devil, Lord preserve us, he heard them in an evil hour, my boy, when his mother was cursing him like this: "My son, my son. May you turn into two birds and fly out of this house of ours and go into the fields and sit among the thornbushes and look for one another and never be able to find each other. So may we see the back of all the troubles you've given us." And, in truth, Silyan, he did turn into two birds and they flew into the

---

41 Translator's note: The following text is adapted from part of a Macedonian folk tale called *Silyan The Stork*. The original written version is in an archaic dialect. This translation only hints at this, but could be adapted as required to reflect the traditional form of story-telling in a given culture.

fields to live in the thornbushes and look for one another, day in and day out, and never be able to find each other, nor see each other neither. And so it was, God's truth, my child. You may not believe it, but I surely do, for it was told me by my grandfather and great-grandfather, too.

Silyan How long is it since I last saw you?

The Mother Don't you know?

Silyan You died.

The Mother Yes.

Silyan I cut you up. Your mouth was open, your face all contorted.

The Mother Yes.

Silyan From joy or pain? (*Pause.*) It was as if I'd brought you into the world. (*Pause.*) We buried you.

The Mother Yes.

Silyan So how come you're here now?

The Mother That's what I wanted to ask *you*.

Silyan What?

The Mother How come *you're* here now? You're the one who came, Silyan, not me. You're invisible.

Silyan Invisible?

The Mother There's no you any more. You're lost. You've come unpeeled like an onion.

Silyan And now what?

The Mother You've brought yourself into the world on your own. Good luck to you.

Silyan   What day is it today?

The Mother   In a few hours it'll be the New Year.

Silyan   New Year? Everybody's celebrating?

The Mother   Nobody's celebrating.

Silyan   Why not?

The Mother   Let's go.

Silyan   Why is nobody celebrating?

The Mother   Everything's changed. Nothing's like it was. (*Going up to the window*) Let's go.

Silyan   Through the window?

The Mother   You can't fall. There's no you any more.

They fly out into the darkness.

From Scene Nine of *The Black Hole* in the 1988 production at The Macedonian National Theatre in Skopje, directed by Paolo Magelli

From *The Black Hole* in the 1988 production at The National Theatre in Bitola directed by Branko Brezovec

PART TWO

Scene Nine

A cold, empty, dirty room. **Svetlé** *and* **Anna** *are lying naked in bed, covered with ragged, patched winter coats. They are wearing fingerless gloves. Enter* **Silyan**. *In all the scenes in* Part Two *his entrances can be through walls, windows, or down chimneys. He floats a few inches above the ground. Or squats on the ceiling. He looks at* **Anna** *and* **Svetlé**. *They can neither see nor hear him. Pause.* **Svetlé** *offers* **Anna** *a cigarette. They light up and smoke.*

Svetlé (*Singing*)

> Love me not, my dear,
> Don't lose your heart,
> For I come from far away, my dear,
> Tomorrow I'll depart
> For foreign lands, my dear,
> For foreign parts.

Pause.

Anna   D'you always shout out like that? (*Pause.*) I've never heard anyone make such a noise. I thought you'd died.

Svetlé   I *did* die.

Anna   You must really get off on it. You're young. I used to shout out like that at your age. I live in a big flat. My husband doesn't make a sound. He's dead inside. They arrested him the first day of the Occupation. They tortured him with electric shocks. He came home like an empty shell. I watched you while you were shouting. I thought

77

you'd had a heart attack. You looked like an animal. A wild animal. Your mouth all twisted. Your face all distorted. Like you were in terrible pain. Like you were having a tooth out.

Svetlé   Show me what I looked like.

Anna   *Opens her mouth, contorts her face and closes her eyes.*

Svetlé   I watched myself in the mirror once. But I missed the vital moment. When the best part came, I had to shut my eyes.

Anna   You went cross-eyed first, and then you shut them.

Svetlé   That's when they look inside.

Anna   I'm afraid to let go. I think I might come apart. Burst like a pumpkin.

Svetlé   Don't hold it back. It comes from God.

She touches her.

Anna   What is it?

Svetlé   You have a body. (*Pause.*) So have I. (*Pause.*) Heavenly bodies. For carving up. How do you feel when you come?

Anna   I don't know. Like warmth, like some force flowing up through me from my toes. Something like that. I haven't really thought about it.

Svetlé   Well, think now.

Anna   That's all you think about.

Svetlé   It's all that's left.

Silyan   Anna!

Svetlé   Ssssshhhhh !

Anna   What's the matter?

Svetlé   Hear that?

Anna   What?

Svetlé   Thought I heard something. I've been hearing voices lately.

Silyan   It's me. Silyan.

Anna   What kind of voices?

Svetlé   Human ones. Like an echo. Like something that was said once before and now comes back again.

Anna   Stop trying to scare me.

Svetlé   It's beautiful.

Anna   It's terrifying.

Svetlé   That's why it's beautiful. We're huddling together here. Of all the billions of people in the world, just you and me.

Silyan   What's going on?

Anna   If only there was some hot water so we could have a bath. And electricity so we could make ourselves a cup of coffee.

Svetlé   D'you often walk by the rubbish dump?

Anna   It's safe there. That's where we hid when the floods came.

Svetlé   Doesn't the rubbish stink?

Anna   It stinks all right. I watch it steaming.

Svetlé   D'you want to be my girlfriend?

Anna Aren't you married?

Svetlé They put my husband on a spike down by the bridge. We can go on dates – fixed time and place, stroll round the rubbish dump, listen to the ravens. (*Pause.*)

Silyan It's got dark. The buses and the workers have gone home. The misery has begun, known in the parlance as our sleeping hours. There's nothing. Just a blur. Like the slime left by a snail.

Anna I've got to go.

Svetlé Stay 'till morning.

Anna My husband'll kill me. He thinks I'm queueing for rations by the barracks. You scare me when you look at me like that. You're scary, you know.

Svetlé Won't I be seeing you again?

Anna No.

Svetlé What's your name?

Anna What's yours?

Scene Ten

Silyan *in* **Sania***'s flat. An army bed instead of the comfortable sofa. A bowl on the floor catching drips from the ceiling.* **Sania***'s kimono is dirty and creased and her black stockings are full of holes.*

Sania Where've you been?

Silyan You can see me.

Sania (*Not seeing or hearing him at all*) At work. 'Till this hour? You said you'd come for dinner. I opened some caviar. What were you doing at work so late?

Silyan You talking to yourself?

Sania Jealous? Yes. How beautifully contrived this all is. You fly by night, like a bat. You read the papers? I like to know what's going on. Oh, do *please* tell me what's going on! The Titanic's going down. You need papers to know that? There. No more foreign affairs, home affairs, culture, sport, or weather forecasts. Nothing. Just you and me.

Silyan Got any whisky?

Sania Got any whisky? You finished it this morning. Want some coffee, tea?

Silyan Yes.

Sania (*Suddenly turns to look behind her. She looks in Silyan's direction.*) What's the matter? I thought there was someone behind me. Someone? Or something. Something? Someone or something alive.

Silyan You see. You didn't believe me.

Sania   Nonsense, Sania. You're too tense. Overdoing things. Imagining things. It's not really like that. You're always so negative. Be realistic. Be realistic.

Silyan   Be realistic.

Sania (*Lifting her kimono*)   I'm wearing what you asked. Chinese silk, French underwear, Balkan breast and leg. Take me. This is a brothel.

Silyan   What's the next item on the agenda?

Sania   We vanish. Cease to exist. This sofa, this room, this town, this language we speak, the square, the people, their habits and customs, all the files, newspapers, dishes and drinks. All swept away. Vanished. Into thin air.

Silyan   You taking those pills I gave you? I'll make you some mint tea. There's an explanation for all this. The mid-life crisis. They've done research on it. You can't go on wearing those rags. Come with me. Get the hell out of this place.

*He tries to reach **Sania**, but doesn't manage to. He holds out his hand towards her. **Sania** turns round suddenly and goes to the window. She draws the curtains and looks out into the darkness.*

Sania   What's the matter? Look! What? Night. Silyan! Ssssshhhhh.

She masturbates and cries.

Scene Eleven

Pero *and* **Magda** *on a hill.* **Pero** *is wearing a creased tail-coat. His hair is in a mess and he looks haggard, aggressive and dangerous.* **Magda** *is wearing black.* **Silyan** *listens to them from the side or is above them.*

Pero   Why did you bring me up here?

Magda   It's high up. Above the excrement.

Pero   Look at the town. Black and beautiful. It burned for three days. The patrols 'll kill us if they see us.

Magda   What's your wife like?

Pero   We couldn't have any children.

Magda   Mine died.

Pero   How long is it since we last saw each other? Ten years? Fifteen? I hope you're not still in love with me.

Magda   It wasn't love...

Pero   It was an illness. I remember what you said. Puppy love. You asked me if I wanted to be your boyfriend.

Magda   And you said "No, thank you".

Pero   And after that you kept looking at me for years. Whenever I'd turn round, wherever I was, there you'd be, looking at me.

Magda   I loved you.

Pero   Oh, yes.

Magda   I fell at your feet and you stuck your nose in the air.

Silyan Life.

Magda Sorry? Did you say something?

Pero Me? I thought you did.

Magda My teeth have fallen out. My breath smells. My husband turned me into a mop. I've got folds around my middle. I used to walk around on tiptoe so as not to wake him. He died in the battle near the nuclear power station. From a poisoned arrow. D'you want to run away with me? I've got money. We can forge the documents.

Pero Where would we go ?

Magd Bangkok. Malaysia, Indonesia.

Pero The borders are closed. We can't run away. Bangkok's in Thailand.

Magda I want there to be no me any more.

Pero Why did you ask me up here? What did you want to tell me? It's death to leave the shelter of four walls. Did you feel that? Another tremor. Constant earthquakes.

Magda (*Pointing in Silyan's direction*) Look!

Pero What?

Magda Those openings through which some amazing light from the other side is coming through. Imagine what it's like on the other side! I want to be there!

Pero What are you on about?

Magda This isn't enough. This is nothing. This is all fixed. I want to be there.

Pero Who sent you after me? You think I'm stupid. You

84

think I don't know who you work for. Wasn't it enough what you did to me? Look at me!

Magda (*Opens her coat. She is naked to the waist.*)   Touch me. I'm clean. I wear a chastity belt.

Pero (*Embarrassed*)   Touch yourself.

Pero *walks away.* **Magda** *looks after him.*

Silyan   We want a name, a past, a future. Some kind of tradition and morality. We want to owe somebody something. We want to expect something. We want to be. Who's going to pay us special allowances for living away?

Magda *contorts her face, opens her mouth, shuts her eyes and lets out a long, loud shout.*

Scene Twelve

*The bedroom in **Silyan's** flat. **Tsveta** in a nightdress. **Makso** is getting undressed. **Silyan** is watching them.*

Makso Take that off.

Tsveta I'm ashamed.

Makso Don't be. Look at it. (*Looking into his underpants*) Like a python down there.

Tsveta I dreamt Silyan came back.

Silyan Tsveta!

Tsveta He's calling me.

Makso God bless his soul.

Tsveta You think he's dead?

Makso If he were alive, he'd have come back by now.

Tsveta How many years is it now?

Silyan What d'you mean, years, Tsveta? It's been no time at all.

Tsveta If he'd been here, things would've been different. Wartime.

Silyan What war? Who are we at war with?

Makso Don't you worry. I'm here. Take that off.

Tsveta I can't.

Makso Look at it. One kiss is all it takes.

Tsveta Does your wife know you're here?

Makso She knows all right. She's listening with one ear glued to the wall.

Tsveta And Silyan's here, too.

Makso If he's here, let him watch this. (*Going up to her*) I want to do it here. On your bed.

Tsveta No.

Makso Tsveta, I've been burying corpses all day. Have a heart.

Tsveta Don't touch me.

Makso But you take tins from me, don't you? Flour, oil – all from me. You live on my stocks. You'd starve to death if it wasn't for me. I'll smear pitch all over you and set you on fire. (*He tears her nightdress and slaps her. He kisses her neck.* **Tsveta** *throws him off and spits at him. Pause.*) Bitch. You'll come crawling to me.

Exit. Pause.

Silyan You're suffering. Who isn't suffering? We'll live a normal human life. We'll work, struggle to make ends meet, freeze things for the winter. We'll have birthday parties and celebrate national holidays. Sunday mornings I'll wash the car and you'll make the lunch. Now I'm another man, a new man.

Tsveta Silyan! Are you here, or are you there? Either come or go. I want to know where I stand!

Scene Thirteen

Pero *and* **Anna's** *flat.* **Pero** *is wearing a dressing gown loose around him, under which his bulletproof vest is visible. He is barefoot and his hair is all over the place.* **Silyan** *is sitting in the place he sat in in Scene Five.*

Silyan   I like your vest. I haven't seen it before. We are all masters of our fate. (*Pause.*) You know what I did when you suspended me? I went to your office. There was nobody there. I phoned Bangkok. On the automatic number that tells you what's on at the cinema. Goes on forever. Once it finishes, it starts at the beginning again. I left the phone off the hook. From Friday afternoon to Monday morning. A sixty-hour telephone call to Bangkok. (*Pause.* **Pero** *is drinking wine.*) Your wine is disgusting. An unusually disgusting wine.

Pero   Who's here?

Pause. **Pero** *looks about. Silence.*

Silyan   Even you've started believing in the supernatural.

Pero   Who is it?

He gets up and goes to the door. He listens. Pause. The door opens and **Anna** *comes in.*

Pero   Where's the food?

Anna   It ran out when I got to the head of the queue.

Pero   Where've you been all this time?

Anna   Queueing for rations.

Pero   Leaving me here alone.

Silyan You're not alone. No one's alone. We're never alone.

Pero Whenever you go out, the room fills up with ghosts.

Silyan An unfortunate set of circumstances. I've got nothing against you personally.

Anna I passed the zoo. The animals were roaring.

Pero It's a danger signal.

Anna That's what Silyan said. That night.

Pero Silyan who? What night?

Anna (*Pointing to the place where the invisible* **Silyan** *is sitting*) He was sitting there.

Pero I don't know anything. I don't remember anything.

Anna You told him our individuality was only a tiny drop in the great sea of the universal. That there is a real world of history.

Pero That's enough!

Anna And that with one move we can be eliminated. You're a prophet. It all happened down to the smallest detail.

Pero Stop it!

Anna Control yourself, Pero. Get ready for the meeting tomorrow. Write something in your diary. Read. Listen to a symphony. You've taken your plug out and now you wonder why you haven't got any electricity. You're not really here, Pero. Absent. (**Pero** *leaves the room.*) Going for some wine? It's turned into vinegar. (*Pause. She looks ahead.*) Are you relatively happy, my dear Silyan? Where are you now? Did you find the dark at the end of the tunnel? If only you could hear me.

89

Silyan   I'm listening.

Anna   If only you could see.

Silyan   I'm watching.

Anna   I know you're listening and watching. You knew it all, even then.

Silyan   What comfort is that now?

Enter **Pero** *with a knife in his hand.*

Pero   Who were you talking to?

Anna   Myself.

Pero   Talking to yourself behind my back?

Anna   What's the matter with you?

Pero   It's terrible that when you make love there are no marks left. (*Going up to her*) Explain!

Anna   What?

Pero   Everything!

Anna   Pero!

Pero   Explain everything. Subjective and objective. Everything!

He lunges at her with the knife.

Anna   Pero! You're frightening me!

Pero   Which doesn't mean we can't butcher you.

Silyan   No-o-o-o!

Pero *turns around in fright and looks in* **Silyan**'s *direction.*

Pero   Who is it?

The knife falls from his hand. He sinks to his knees and starts shaking. **Anna** *puts her arms around him.*

Scene Fourteen

The street. **Makso** *is walking with* **Silyan** *beside him. Suddenly shooting breaks out.* **Makso** *tries to find shelter. He has been hit. He looks down at his body.*

Makso   Curfew. Don't shoot, brothers! Brothers!

Silyan   Makso!

Makso   Help!

Silyan (*Trying to reach Makso but not managing to*)   Who was shooting?

Makso   Don't leave me. (*He takes money out of his pocket and scatters it about.*) I'll give you guilders, florins, marks, dollars. Don't leave me. Just one injection 'll save me. One pill. Is anyone listening? I can't die. This is my street. My territory.

He falls to his knees and begins to crawl on all fours. He goes towards **Silyan**. **Silyan** *retreats.*

Silyan   Now's the moment. We'll get a loan. Steal. Borrow. We can't reach our full potential here. We'll go to Germany. Spread out. We'll hunt kangaroos. Australia. Toronto, Quebec, Montreal. We'll have a good journey. Where're we going? Wherever it is we're going.

Scene Fifteen

Silyan's *flat. A withered Christmas tree stands in the middle of the room. The needles have fallen off and only the bare branches remain.* **The Father** *is blind. He is facing the television, which is now only a frame and a cathode tube with a hole in it.* **Tsveta** *is looking out of the window.* **The children** *are asleep.* **Silyan** *is above them and watches them.*

Silyan   Is this exile or asylum? Past or future? Reward or punishment? Have *I* been planted on the here and now, or *the here and now* have been planted on me? Finery. Frippery. Frumpery. Trumpery. Chivalry. Gallantry. Pleasantry. Dysentery.

The Children *wake up with a start and look in front of them.* **Tsveta** *looks at them, then goes and settles them down again.*

The Father   What's the matter?

Tsveta   They woke up with a start. They must've been dreaming about something.

The Father   Their father. Now I'll never see him again.

Tsveta   Don't think about it.

The Father   Of all the drivers around, why did they have to pick on me?

Tsveta   Fate.

The Father   I put the tow-rope around the unknown hero's neck.

Tsveta   One statue less.

The Father   I built it. That's where I evoked memories.

Where they gave me flowers. I look out through the window and there's the ex-unknown hero, his gun in his hand, being dragged through the dust. He was looking at me.

Tsveta It just seemed like that.

The Father He was looking me straight in the eye. He made me go blind.

Tsveta Somebody else finished the job for you. Actors will give performances in front of a new statue. Actresses will stroll about with the officers. Boys and girls will set doves free into the air.

The Father (*Going up to the window*) What's it like outside?

Tsveta (*Looking out of the window*) The square. Empty. A few bodies hanging from the lamp-posts. The shop windows are broken, the shops looted and dark. There's a group of casualties going by. Escorted by people in uniform on ponies. They look like the barbarians. The snow's dirty. They're pulling sledges covered with tarpaulins, with blood coming through. New Year.

The Father Read me my newspaper cutting.

Tsveta The children tore it up.

The Father What are my chances?

Tsveta You've lost a lot of blood. You've got a rare blood group.

The Father Silyan's the same group.

Tsveta Where's Silyan now?

The Father Where's Silyan now?

Silyan Where's Silyan now?

The Father   See whether he's coming.

Tsveta   He'll come, wherever he is. Before I've finished this sentence, there he'll be, bursting through the door. Talk of the devil. He'll come. He's nearly here. Here he comes.

Long pause. Silence.

Silyan   [42]Oh mother of mine! Oh father of mine! Oh my dear little boy and my dear little girl! And you, my dear, dear wife... Will you see me in your dreams in this wasteland, with not so much as a bird singing? Oh, that I had been cut down in my prime, Mother, that I had been buried in the churchyard, and you, Mother, had come to my grave, to light a candle for me and give alms for the dead! But I am to die here, Mother, in this wasteland. Eagles and crows shall feast on my flesh. Oh, why was your curse so dire that I am come to this? Is this bare land the underworld? Ah, woe is me, for I shall see no deliverance, no homecoming. I pray to God to take me back there once again. Oh God, grant my wish and I swear to serve Our Lady three years in the monastery. I beseech Thee, do not take my soul 'ere I become a man again!

The window suddenly flies open. Some amazing light comes through from the other side. **The Children** *wake up with a start. Everybody on stage suddenly turns to look behind them at the light. A tense silence.*

C U R T A I N

---

42 Translator's note: The following text, like that spoken by the Mother on page 30, is adapted from part of a Macedonian folk tale called *Silyan The Stork*. The original written version is in an archaic dialect. This translation only hints at this, but could be adapted as required to reflect the traditional form of story-telling in a given culture.

SHADES OF BABEL

a play by Goran Stefanovski (1989) Translated from the
Macedonian by Patricia Marsh Stefanovska

For Pat

Poster for the 1990 production of *Shades of Babel*
by the Skopje Dramski Teatar, directed by Slobodan Unkovski

Characters

Rina, 37

Damian, 33

Todor, 50

Blaga, 40, his wife, Damian's sister

Marta, 17, their daughter

Petar, 60, Damian and Blaga's father

Viktor, 55

Nevena, 55, retired actress

Marko, 40, Todor's aide

Scene One

A sunny autumn morning. Tables outside a small café. **Damian** *is sitting at a table playing chess with himself, using a chess manual. Enter* **Rina***, smartly dressed, wearing dark glasses, carrying a suitcase. She sits down at another table and takes off her glasses.*

Rina   Good morning. (**Damian** *turns round and stares at her. Pause.*) Coffee, please.

Damian   I don't work here.

Rina   Who does?

Damian   It's closed. (*Pause.*) There's a restaurant at the end of the street. (*Pause.*)

Rina   Thank you. (*She puts on her dark glasses and gets up. Pause.*) What about you? (**Damian** *looks at her uncomprehendingly. Pause.*) What're *you* doing here?

Damian   The café belongs to my sister.

Rina   So why don't *you* make some? (*Pause. They look at each other.*) Coffee.

Damian   I don't know how… (*Pause.*) What it'll be like. I can't promise anything.

Rina   I'll risk it. (*She sits down again. Pause. They look at each other.*)

Damian   Turkish. (*Pause.*) There's only Turkish coffee.

Rina   Great.

Damian *looks at* **Rina***. Pause. He goes inside the café.* **Rina**

lights a cigarette and smokes. **Damian** *comes back with a tablecloth and puts it on* **Rina**'s *table.*

Rina   Nice day. High sky.

Damian   You came in on the nine o'clock train?

Rina   No secrets here, then.

Damian   Small town. Nothing much happening.

Rina   Idyllic.

Damian   Cut off from everything. Nothing worth seeing.

Rina   Not even the church?

Damian   Except the church.

Rina   Is it open?

Damian   The caretaker lives nearby. He'll open it up for you. If he's still alive. The path up there is all overgrown. Never used.

Rina   Clear it.

Damian   There isn't the money.

Rina   You wouldn't make much of a tourist guide. (*Pause.*) You said "only" Turkish. Why the "only"?

Damian   No cappuccino, filter, that kind of thing.

Rina   Do I look fussy? (*Pause.*) I am.

Damian   I was right, then.

Rina   No. (*Pause.*) When I can choose between cappuccino, filter, that kind of thing, and Turkish coffee, I always choose Turkish. (*Pause.*)

Damian How long are you staying? (*Pause. They look at each other.*) There's nowhere to stay here. The hotel's a ruin.

Damian *goes to get the coffee.* **Rina** *gets up and goes to his table. She looks at the chessboard and at the open book beside it.* **Damian** *appears with the coffee.*

Rina Who's winning?

Damian The best man.

Rina Which one is he?

Damian Him. I'm both the winner and the loser. I'm learning openings.

Rina The Queen's gambit. Used at the world championship match in Buenos Aires, 1927. (*Pause.* **Damian** *looks at her in amazement.*) Alekhine versus Capablanca. (*She looks at* **Damian** *and laughs in a merry childlike way. She takes the coffee from his hand.*)

Scene Two

The spacious living room of an old house. **Petar**, *a dishevelled invalid, with a book in his hand, slowly makes his way from the bathroom, through the living room, to his bedroom. He closes the door behind him. Pause. The front door opens. Enter* **Damian** *and* **Rina**. **Damian** *is carrying her suitcase.*

Damian This is where I live. (*Pause.*) Where've you come from?

Rina England.

Damian Ah.

Rina Been there?

Damian I hitchhiked across Europe once. I spent three days in London. Slept in a karate hall. Gym during the day and dormitory for passing travellers at night. Near Charing Cross. Long time ago, it was. Seems like it happened to someone else. I never go anywhere now.

Rina A long time ago, I used to live here. In the old part of town.

Damian It's not there any more.

Rina I left when they started knocking it down. I ran off with a foreigner.

Damian That was brave of you.

Rina It's not brave to do what you must. It was brave of me to come back. (*Pause.*) To the scene of the crime.

Damian Welcome home.

Rina Thank you.

Damian   Where's all your luggage?

Rina *points to her head.*

Damian   Want a game?

Rina   Long time since I've played.

Damian *sets up the chessboard. They begin to play.* **Rina** *moves her pieces quickly, hardly looking at them.* **Damian** *is perplexedly trying to follow her moves.*

Damian   What happened to him? (*Pause. They look at each other.*) The foreigner?

Rina   We got divorced. (*Pause.*) We lived in various places. Seven years in Brazil.

Damian   What were you doing in Brazil?

Rina   You want my secret straightaway. (*Pause.*) We were in the jungle. In a gold-diggers' camp.

Damian   Where?

Rina   Those places don't have names. The nearest town was Boa Vista. Two hours away on a Cessna Skymaster. You pay for everything there in gold. Beer – half a gram. Gun – 17 grams. Boots – 20 grams. (*Pause.*) How d'you think you dig for gold? You think you find it in gold bars? First you wet the ground. Then you pump up the mud. The gold dust collects on the felt in the chute. The Indian women go about with bare breasts. (*Referring to the chess board*) Check. The men hunt with spears and blow-pipes.

Damian   What d'you do, otherwise? (*Pause. They look at each other.*) For a job?

Rina Checkmate. (*Pause.* **Damian** *looks at the chessboard in bewilderment.*) Otherwise, I'm an actor.

Damian You're the first woman I've met who can really play chess.

Rina You're not the first man I've met who really underestimates women.

(*The door to* **Petar***'s room opens.* **Petar** *appears at the door.*)

Damian This is my father. Rina. A friend of mine.

Rina Pleased to meet you.

Damian My father can't speak.

Petar *and* **Rina** *look at each other.*

Scene Three

The café. **Blaga**, *dressed in a fur coat and wearing a lot of jewellery, is counting money.* **Damian** *is playing chess.*

Blaga If the hotel isn't good enough for her, she can go to some other town.

Damian I'm not a child. (*Pause.* **Blaga** *looks at him.*) I've got the right to invite anybody I like into my own home. She wouldn't have it at first.

Blaga But she would in the end. (*Pause.*) Half of that house is mine.

Damian She's sleeping in my half.

Blaga So? Who is she?

Damian She's been living abroad.

Blaga Where abroad? (*Pause.*) How was last night?

Damian We played chess.

Blaga Did you let her have it?

Damian I managed one stalemate.

Blaga Did you get fixed up? (*Pause.*) For a re-match? (*Pause.*) Why would she come back? Nobody comes back to this place.

Damian You smell like a perfume counter.

Blaga And you stink of sweat. You've been wearing the same shirt for years. I can't remember you in any other one. Have you *got* another one at all? Everything's changed, my dear Damian. Nothing is like it was.

Damian How was it?

Blaga Thank your lucky stars you went off your rocker when you were still young. You don't even know which month it is.

Damian October.

Blaga Day?

Damian The forty-second.

Blaga How's Dad?

Damian Come and see.

Blaga Marta's driving me crazy. She's asking me for money to go to Tibet. Somebody's stuffed her head full of ideas. That's the way it goes. First the head, then the stomach. Talk to her. She trusts you. I'm having a sauna built at home. We agreed on the price, now they want to change it. What're you all hunched up for? Hiding? (*Pause.*) He goes and falls for some tart of a woman. Don't you go falling in love, y'hear?

Pause. She throws him a wad of banknotes and sends his chessmen flying. She goes out. **Damian** *puts the money in his pocket.*

Scene Four

Marko *and* **Todor** *in a huge underground concrete space. A pile of shiny yellow metal barrels in the centre.* **Marko** *opens a bottle of champagne.*

Todor/Marko: (*Singing to the tune of the refrain of The Internationale*)

> "Oh arouse now, arouse now,
> And hold yourself erect,
> For Brigitte Bardot waits for you
> In her suspender belt."

Todor Get these barrels cemented up straightaway. Who knows what's in them?

Marko Who cares! They don't want them and we don't mind them. (*Raising his champagne glass*) Cheers.

Todor We've turned into an international rubbish dump.

Marko The dregs always fall to the bottom.

Todor Multinational shady dealings. A Swiss firm representing a Hong Kong firm, representing a Japanese firm.

Marko We take the barrels, they solve our problem with the car park. This national calamity. This armour-plated, seven-storey monster. We move the Balkans into Europe. We rise from the ashes like a phoenix. We turn the car park into a fun palace with neon-lit bars, boutiques, hamburger joints, slot machines, robots, computers. Snooker tables. A casino. Bread and technology. Video. Stereo. Money, money! Whole families coming to pray to the new God on Sunday mornings.

Todor All we need now is the electricity.

Marko We'll ask for a power station as part of the contract.

Todor You don't know the meaning of the word 'conscience', do you? (*Pause.*) That's a compliment.

Marko Thank you. Your daughter, Marta, was seen in the railway station buffet again after midnight in the company of Gypsies and drunks. There was a knife-fight. Marta watched and clapped.

Todor Who saw her?

Marko I did.

Todor Then say "I saw her", not "She was seen"!

Marko It's more official-sounding. Your wife, Madame Blaga, has made her regular food-money drop to her brother, Damian. The girl sleeping at Damian's is a returnee from abroad. Her name is Rina.

Todor Rina?

Marko Rina.

Todor Rina?

Marko Rina!

Scene Five

Todor *and* **Rina** *in* **Damian's** *house.*

Rina   What d' you want?

Todor   *I* ask the questions around here. What're you doing in this house?

Rina   I'm here quite by chance.

Todor   Sleeping in the room my wife grew up in?

Rina   There's a wedding photo of you on the wall. I turned it over.

Todor   Why've you come?

Rina   I've come back.

Todor   What d' you mean, "come back"?! This isn't your town any more. This is *my* town. I have a happy marriage. A seventeen-year-old daughter.

Rina   *I* was seventeen.

Todor   I hold public office, I have a whole host of responsibilities. I won't allow anyone to rock the boat. If you've come to blackmail me, I'll break your neck.

Rina (*She takes a newspaper cutting out of her handbag and hands it to* **Todor**.)

Todor   The multi-storey car park.

Rina   It was in the column called "Believe it or not!".

Todor   You vowed you'd come back some day. "To cut off that tiny thing between my legs". I haven't come here to negotiate – just to warn you. Put one foot wrong, and it's "bye, bye, baby". Isn't that what they say in your precious England?

Scene Six

Damian *and* **Rina** *in a restaurant. They have just had dinner.*
They are drinking some wine.

Rina I found my mother's grave. I told her everything.
I cried a little. I've prayed for her soul in all the churches
I've come across. She was the prompter in the theatre. She
helped the actors when they forgot their lines.

She pours him some more wine.

Damian I'll get drunk.

Rina That's the whole point of drinking. I was looking at
the Madonna with the Beard today. (**Damian** *looks at her*
uncomprehendingly.) In the church. The damaged fresco.
You know the one.

Damian No.

Rina Of course you do. It's world famous. It's in all
the books.

Damian They didn't teach us anything at school.

Rina The church is right here under your nose.

Damian I never had the time. I was globe-trotting.
Charing Cross.

Rina (*Pause.*) What did you study?

Damian Electronics.

Rina Got a job?

Damian I don't even bother looking for one.

Rina What d' you live on?

Damian I fix electronic scales. I make them steal 50 grams of whatever they weigh. The butchers used to hit the scale with their fingers – now they're in league with science.

Rina Why don't you get out, go abroad?

Damian Everybody asks me that. I had an offer to work in Canada. 50,000 dollars a year. A development firm.

Rina You hate this place. Why're you still here?

Damian I was born here.

Rina You don't have to die here.

Damian Makes no difference where I die.

Rina It does make a difference where you live.

Damian Where should I live?

Rina Somewhere where you feel good.

Damian Why should I feel good?

Rina Why should you feel bad? Or do you feel good when things are bad?

Damian I don't think about it. I'm only interested in chess.

Rina I've got no right to judge you. I know as much about why I came back as you do about why you don't leave. (*Pause.*) But other people *do* go. Something makes them. They don't waste time wondering what it is. (*Pause.*) This used to be a place of power.

Damian I hadn't noticed.

Rina Which has now become a place of powerlessness. (*Pause.*) Why?

Damian Ask me an easier one.

Rina What's two and two? (*She giggles merrily.*) I'm very improper. Everybody around here is dignified and serious.

Viktor *comes over to them. He looks unkempt. He has a briefcase under his arm and a wreath in his hands. He looks around him nervously and timidly.*

Viktor May I? (**Damian** *looks at him in amazement.* **Viktor** *sits down without waiting for an answer.*) Thank you.

Damian There's a table free over there.

Viktor It's cold. I'll have tea with rum. (*Pause.*) I drink nothing but tea with rum in autumn and winter. With lemon, if they've got any. Usually they haven't. I bring my own lemon and put it in their tea. I'm Viktor.

Rina Pleased to meet you. Rina.

Viktor "As you sow, so shall you reap." I know some facts to make your hair stand on end. It's the anniversary today. I always go to the cemetery. Never miss. I've got documents to show he was murdered.

Rina Who?

Viktor (*Opening his briefcase and taking some papers out*) These are photocopies – the originals are in a safe place. It was *our* side killed him. They got the order. They say he was trying to escape across the border. They shot him in the back. Now they honour his memory. Don't believe anything. It's all lies. The grave's empty. They threw his bones to the dogs. He knew Esperanto – he was a man of learning. Someone had a grudge against him, so that was it – a farce of a tribunal and bang! They kept it quiet for years, but now it's all coming out. The cesspit has been opened up.

Damian   What're you talking about?

Viktor   Blackie.

Damian   Blackie who?

Viktor   Our Blackie. An accident? There's no such thing. It's been shown that babies dream before they're born, in their mothers' wombs. What do they dream about, I ask you? What can unborn babies dream about? If not the past. I don't know what it's like in other places, but here the poor things must dream about looting, rape and slaughter.

Damian   I don't understand.

Viktor   No wonder. This place is cursed. All kinds of weird things build up here. One on top of another, another on top of yet another. And another and another. And then things are weird. Of course they're weird! You can have these (*Leaving the documents on the table*). I've got copies. I send them to various places. Reuter's, United Press International. Not to mention *our* lot. They don't print them. So it must be hot stuff! And then there's your Dad! What about *his* story?

Damian   What story?

Viktor   How should I know? We all have a story here. *He* must have one.

Viktor *gets up and leaves them.* **Rina** *and* **Damian** *watch him go*.

Damian   That's why I sit at home and play chess.

Rina   That's why it's not the answer.

She pours him some wine and laughs her merry childlike laugh.

Scene Seven

The church. **Damian** *is looking at the frescoes.* **Nevena** *comes up behind him. She is a timid, indecisive woman of 55.*

Nevena   You're looking at the Madonna.

Damian (*Turning, startled*)   With the Beard. It's a famous fresco. In all the books.

Nevena   My name's Nevena. I used to work in the theatre. You're young, you wouldn't remember me. They sent me to see you. (*Pause.*) There's been no word from my brother these ten years now. One evening he said he was going to buy cigarettes and he disappeared. I knew that kind of thing happened, but I never thought it'd happen to *me*. Once we heard he'd been seen in Trieste. Then that he'd drowned in the Bay of Salonica.

Damian   What can *I* do about it?

Nevena   We'll be eternally grateful. I've got a list. We decided it was best if we didn't all come, so they sent me. My next-door neighbours, good people, they've lost their dog. They've posted notices about it everywhere, but no luck so far. Next door to them there's a very sick man. The doctors have given up on him. He just lies there and can't seem to die. Perhaps you could see if there's a cure. And an end to all these high prices. We're being skinned alive.

Damian   Perhaps *who* could see?

Nevena   You and the girl. (*Pause.*) On the tower.

Damia   What tower?

Nevena   The multi-storey car park.

Damian   How are *we* supposed to help?

Nevena   You should know. They say she has the power of healing. The lame and the blind are getting together in the villages to ask her help. They've recognised her. She has the healing touch. Can foretell the future.

Damian   Somebody's been having you on.

Nevena   If you *can* help us, it'd be a sin not to.

Scene Eight

Night. The living-room in **Damian's** *house.* **Rina** *is grinding coffee by hand. Her hair is wet – she's just washed it.* **Damian** *comes in in his pyjamas.*

Damian   What time is it?

Rina   I had a shower. Did I wake you up?

Damian   I couldn't sleep.

Rina   Full moon. Want some coffee? I grind it by hand. My grandmother's grinder.

Damian   You carry it around with you?

Rina   Yes.

Damian   Isn't it heavy?

Rina   It is. (*Pause.*)

Damian   They're asking about you. I don't know what to tell them. They think you have supernatural powers.

Rina (*Giggling*)   Poor things if they look to me as their saviour! (*Pause.*) What did your father do?

Damian   Worked in the local council offices.

Rina   What's the matter with him?

Damian   I don't know. (*Pause.*) Not exactly. Something with his brain. (*Pause.* **Rina** *looks at him.*) Some disease. A car crash.

Rina   I looked at the coffee grounds in your cup. Know what I saw?

Damian   I don't like people looking at my coffee grounds, or reading my palm, or interpreting my dreams, or telling me my horoscope. I like simple operations, precise results and clean slates.

Rina And to sleep at night. Only the gods can do that. (*Pause.*) No television? The window on the world?

Damian (*Pause.* **Damian** *looks at her.*) Good night. (*He turns to go. Pause. He comes back.*) There are too many pictures. I can't watch that fast. I haven't got a radio, either. I can't listen that fast. Arab laments, American commercials, the Kremlin clock, unknown languages – all mixed up together. In the space of a quarter of an hour they manage to squeeze in a bit of a symphony, the news, a few ballads, some household hints, commercials, a children's programme and more news. (*Pause.*)

Rina We *are* fragile, aren't we? What do you want?

Damian The rules of the game.

Rina You only get that in the theatre. (*Pause.*) But they've knocked it down. (*Pause.*) Isn't that terrible? Life is slow and stark. You don't know who I am. I don't know who you are. You make love with someone and the next day they pretend they don't know you. But in the theatre there is order, connection and logic. A move once played cannot be played again. Speech is full-blooded and precise. One person speaks, the others listen. There's a beginning, a middle and an end. This is the exposition. (*Pause. They look at each other.*) The introduction.

Damian To what?

Rina Our play. Which can't begin without a moment of tension at first. (*She kisses him, then laughs merrily. Pause.*)

What were you in your previous life? You were killed in a village inn. With a broken bottle. There's a tower in your coffee cup.

Damian I don't want to hear about it.

Rina Don't listen, then. A great cylindrical tower. Like a castle. The upper storeys are lost in the clouds. You can't see the top. There is scaffolding down below supporting the structure. Pulleys for taking up the stone, thousands of bricklayers and stone-cutters. A young man and woman are trying to find each other among the floors of the tower. She's wearing a black petticoat. He a sleeveless t-shirt. They look out in dismay. Is someone coming for them? (*Pause.*)

Damian Like the multi-storey car park.

Rina The car park?

Damian (*Pointing out the window*) That monster looming out of the darkness.

Rina It looks like a shell. A fossil.

Damian There are all kinds of tales about it. (*Pause. They look at each other.*) Nonsensical rubbish. Some woman left a bag there with a blunt razor-blade in it. When she found it, the blade was as sharp as new. Meat left there stayed fresh.

Rina Like the Egyptian pyramids. (*Pause.*) Teeming with life. (*Pause.*) Of the dead. And the unborn.

Damian Egypt?! Pyramids?! You mean poverty and misery. People consoling themselves with stupid fantasies. Poor devils.

Rina Why isn't the car park finished?

Damian I don't know.

Rina Yes, you do. (*Pause.*) You said "I don't know" as if you knew.

Damian Bad investment, inaccurate calculations, cheap cement, wrong iron. It's been going on for years. Nobody knows what's going on any more. Rumours, denials, new rumours. I don't take part in those rituals. I stand to one side. I learn the finer points of chess. I don't want to think about that absurdity.

Rina It thinks about you. (*Pause.*) Have you been up to the top?

Damian No.

Rina Why not?

Damian No wish to.

Rina Or too afraid?

Damian What's there to see up there?

Rina What's there to see up there? (*Pause.* **Rina** *looks at him. Paus*e.) D' you like me?

Damian I was with one girl for two years. Her name was Lena. We exchanged rings, but I couldn't go through with the engagement party. Now she has two kids and ignores me if we meet on the street. She hates me. Or still loves me. (*Pause.*) I knew who you were as soon as I saw you. I thought to myself, here she is, she's come. I like you being an actress. Actors are always changing costumes. They're forever new. (*Pause.*) This is so banal. I'm talking too much.

Pause. He kisses **Rina**. *They look at each other.* **Damian** *shakes his head. He puts his hands over his eyes.*

Scene Nine

Night. A floor on the unfinished multi-storey car park where work stopped long ago. The lights of the town can be seen below. A wind is blowing. **Damian** *is wearing a raincoat and scarf. He is looking out into the distance. Suddenly a man appears with long hair and a beard, cartridge belts across his chest. He is played by the same actor who plays* **Marko**, *but this is not at first obvious, if at all.* **Damian** *looks at him in dismay.*

Marko You've come. He'll be here soon. It's a two-hour walk from here to Viryani. We'll be there by sunset. Then it's only another half-hour to the border. The corpse is rotting, the worms are coming out. We crush each other like lice. Who would've believed it'd come to this? I'll get it over with and then get drunk. But not on that wine from last night. It split my head apart. Like I'd been drinking bile. I don't know who this man is. But then, who cares anyway?! We're all bloody under the skin.

Pause. The actor who plays **Petar** *appears. He is totally changed and wearing an old-fashioned travelling coat. He is young, well-groomed, and wearing a hat.* **Damian** *is completely dumbfounded.*

Petar Are you the escort?

Marko Yes. Me and him.

Petar (*Pause. He looks at* **Damian**.) Is it you?

Marko (*To* **Damian**) You know each other? (*Pause. To* **Petar**) You must have been mistaken.

Petar (*To* **Marko**) Let's go.

Marko First the money.

121

Petar   When we get there.

Marko   Before we start.

Petar   That wasn't the agreement.

Marko   I agree the agreement.

Petar *gives him the money.* **Marko** *counts it.*

Petar   How far is it to the border?

Marko   A couple of hours.

Petar . We'd better get a move on.

Marko   No need. (*Pause.*) I'm going to kill you. (*Pause. They look at each other.*) You betrayed us.

Petar   The traitors are the ones who sent you.

Marko   They're paying. (*Pause.*) I'm supposed to kill you over the border. But I'll kill you here, so we don't walk all that way for nothing. (*Pause.*)

Petar (*To* **Damian**)   You'll have to get by on your own now. (*Pause.*)

Marko (*He and* **Petar** *are looking at one another.*)   Run. I can't do it standing still. (*Pause.*) Run for it.

Petar   Where?

Marko   Nowhere. Just run.

He pushes **Petar**. **Petar** *looks at* **Damian**. *He tries to run away, but* **Marko** *is on him. He murders him.* **Marko** *turns towards* **Damian**, *slowly wiping his knife on his trousers. He goes.* **Damian** *stands aghast.*

Scene Ten

The living-room of **Damian's** *house.* **Marko** *is standing at the door.*

Marko Hello. Damian not here?

Rina No.

Marko Where is he?

Rina I don't know. (*They look at each other.*) Can I give him a message?

Marko (*They look at each other.*) I'll wait for him. (*He comes in.*)

Rina I don't know when he'll be back.

Marko I'm in no hurry.

Rina He's probably down at his sister's café. You could try there.

Marko I'll wait here. (*He sits down. Pause. They look at each other.*) Mind if I smoke? (*Pause. They look at each other. He takes out his cigarettes and offers her one.*) Would you like one?

Rina No. Thank you.

Marko You don't smoke?

Rina I've just put one out.

Marko Have another.

Rina No.

Marko Go on. (*Pause. They look at each other.*) Ashtray. (*Pause.*) There's no ashtray.

Rina *hands him an ashtray.*

Marko   I'm Marko. You're Rina. (*They look at each other.*) You're not bad-looking.

Rina   I've got to go. Try the café.

Marko   What for?

Rina   I'm going out.

Marko   That's all right. (*Pause.*) I'll look after the house. (*They look at each other. He takes out a revolver and puts it on the table.*) Beretta. (*Pause.*) The car park! (*Pause.*) What were you doing in the car park? (*Pause.*) How did you get into the basement?

Rina *gets up and fetches her handbag. She takes out a pistol and puts it on the table. She gets out a cigarette and lights it.*)

Rina   Browning.

Marko   My kind of woman. (*Pause. He puts his hand out.* **Rina** *pulls the pistol towards her.*) Got a licence?

Rina   Yes.

Marko   Let's see it. (*He takes a good look at the pistol.*) Oh, it's a toy one!

Rina   Get out.

Marko   Shout at me.

Rina   Out.

Marko   Louder. Really shout at me.

He gets up and so does **Rina**. **Marko** *puts out his hand and touches her hair, then her face, coming to her lips.* **Rina** *kicks him hard below the belt.* **Marko** *keels over and collapses on his* *knees on the floor. Pause. Enter* **Marta**, *a beautiful seventeen-year-old girl.*

Marta   Is he proposing to you?

Rina   He's looking after the house.

Marko *gets up. He gives* **Rina** *a menacing look and exits.*

Rina   Who's he?

Marta   Marko. The local playboy. He comes on to all the girls and they all give in. He comes on to me and I don't. I'm Marta. You're Rina. Damian's told me about you. He's my uncle. You're from London?

Rina   No.

Marta   Damian said from England.

Rina   England isn't just London.

Marta   Where d' you live, then?

Rina   In a village near Stonehenge. 60 miles from London.

Marta   An hour and a half's drive. Not too far. You're an actress. Divorced. Is there a theatre in this village?

Rina   In a town nearby.

Marta   You don't wear make-up. I had my hair dyed green this summer. I'd like to go to London. There's a life to be made there and somewhere to go in the evenings. I'd like to work in a fashion boutique. Do a modelling course. Did you fly over? How much is the plane now? It must be really expensive. I've got to get out of here. This is no place for young people. It's like a morgue. A never-ending funeral service. Something always being lamented over. I took an overdose of sedatives last year. I can't stand this place any more. Take me with you! When are you going back? They say you're a sorceress. They say that, though it was a sunny day today, you left no shadow behind you. I'd like people to talk about *me* like that.

Petar's *door opens and he comes out with a cigar in his hand.* **Marta** *goes up to him and takes his arm. She leads him to the centre of the room and puts his cigar in his mouth. She lights it for him.*

Marta (*To* **Rina**)   He loves smoking. It's not good for his health, but he hasn't got much health left, anyway. (*To* **Petar**) How are you, Granddad? You get younger every day.

Petar *moves one finger very slightly.*

Marta   What d' you want? The photos? (*She brings him a shoebox full of photographs. She shakes it about and opens it.*) I keep telling Damian to buy an album so we can put these photos in some kind of order. This is chaos. No way of knowing who's who and what's what. (*She guides one of* **Petar**'s *hands to pick up one of the photos.*) Here's you and Grannie in the garden. What kind of tree is this? An apple? No? Pear? (**Petar** *nods.*) You're watering the ground in front of the house. A summer afternoon. The sun's setting. You've just got up from your nap, had your cup of coffee and now you've shaved and splashed on some after-shave. I remember this waistcoat. You used to produce sweets and marbles from the little pocket. (*Pause.*) Who are these people? These places? This woman? It doesn't say anything on the back. How will we ever know now? Here's you in your safety helmet on the multi-storey. (*Pause.*) My grandfather was an architect. Head of Urban Planning. He had a stroke. Ictus apoplecticus. His speech got all garbled. He mixed up the names of things. Said 'potato' when he meant 'meat'.

Nobody could understand a word he said. His favourite expression was "Hunderd dievils inteered". Soon he stopped talking altogether. It's pretty commonplace around here. Ask them anything and they'll start to stutter, go red and roll their eyes.

Rina He was in a car crash?

Marta That's what Damian told you. He plays the innocent. Turns a blind eye. He drinks like a fish, but it doesn't show. Strictly vodka, so it doesn't smell. You been in his room? The TV's on twenty-four hours a day. Without the sound. He sits and stares at it. He doesn't watch it. Just keeps changing channels. This divorcee got him between her legs. He would've married her, but she squeezed him dry and ran off with a sergeant. I found his diary. He just writes in the date. No text. Bare dates. Now he plays chess. People here turn from grown-up children into pensioners overnight. (*Pause. She looks at a photograph.*) This is from my sixth birthday party. I'm sulking. I didn't want to have my picture taken. My Dad slapped me a couple of times and here he is holding me in place by the shoulders. I don't remember any of it, but here's the picture. So it must have happened.

Enter **Damian**. *He sits down. Pause. He looks at* **Rina**.

Marta You look as if you've seen a ghost.

Damian Why's he smoking? He's not supposed to smoke. Why's he looking at pictures? He cries when he looks at pictures. Go home.

Marta Why should I?

Damian Because I say so.

127

Marta   I don't understand why you're nice to me when you're nice. And why you yell at me when you yell.

Exit **Marta**. *Pause.* **Damian** *looks at* **Rina**.

Damian   I went up. (*Pause.* **Petar** *starts coughing. He coughs for a long time.*) The stairs have no walls. A bare skeleton. (*Pause.*) There's nothing there. Dust and bird-droppings.

Rina   Weren't you scared?

Damian   What of, when there's nothing there?

Rina   Weren't you afraid there might be something?

Damian   I knew there was nothing there!

Rina   So why did you go up there, then?

Damian   To get a view of the town.

Rina   And?

Damian   I did.

Rina   Why are you shouting?

Damian   I'm not. (*Pause.*) I am *now*, but I wasn't a moment ago.

Rina   Tell me, Damian. (*Pause.*) Please.

Damian   I saw a murder.

Rina   That's it! (*Pause. They look at each other.*) That's my boy.

Damian   A young man with a beard and cartridge belts. First he sharpened his knife. Then he murdered this traveller. I'm a child of science, of numbers. I don't believe in life after death.

Rina   You're pale.

Damian   I saw real people. Like I see you now.

Rina   I knew it. (*Pause.*) I knew it was like that. That it must be like that. (*Pause. She touches him gently with one finger. Like a healer.*) D' you want me to go away?

Damian   No.

Rina   You want me to stay?

Damian   No.

Rina   What do you want?

Damian   To play chess. (*Pause. They look at each other.*)

Rina *gets up and puts on her raincoat.* **Damian** *watches her.*

Damian   Don't leave me.

Rina   Don't *you* leave *me*!

Rina *takes the cigar out of* **Petar**'s *mouth and shakes the ash off into the ashtray. Then she puts it back in his mouth and goes out.*

Damian   Rina! (*Pause. To* **Petar**) "Daddy's at work. He's building a tower which will reach up to heaven. The whole world will envy us. This place will become a flowering garden. Life will be a song." (*Pause.*) The one they murdered looked like you. I don't understand any of this. There must be a simple, logical explanation. (*Pause.*) I have the faculty of speech. I put sentences together with a subject and predicate. With a logical stress. I can shout, I can whisper. I don't have your illness. I'm not going to go dumb. (**Petar** *moves his head.*) What is it? (**Petar** *moves his head. Pause.*)

What d' you want? There must be a simple and logical explanation.

They look at each other. **Petar** *kisses* **Damian** *on the cheek. He gets up and slowly goes into his room.* **Damian** *pulls over the chessboard and sits over the chessmen. Pause. He takes his head in his hands. Pause.* **Marta** *comes back and sits on the floor in front of* **Damian**. **Damian** *strokes her hair.* **Petar** *comes back and sits next to them. Enter* **Rina**. *She stands behind them as if posing for a family portrait.*

From the 1990 production of *Shades of Babel*, Dramski
Teatar, Skopje

(From left: Stevo Spasovski, Sofi Matevska-Kunovska, Nenad
Stojanovski, Ljiljana Bogoević-Jovanovski)

Scene Eleven

The car park basement. **Marko** *and* **Blaga** *are leaning against the barrels. They have been making love. They are smoking.* **Blaga** *is holding up a finger for him to catch with his hand. He does it several times.*

Marko   When the problems started, an international team of experts came. They said building was impossible.

Blaga   But you went on. What could they tell *you*? Why should they know more than *you* do?

Marko   Rina ran off with one of the engineers. She went to bitch about us around the world. What does she want now? Why's she come back at this particular moment? I'm not the one who's asking. There's multinational capital involved here.

Blaga   What's she done?

Marko   Poked her finger in some shit.

Blaga   What's in these barrels? Stop talking about her. Talk about me. Or do you men prefer women who kick you in the balls?

Marko (*Catching her finger quickly*)   I must get back the speed little kids have, catching flies. Without thinking. Without dilemmas. *I* first have to establish that what I'm seeing is indeed a fly, then work out how to catch it, then prepare to attack, then lash out with my hand, then gape stupidly as the fly gets away.

Blaga (*Singing*) "Don't be looking at my rags and tatters
                         It's my little fanny here that matters."

(*Pause.*) Take me away from here. I can't stand these strikers and demonstrators any more, people queuing for bread from daybreak, checking the dustbins for anything worth having, sweating in the buses, smuggling panties and petticoats across the border, buying foreign currency in basements, driving half-cars, lugging leeks and aubergines home to freeze for the winter, squatting outside supermarkets drinking cheap brandy and beer at eight o'clock in the morning.

Marko   They're born, they breed, then they die, never knowing that democracy, constitutions and elections were invented for *them*. I protect that fragile soap bubble called order. And I don't know any more what I'm protecting, or who from. (*Pause.*) Once again?

Blaga   Only *once* again? (*Pause.*) But you have to look into my eyes. You're not allowed to think about *her*.

Scene Twelve

Nevena *and* **Rina** *in a cake shop café.*

Rina How do you like it there? Is it very regimented? (**Nevena** *mutters something incomprehensible.*) Sorry?

Nevena I don't want to talk about it. (*Pause.*)

Rina Would you like another cream puff?

Nevena When we forgot our lines, we used to turn to your mother in a panic. She was going to call you Angelina at first. After the beautiful girl in the folk songs who had such a cross to bear with her sick brother. She used to breastfeed you in the wings during performances. Once you started crying. We were in the middle of the performance and you're screaming away in the wings. We were at a loss what to do. Then I saved the day by saying "Oh! The neighbours' baby's been born!" The audience started clapping. They were clapping *you*. The first time you saw me killed on stage, you wet your pants. Once, later, when you'd got over your terror, you shouted from the auditorium "She's not dead, she's not dead. She'll get up again."

Rina You were my favourite actress. I grew up under that stage. I had a little den under the rotating bit. I used to watch you walking around through a crack in the boards. I heard you speaking your lines. I cried when you cried, I laughed when you laughed. I had dolls, jars of paint, a peacock feather.

Nevena Now it's all covered with a thousand tons of cement.

Rina I know all your roles by heart.

Nevena   I've forgotten them all. That's all dead.

Rina   Where are the other actors?

Nevena   They split up. Some died, some went to other theatres. I'm the only one left of the old guard.

Rina   I've got money. I've been saving for years. We'll make a new theatre.

Nevena   My little girl.

Rina   Where are all those movements you made, those passions, those sighs, those sentences, those monologues? They're still here somewhere, in this air, in this space. Things like that don't just vanish. There's no order left in what we do any more. Our exits and entrances, our lines, our cues, our costumes and props – everything's got mixed up. The production has fallen apart. (*Pause.*) Would you like another cream puff? (**Nevena** *mutters something incomprehensible.*) Sorry?

Nevena   There are noises coming from the tower at night. Sometimes I think it's the wind. Sometimes I think it's human voices.

Scene Thirteen

The car park. **Damian** *is tense, looking about him. Pause. Silence. Suddenly a woman and a girl appear, the same actors who play* **Blaga** *and* **Marta**. *They seem to be on a battlefield, in a war. They are dirty and in rags.* **Blaga** *is carrying a baby in her arms.* **Marta** *is blind.*

Blaga   Excuse me, sir. Where's the front?

Damian *laughs nervously.*

Marta   Which front?

Blaga   Is there more than one?

Marta   When they're shooting, you know. Now there's some kind of odd truce. We can't work it out.

Blaga (To **Damian**, *as if anticipating his question*)   Who are we?

Marta   People.

Blaga   She's blind. They gouged her eyes out. She's latched on to me like a leech.

Marta   Would you like some olives, cheese, butter, tobacco, opium? Which side are you on? We do business with all the armies. We do funny acts for them, too. Would you like to see one? (*Pause.*) The baby's dead.

Blaga   Liar.

Marta   It's a bastard.

Blaga   Bitch.

Marta   She can't decide where to bury it. The situation changes every day. Different occupying armies overlap. Some are advancing, others retreating. Then the other way round. You can't find a quiet piece of ground for a grave. Would you like her to dance for you? Dance. The gentleman wants you to dance for him.

Blaga *gives the baby to* **Marta** *and starts dancing.*

Marta   That's the dance she does for the soldiers. I can't see. Is she pretty, sir? Would you like to have her?

Blaga   Don't listen to her, sir, I'm not like that.

Marta   Yes, she is, sir. Yes, she is. We take any kind of currency.

Damian *starts to leave.*

Marta   Now you've frightened him off. Get your clothes off. (*To* **Damian**) She'll have anyone. She's just playing the innocent in front of you.

Blaga   Don't believe her, sir.

Damian *starts to go again.*

Marta   Watch where you step. There are mines.

Damian *stops in his tracks. He turns towards them. He laughs helplessly. They laugh at him.*

Scene Fourteen

The living room of **Damian's** *house.* **Damian, Marko** *and* **Todor. Marko** *and* **Todor** *are in their Sunday best.* **Damian** *is drunk.*

Todor   Next time, take a camera with you and get a picture of yourself with the ghosts. I'm fed up with all this science fiction. Those fabrications have been denied once and for all in the daily papers. Half of Europe is making a laughing-stock of us about that damn car park. Bloody vampires appearing there is the last thing I need! People are superstitious. Don't you get taken in. You ought to be showing up those superstitions for what they are, not spreading them. We had noble intentions. We wanted prosperity for this area.

Marko   There are three categories of tales doing the rounds. Land, sea and air ones. That the car park will sink into the earth and take us with it. That it will spout water and flood us. That it will soar up into the air and drag us with it.

Todor   That the Four Horsemen of the Apocalypse will land on it and the end of the world will begin from here. Then at least we could say *something* began here. What did we do wrong? We built a modern car park with seven storeys.

Damian   There are no roads to this place. The one there is is full of holes and blocked with sheep, donkeys and ox-carts. We have one petrol pump. When you need some petrol you get some kids to go and get the pump attendant to come. He arrives in his pyjamas.

Todor   We were thinking of the future. The future wasn't thinking of us. Sooner or later the economy will recover, motorways will be built, industry will thrive. And we'll be first. Nobody else has a multi-storey car park – we've got one with seven floors. Then who was it who planned ahead? Who was that far-sighted?

Damian Why isn't it finished?

Todor Ask your father. Ask those consultants, professors, M.A.s and Ph.D.s of his. They're the ones who gave the go-ahead. "You want the donkey to fly? It can fly. With its saddle on? With its saddle on." Illiterate scum. They used up all the money for nothing. And now they're the saints and we're the sinners. How about that?! You think I enjoy looking at that hollow tooth out there? I dreamt of a gala opening, cutting the tape, floors full of guests, girls in national costume, fireworks, a big celebration dinner with roast lamb. We knocked down the whole of the old town to clear that building space. We moved the people out. *I* used to live there, too. *I* have happy memories, too. I used to teach the younger ones how to smoke, swear and spit through their front teeth. I used to lie in wait for them outside the school and frisk them. I used to scalp tickets in front of the cinema.

Marko (*To* **Damian**) You never so much as left the house until yesterday – now you're like a mole popping up all over the place.

Todor Where's Rina?

Marko What have you two been doing in the last few days? Apart from screwing, that is. Don't tell me you haven't been screwing. What does she want from you? We know everything.

Damian   What do you know?

Marko   (*Grabbing* **Damian** *by the throat*)   Want me to tell you?

Todor   Marko.

Marko   I can't help it. He thinks this is all a game.

Damian   I love her.

Marko   You picked a good one! She left a lasting impression in this town. The only ones who hadn't screwed her hadn't reached the front of the queue before she left.

Todor   I know the story she told you. It would have happened the day before we knocked down the theatre. The place is besieged by bulldozers and heavy machinery. That evening Rina comes to the stage where she means to spend the night. She wants to say farewell to the life she's known. She weeps a river of tears over the flood of memories that come to her. I suddenly appear out of the darkness. I smell of wine. She runs away, scratches, fights. I don't manage to satisfy my base passions, so I take my revenge by locking her up under the stage. She is still there the next morning when they start the demolition. (*Pause.*) Poor unprotected innocence. It's true – I did appear out of the darkness. But she was expecting me. That was one of the better nights of my life.

Enter **Blaga**, *drunk. She puts her arms round* **Todor** *from behind. Pause.*

Todor   We're having a chat with your brother. He's been seeing visions in the car park. You all have nightmares and then say *we're* to blame. Why the devil can't you have some *nice* dreams for a change, like normal people?! Why don't

139

you dream about coconut palms, white rum cocktails and naked ladies on tropical islands?

Blaga Are you going to knock down the multi-storey car park?

Todor Get up a petition. Don't forget to enclose a stamped addressed envelope. What do we put in its place, may I ask? Plant pumpkins? We're going to turn it into a pleasure dome. Damian's going to service the pinball machines and the jukeboxes. Do computer horoscopes. Measure people's bioenergy.

Blaga I heard this joke. How can you make a dog say "Miaow"? You kill the dog, skin it and put it in the freezer till it's rock hard. Then you take it out and slice it with an electric saw. And the dog goes "Mi-aow, mi-aow". (*Pause.*) You didn't get it, or you don't think it's funny?

Enter **Rina** *and* **Nevena**.

Todor New guests in the hotel.

Rina Are you Reception?

Todor How were the coffee and cream puffs? (*Pause.* **Rina** *looks at him.*) We want you to feel at home here. A little bird told us about your idea to get up a petition to reopen the theatre. Start up a drama society. There's an old saying: the old woman combs her hair while the village burns. Have you heard it? Some old woman was combing her hair while the village was burning.

Rina And?

Marko And she burnt to death with her hair combed.

Enter **Marta**, *her hair dyed pink. She is carrying a cake shaped like a tower with several storeys.*

Marta   What a silence. The angels must be passing over. (*Pause.*) How do you like my new hairstyle?

The door opens and **Petar** *comes in with a book in his hands.*

Marta (*Singing*)   Happy birthday to you, Happy birthday to you, Happy birthday, dear Granddad, Happy birthday to you.

Everybody claps. **Petar** *sits down.* **Marta** *puts the cake on his lap and lights him a cigar.*

Todor/Marko (*Chanting*)

> "Petar White
> Will ne'er go right
> Would you know the reason why?
> He follows his nose,
> Wherever he goes
> And that stands all awry."

They clap themselves. Pause. **Petar** *gives the book to* **Marta**. *He points to the place on the page.*

Marta   You want me to read? (**Petar** *nods.*) "And the whole earth was of one language, and of one speech. And it came to pass, as they journeyed from the east, that they found a plain in the land of Shinar; and they dwelt there. And they said one to another, Go to, let us make brick, and burn them thoroughly. And they made brick for stone, and slime had they for mortar. And they said, Go to, let us build us a city, and a tower, whose top may reach unto heaven; and let us make us a name, lest we be scattered abroad upon the face of the whole earth. And the Lord came down to see the city and the tower, which the children of men builded. And the Lord said, Behold, the people is one, and they have all one language; and this they begin to do: and now nothing will be restrained from them, which they have imagined to do. Go to, let us go down, and there confound their language, that they may not understand one another's speech. So the Lord scattered them abroad from thence upon the face of all the earth: and they left off to build the city".

Pause. **Petar** *claps his hands slowly.*

Rina   Come on, Nevena. (*Pause.* **Nevena** *looks at her in fear and confusion.*) Throw some pearls before swine. Give us a performance. (**Nevena** *looks straight ahead in panic.*) A mother who has lost her children and is tearing her hair out. A woman whose heart is struggling with her reason. A girl tied to the railway tracks – the train's coming – a young man is charging up on his horse to save her. Or something happy, hopeful. (*Pause.* **Nevena** *doesn't say a word.*) After so many years on the stage? Where is that diction, Nevena? Where is that voice?

Nevena *looks dumbfoundedly straight ahead. She glances at* **Petar**, *who is looking at her tensely. Pause.* **Nevena** *runs out of the room. Pause.* **Petar** *buries his face in the cake. He goes out. Pause.*

Todor   See what you've done?!

Rina   Me? What *I've* done?!

Todor   You came here to give us some theatre? Your bloody theatre and your bloody petition and your bloody society – they make me want to puke!

Rina (*She takes out a pistol and points it at* **Todor**.)   If we produce a pistol at the beginning of the play, it's only right we should use it.

She shoots at **Todor**. **Todor** *collapses.* **Damian** *puts his hands over his eyes.* **Blaga** *screams.* **Marta** *laughs. Pause.* **Todor** *feels his body. There is no bullet-wound. Exit* **Rina**.

Todor (*Shouting after her*)   That's right, run, you little bitch!!!

Damian *opens his eyes. He takes a bottle of brandy and tries to hit* **Todor** *with it.* **Marta** *takes the bottle from him and takes great swigs from it. She makes to go out, then collapses on the floor.*

Scene Fifteen

A bench on a railway station platform. **Viktor** *is lying on some newspapers, dressed in a jacket. He is eating sunflower seeds. Enter* **Damian***. Pause.* **Viktor** *motions him to sit down.* **Damian** *sits down.* **Viktor** *offers him some seeds.* **Damian** *declines.*

Viktor   We should make the most of these last sunny days. Who knows what the winter will be like. (*Pause.*) Somebody tried to assassinate Todor. Failed. Not even a cannon could fell him, it seems. (*Pause.*) They think it was me. As usual. But we'll survive this, too. (*Pause.*) Not playing chess any more?

Damian   Have you ever been up the tower?

Viktor   It's not a tower. It's a reinforced concrete multi-storey car park. That cauldron's still on the boil. Mind you don't get scalded. I was the chief statistician. I worked with your father.

Damian   That's why I'm here.

Viktor   Yes, indeed. I was the best student of my year. A Wunderkind.

Damian   There are some weird things going on up there.

Viktor   The same law of numbers applies to Man as to Nature and to the Earth and to the Universe.

Damian   Visions appear.

Viktor   I fell twice from up there. Three times, actually, though the third time was more for show. I fell twice good and proper. Once from the top, once from the fifth floor.

Something was stopping the work from going ahead. We put in the foundations and hit an underground spring. Erosion all over the place. We put in a cube of reinforced concrete. It started resonating in a strange way. Hypertrophied acoustics. Unknown frequencies. I told your father not to bother about it. Sir, I said, let's just turn a blind eye. If it's not working, it's not working. No! He wanted a reason, logic. They cooked our goose. I pee blood now. We built through the night. Somehow, anyhow. We lost a lot of men. We got through all the money loaned. My wife left me.

Damian   There was a theatre under there.

Viktor   So? Under that theatre there was another theatre, and under that – a church, and under that a pagan temple. (*Pause.*) They didn't agree to my proposals. If we're going to build anyway, why just seven floors? Why not fifteen? Twenty? Seven's a mean sort of number. Provincial.

Damian   I'm sick of all these double meanings! I can't stand it any more! It's like this because it's not like that, and if it *had* been like that, heaven knows what it would have been like! Tell me loud and clear what's going on!!

Viktor   There's a curse on the place. Blackie's ghost. That's what's going on. (*Pause.*) Sing. Sing something. It's being taped.

Damian   What's being taped?

Viktor   Everything's being taped. You installed the bugging machines for them. (*Pause.*) In the post office?

Damian   What?

Viktor   All right. It wasn't you, then, it was me.

Damian   I've got nothing to do with them.

145

Viktor   I haven't got a phone. (*Pause. He checks* **Damian's** *jacket lapel for hidden bugs.*) Once bitten, twice shy. Just taking precautions. That funny, familiar feeling of uneasiness. Do *you* write Todor's speeches? (*Pause.* **Damian** *looks at him in amazement.*) You can outdo yourself when you really want to. (*Pause.*) I got Rina's file. She used to be a ticket-collector on the underground railway. (*Pause.*) Supposedly. Cover. (*Pause.*) Here top left, first molar, it hurts when I drink something cold. And there's no tooth there. It must be some reaction from the one next to it. (*He winks at* **Damian**.)

Damian   I don't follow you.

Viktor   Thank God *someone* doesn't! Know who Angelina's sick brother was? That Doychin? Blackie's brother. I'm their cousin. On my father's side.

Damian *gets up and goes.* **Viktor** *watches him and eats some seeds.*

Viktor   The truth hurts.

Scene Sixteen

Damian *comes into the car park. A middle-aged man is lying in a deckchair. He is played by the same actor as* **Todor**, *though he is unrecognisable. He is wearing a suit with a bow-tie and a straw hat on his head. He is drinking champagne.*

Todor   You're just what the doctor ordered. A compatriot, I believe. I heard you talking at breakfast. Going to America? Everybody's going to America. I'm feeling seasick. All this water is too much of a good thing. The ocean. The open sea. Waves billowing for days on end. The sun is murderous. I bought this straw-hat on the ship. It doesn't help. (*He takes off the hat.*) You don't find it oppressive? (*He takes a handkerchief out of his pocket and puts it on his head like a reaper.*) Now I look like a reaper. A tobacco-picker. I'll get garlic and vinegar for my lunch. My grandfather met his death somewhere around here.

Damian *turns to look behind him.*

Todor   God knows where. The steamer sank on his way back from working overseas. I'm following in his footsteps. (*Pause.*) I've had a full life. Power, authority, glory. Receptions, hunts – wild boar, stags, zebras, rhinoceroses. A glass of champagne? They used to serve us with this stuff. We didn't even look at them. Servants. Trustworthy people. Like shadows. There to fetch and carry. Not seen, not heard. With white gloves. The people loved us. Little marks of respect wherever we went. They put whole cheeses in the boots of our cars when we weren't looking. Eels. Flowers. Milk and honey.

Damian *looks at him blankly. Pause.*

Todor   Riches to rags. Didn't you see it on the television? Political liquidation. Moral death. I know what it means. I did it to others before me. There was panic in our ranks. Suddenly no holds barred. (*Pause.*) I left. There was no point in staying. They'd have taken in the ones who used to be seen in my company. I'd be nameless. No documents. Cut out of all the photographs. They'd turn their heads away from me. Nobody'd come to see me, I wouldn't go to see anyone. I'd wake up at night and pinch myself to see if I was alive. This is my swan-song.

Enter **Viktor** *dressed as a photographer from the 1900s, his hair sleaked down with brilliantine, granny sunglasses, well-groomed moustache. He is carrying a big old-fashioned camera on a tripod.*

Viktor   I'm sorry I'm a bit late. They kept me below decks. I was taking pictures of our migrant workers. They haven't even got there yet and they want their picture taken. Some of them will never make it alive. Scurvy. Fever. Delirium. (*He looks at* **Damian**.) I haven't had the honour of making your acquaintance. Perhaps you might like an artistic photograph? I guarantee you'll look better than the real thing, at least three times better. Quick and prompt service. Reasonable prices. (*He sets up his camera. He combs* **Todor**'*s hair and puts some powder on his cheeks. He poses him for the photograph.*) I'm starting an agency for metamorphosis.

Damian *looks at him uncomprehendingly.*

Viktor   Complete spiritual and bodily renewal. The Chameleon Salon. We do new hairstyles, pedicure, manicure, massage. We look at the colour of the eyes and decide on the colour of the shoes, the cut of the clothes. We give injections of self-esteem and determination. A family coat-of-arms, a noble title. We hire out admirers by the hour. Young girls to follow you, gaze at you and admire you. (*He looks at* **Damian**.) You look like a good candidate. Have you got a hole in your sock?

Damian *looks at him blankly. Pause.*

Viktor I can see it in your eyes. The big toe is sticking out like a potato. It's chafing on the shoe. It won't let you stand up straight like a man. (*He is finishing preparing* **Todor**. **Todor**'s *cheeks are as white as a dead man's.*) Now you're ready. Ready for eternity. (*He puts* **Todor**'s *head in an odd, unnatural position.*) Eyes this way. Keep them open till you see the birdie.

Viktor *goes behind the camera and covers himself with a black cloth.*

Todor (*Looking at* **Damian**)   Help me. I lack the courage. (*He takes out a pistol.*) Throw my body into the sea.

Todor *shoots into his mouth and collapses.* **Damian** *gapes at him in disbelief.*

Scene Seventeen

Rina *and* **Nevena** *in the car park.* **Nevena's** *face is powdered and her cheeks rouged. She is wearing the theatre costume of the heroine in a melodrama, Tsveta in Macedonian Blood Wedding by Chernodrinski.* **Rina** *is dressed in a man's black suit. She is wearing a lot of makeup.* **Petar** *is sitting on a chair as the audience.*

Rina   Let's try it. This is the stage. Petar's the audience.

Nevena   How do I look?

Rina   Like a rosy red apple.

Nevena   I've forgotten everything.

Rina   You'll remember. Remember the scenery? A big field. Haystacks. You were standing stage front, gazing into the audience. Spasé came up behind you and made you jump. (*She goes up behind* **Nevena** *and startles her.*) Boo! (*Pause.*) You jumped. Remember?

Nevena   No.

Rina   Try to remember. Boo! You said "Goodness gracious!" And ran over to the other side of the stage.

Nevena   There's no stage here.

Rina   Imagine it. Let's start. Stand here. (**Rina** *goes back. Then she comes up behind* **Nevena**.) Boo!

Nevena (*Jumps*)   Goodness gracious!

Rina   What 're you doing here, me darlin'? (*Pause.*)

Nevena   Then what?

Rina (*Like a prompter*)   Ooh, you rascal...

Nevena   Ooh, you rascal... (*Pause.*) I can't remember.

Rina (*Prompting*)   You scared me to death.

Nevena   Ooh, you rascal! You scared me to death!

Rina   Come on, silly. Are you such a timid little thing?

Nevena   My heart jumped into my mouth.

Rina   Bravo. (*Playing Spasé again*) Did I really give you such a fright?

Nevena   Why, indeed you did! Anyone would have been frightened in my shoes.

Rina (*Going up to* **Nevena**, *who pulls away*)   What are you running away for, my frightened little quail?

Nevena   What else am I to do with a devil like you?

Rina   Don't be afraid, I won't eat you. I'm not a wolf nor a bear. (*Grabbing her by the hand*) Stop!

Nevena   Go away! I'll scream!

Rina   Wait, me darlin', wait. I want to ask you something.

Nevena   Let me go! Let me go!

Rina   Tell me, darlin', shall we be wed?

Nevena   Let me go, man, someone'll see us.

Rina   There's nobody about. I won't let you go till you give me your answer. Tell me, do you love me?

Nevena   No, I don't.

Rina   I love you and I'll die if you won't be mine. I have a great yearning in my heart for you.

Nevena   So had I 'till you gave me such a fright and stopped my heart from beating.

Rina   Forgive me, my dearest, forgive me. I only did it in jest, only in jest.

Nevena *and* **Rina** *embrace.* **Nevena** *is crying.* **Petar** *is clapping.*

Nevena   It all came back.

Rina   It was all there.

Enter **Damian**. *He thinks he is seeing more ghosts.*

Damian   And you are...?

Rina   Us. And you are...?

Damian   Me. Who are you?

Rina   Who are you?

Damian *touches* **Rina** *to make sure she is real. He smudges her makeup. They look at each other.*

Scene Eighteen

Todor, **Blaga** *and* **Marko** *in the car park.*

Blaga   We ought to light a big bonfire here. To bring the air pressure down. Bring people some relief. We could douse the upper storeys with petrol. A great purification. A spectacle for the masses. Something really impressive.

Marko   Then the ghosts would burn up.

Todor   You believe in them?

Marko   It'd be useful if they *did* exist. Then we could take them in and get them to work for us. Tell us everything that's been going on and what's to come.

Blaga   We're so high up!

Marko   Imagine if Rina were suddenly to decide to jump off here. (*Pause.*) To her own and everyone else's general satisfaction. That would have no end of advantages. We could compose a moving report on it. Returned to her place of birth after many years. An unhappy love affair. Derangement. Clear motivation. Case closed.

Todor   We would pay the funeral costs.

Marko   You've always been such a generous man.

Marko/Todor (*Singing*)
       "Rock-a-bye Rina on the tower-top,
       When the wind blows the tower will rock,
       When the tower breaks the whole thing will fall –
       Down will come Rina, tower and all."

Marko   Sssh!

Todor   What's the matter?

Marko   I think I heard something.

Todor   What? (*They listen.*)

Blaga   I want to go home.

Marko   Did you hear that?

Todor   Yes.

Marko   There.

They look into the darkness. **Marko** *gets out his revolver.*

Todor   Something moved.

Marko   It looked like somebody running across.

Todor   With a flag.

Marko   Or a gun.

Blaga   Stop frightening me.

Todor   It's just the play of the shadows.

Todor *falls to his knees in panic.* **Marta** *emerges from the dark.*

Blaga   Marta!

Marko   We nearly killed you.

Todor   What're you doing here?

Marta   I came to say goodbye. (*Pause.*) I'm going.

Blaga   Where?

Marta   Rina doesn't want to take me with her. She says I have to solve my own problems for myself. I wanted to slit my wrists, but I thought better of it. My decision is simple and final. Consider me gone.

154

Todor   Why did you come up here?

Marta   I pissed on your tower. (*Pause.*) I shall always have fond memories of this erection between heaven and earth.

Todor   Marta!

Marta   Thou shalt not take my name in vain!

Scene Nineteen

The railway station waiting-room. **Damian** *and* **Rina** *are sitting on separate benches. Pause.*

Damian He took out a gun. He said "Throw my body into the sea". He shot himself in the mouth. He collapsed. I closed my eyes. When I opened them again, there was nothing there. He looked like Todor, but it wasn't him. I understand everything they do and say, and yet I don't understand. Like in a dream.

Rina That's the third time you've told me about that. Tell me a happy story.

Damian We've run out.

Rina When do you expect to have some more in?

Damian Come back next week.

Rina I know one. (*Pause.*) The Moor had conquered the city. Every day he demanded two ovens full of bread, a fattened calf, a keg of brandy, two barrels of wine, a young bride for the daytime and a maiden at night. He would have his way with them and then put them to the sword. They drew lots and in time the lot fell on young Angelina. What was she to do? She had a brother called Doychin[1], but he was bed-ridden. Nine years in all he'd been sick.

Damian Not sick, wounded.

Rina It's not very clear in the story.

---

1 Doychin is a famous figure from Macedonian folk song, a man who had been bed-ridden for nine years with a wound that never healed but who rose from his bed to slay the Moor who threatened his people.

Damian   Badly wounded.

Rina   The songs mention festering wounds, but I think he had something wrong in the head. His sister had been sweeping the yard for him all those years, pandering to his every whim, making him broths and custards. And she was quite right to expect him to get up now and defend her. Kill the Moor. (*Pause.*)

Damian   And? (*Pause.*) Did he get up?

Rina   He did. He asked for his sword, his double-edged sabre, he girded his loins with three hundred layers of bandages, and he set to. He killed her.

Damian   Who?

Rina   Angelina.

Damian   You mean, the Moor.

Rina   I mean Angelina. The Moor is still alive and well. (*Pause.*) He's indestructible. Doychin's made a pact with him. They don't interfere with each other, don't get in each other's way. Angelina is his problem. She sees his weakness. She is the witness to his illness. She expects him to help her. (*Pause. She takes his hand.*) "And fetch me my sabre sharp, these nine years have I let it lie. My sabre yet is rusted".

Damian *fires at her with her pistol.* **Rina** *collapses. Blood trickles from her mouth.* **Damian** *looks at the blood in amazement.* **Rina** *laughs.*

Damian   I went down into the basement of the car park. You know what's in those barrels? Chemical waste. Active toxic waste. Ethyl hexyl acrylate. It can go through stone, iron and concrete. Soon there'll be dead fish floating belly-up down the river. We'll be washing in sulphuric acid.

Teams of experts will come in those spacesuits to measure the pollution level. They'll evacuate us for an indefinite period of time. I've been looking for the shade all my life, now I'm naked in the middle of a football pitch. Damian! A kind of lizard. With the aid of his pigment cells he can change his green skin to melt into the background.

He throws himself at **Rina** *and embraces and kisses her violently. She fights and runs. There is a long struggle. Finally* **Damian** *leaves her alone.* **Rina** *is crying. An unpleasant pause.* **Rina** *takes out a big jacket. She puts it round* **Damian**.

Rina From the theatre wardrobe. Nevena kept it. Put it on.

Damian *looks at the jacket.*

Damian The deceased was a big man.

Rina If I were you, I'd do something.

Damian If I were you, I'd know what.

Rina Stop feeling sorry for yourself.

Damian I'm feeling foolish more than anything.

Rina This is the first day of the rest of your life.

Damian Someone else will write my play. I don't understand it. I don't deserve it.

Damian *tenderly touches the blood on her mouth with his finger.* **Rina** *smiles and closes her eyes.*

Scene Twenty

The restaurant. **Damian** *and* **Viktor** *are drinking together.*
Viktor *is wearing hospital pyjamas. He is in a good mood.*
Damian *is looking around nervously and apprehensively all the time.*

Damian   I understand now.

Viktor   What?

Damian   Holograms. (*Pause.*) What I'm seeing are holograms. Laser technology. Optical electronics. A monochromatic laser beam. A great density of energy achieved in a small, restricted space. A three-dimensional image.

Viktor   One chap used to see pink elephants. (*Pause.*) His liver packed up. (*Pause.*) They hit me on the head with a pipe. I don't know who or why. This is the third time I've got out of the hospital. The pissoirs haven't got any pipes. You piss on the wall, the wall pisses on you. It's so funny. Such a laugh. I'm glad I'm still alive. Life is sweet. (*Pause.*) I'm not allowed to drink alcohol. I drink tea with rum. I got drunk once two times today – and twice once.

Damian (*Closing his eyes*)   When I close my eyes, I see the visions.

Viktor   Don't close them, then.

Damian   Like dogs let off the leash. I see a snake. I collapse. My teeth fall out. My Dad says to us before going to sleep, "Kids, remember where you leave your shoes. So, if you have to get out in the middle of the night, you won't waste any time looking for them." Someone is coming to throw us out. I'm a terrified old man, sitting in front of the door, beads in my hand, a cap on my head, rheumatism in my bones. Keep your head up, look blank and whistle to yourself.

Viktor   Be grateful you understand yourself.

Damian   This place shall never more be inhabited, neither shall it be dwelt in from generation to generation: neither shall the Moor pitch tent here; neither shall the shepherds make their fold here. But wild beasts of the desert shall lie here; and our houses shall be full of doleful creatures; and owls shall dwell here, and dragons in our pleasant palaces. And the time is near to come.[2]

Viktor (*Raising his glass*)   Let's drink. (*Pause.*) To the soul of that woman who jumped off the tower. Did you hear about it? Some woman, who'd come back to her homeland after many years, went and killed herself. She'd had an unhappy love affair. She threw herself off the multi-storey car park. That's what the official announcement says. Who knows what really happened? Maybe she was pushed. Or killed and pushed. When you don't know what happened, always think the worst. *That* was what happened.

Damian (*Laughing in a merry childlike way*)   Hunderd dievils inteered. (*Pause.*)

He giggles. **Viktor** *looks at him in amazement.*

---

2   Adapted from Isaiah 13;20-22

1990 production of *Shades of Babel*, Dramski Teatar, Skopje
(From left: Blagoja Čorevski, Nenad Stojanovski)

Scene Twenty-One

Damian's *house.* **Damian**, **Marta**, **Nevena** *and* **Petar** *dressed in their best funeral clothes.* **Petar** *is smoking a cigar and putting his photographs into an album.*

Nevena   What a marvellous funeral! Fit for a queen. The whole town turned out. (*Pause.*) I can't understand it. She was so full of joy, so full of life. (*Pause.*) She bought your Dad an album. To put his photos in.

Marta   Now you'll be going back to your usual things, your usual life. The murderers to their murders, the chessplayers to their chess openings. The Lasker defence. The Carlsbad variation. The development of the knight on F4. The Queen's Indian Defence.

Nevena   She wanted us to build a new theatre. Your Dad was to have done the plans. We were going to do a play to explain our lives, the chaos we see. Define the point of what we want to say. Find a strong idea. Sound story. Fully developed characters.

Marta (*She puts on* **Rina**'s *raincoat and dark glasses. She picks up* **Rina**'s *suitcase. Pause. Silence.*)   It's time.

Nevena   I'll drop by again, lend a hand.

Marta   Take care of yourselves.

Marta *and* **Nevena** *go out. Pause. Silence.* **Petar** *is putting his photos in the album.* **Damian** *laughs in a merry childlike way.*

Damian   The snow crunches under our feet. Icy cold. We snuggle down under the blankets. Who wants to be outside? We want to be home in the warm. I wave that little paper flag for the May Day parade. A lake, pedalos. I'm learning to swim, the sky is scorching hot. You can hear Mexican dance music from the open air café. In the autumn we learn cursive handwriting. I have a temperature and I'm proud to be the centre of attention, everyone worrying about me. The air is thick. I know everything, but nobody believes me. When will I grow up? (*Pause.*) A Balkan meadow, scorched grass, sweaty people. A boy running over a bridge. Crying for his father, who's hurrying along, balancing a couch on a bike, and won't take the boy with him. (*Pause.*) I'm old and tired. (*Pause.*) Adam and Eve and Pinchme went down to the river to swim. Adam and Eve were drowned. Who was saved? Pinchme. (*Pause.*) We are all in the dumps. For diamonds are trumps...

Petar   The kittens are gone to St Paul's. (*Pause.* **Petar** *puts a cigar in* **Damian's** *mouth and lights it.*)

> The babies are bit,
>
> The moon's in a fit,
>
> And the houses are built without walls.

Pause. They sit and smoke in silence.

CURTAIN

SARAJEVO
(TALES FROM A CITY)

a play by Goran Stefanovski Stockholm/Canterbury 1992/93

This play is intended to be a candle lit for the health of the soul of the city of Sarajevo. It is dedicated to the heroic struggle of the people of the city in their tragedy and to one Haris Pašović.

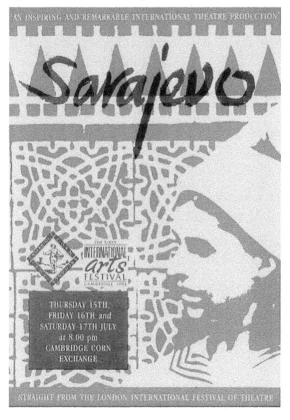

Poster from the tour of the Antwerp 93 production,
directed by Slobodan Unkovski, at the Kirin
International Arts Festival in Cambridge, UK

Characters[3]

Sara: Researcher and Architect / UNHCR nurse / Hasanaginitsa / Linn / Refugee / Rabbi

Rudi: Postman / Officer 1 / Diplomat / Steward / Santa Claus / Skinhead / Major Tankosich

Gorchin: Fireman / Prince Constant / Hasanaga / Rocker / Gavrilo Princip

Hamdia: Historian/ Custodian / Poet / Beg Pintorovich / Ivo Andrich / Josip Broz Tito

Fata: Housewife/ Dubrovnik and Vukovar Chorus / Storyteller / Clouds Chorus / The Caretaker's Wife/ Orthodox Priest

Sulyo: Cleaner / Soldier Blue / Roofs Chorus / Cook / Asylum Caretaker / Uzeir the Skyscraper

Azra: Doctor / Dubrovnik and Vukovar Chorus / Mother-In-Law / Cello Player / Window Woman / Imam

Muyo: Taxi Driver / Officer 2 / Small-Time Smuggler / Momo the Skyscraper / Tram

Maya: Journalist / Dubrovnik and Vukovar Chorus / Migrant Birds Chorus / Water Chorus / The Wife / Catholic Priest

---

3   Language Editor's Note: I have anglicised the names to approximate the correct pronunciation, thus Hamdija becomes Hamdia, and Suljo Sulyo. However, I have left the name of the city of Sarajevo with a *j* as this is the conventional spelling, although the pronunciation of *j* is like *y* in English.

Scene 1

The future

Sara *arrives on the hills around Sarajevo.*

Sara   My name is Sara. I am a researcher.
Architecture is my profession, and music is my love.
I am a loser and a refugee.
I come from the gloom of Europe,
from what once had dreams of being united,
but is now only a series of lonely, uneasy and small
tyrannical city states.
Our life is uncomfortable, our future shaky,
our cities grey, violent and dirty,
the people unhappy and in fear,
the ozone hole larger, the toxic waste worse,
the acid rains regular.
I have had, like a child,
a vision and a dream of a godlike project.
I want to build an invisible city,
a city of the mind,
a new city of human measure.

Scene 2

Sara *meets* **Rudi,** *the postman,*
who turns out to be something very different.

Enter **Rudi**.

Rudi   Hello!

Sara   Hello!

Rudi   Who are you?

Sara   Who are you?

Rudi   I'm Rudi. I'm a postman.

Sara   Postman?

Rudi   Don't I look like a postman?

Sara   Have we met before?

Rudi   Everyone's met me before. I walk up and down the highways and byways of Sarajevo. I deliver telegrams with best wishes for birthdays and marriages, condolences for deaths, pensions for the pensioners, newspapers and magazines, parcels and packages, telephone bills, love letters and presents. I steal the stamps from the letters. I have quite a collection. Where are you going?

Sara   To the city.

Rudi   The city? There's no more city there. It's all rubble. What are you looking for?

Sara   The soul.

Rudi   Aren't we all? What soul?

Sara Of the city.

Rudi Nothing less than that?

Sara Nothing less will do.

Rudi It's probably been killed. I don't mean to be rude. Didn't you read the papers, didn't you watch TV? It's gone. Finished. Sarajevo is no more.

> The city was a beauty once –
> now it's raped.
> It had streets once –
> now only dead ends.
> It had people once –
> now only shadows.
> It had houses once –
> now only ruins.
> It had gardens once –
> now only graveyards.
> It had a face once –
> now only scars.
> It had a mind once –
> now only madness.
> It had stars once –
> now only black holes.
> It had itself once –
> now it has me.

Sara (*Recognising him*) It's you again. I should have recognised your stink.

Rudi Nobody likes me. Why am I so unpopular?

Sara You are the messenger of the Savage God, the City Eater, who started his menace in these parts of the world.

He is a shape with lion body and the head of a man, a gaze blank and pitiless as the sun. He slouched from here towards Bethlehem to be born.

> Your master, the City Eater,
> the town devourer,
> the beast behind Chernobyl,
> Ossetia, Chechnya and Nagorno Karabakh,
> Armenia and Azerbaijan,
> Northern Ireland,
> The Basque Country,
> Flanders and Wallonia,
> And Catalonia.

He tries to attack her, but she is ready to defend herself. He gives up.

Rudi   You are confused. So was the soul of Sarajevo as it hovered over the waste. They say that it was divine and spoke many languages. They say it was female and male and inanimate and used to hide in many persons and auras. But where are they now? And where is it now? Gone. All gone.

Sara   Get lost!

Rudi   I've been watching you, girl. Why don't you leave and find new pastures on the shores of Sumatra, perhaps, or Borneo? Times have changed. No more cities and no more souls. Do you expect a miraculous rebirth? Do you think the bird will rise from the ashes and fly again like the Phoenix? None of that! There will be no divine apparitions.

All of a sudden a rainbow appears in the sky.

Rudi   Do not believe it. It is all false. Utterly false. A lie.

They look at the rainbow.

Scene 3

A shelter

A passage between two houses. It is half dark. Eight people come into it from the street, carrying **Sara***'s body. There is shelling going on outside and general commotion.*

Rudi   She's dead.

Gorchin   She's beautiful.

Azra   She's not dead, she's unconscious.

Fata   God knows where her mother is.

Maya (*Reading a newspaper*)   Look at this. I wrote this.

Muyo (*Looking towards the street*)   Come on then, stop it. I've got work to do.

Sulyo (*Singing*)   "Mošćanice, vodo plemenita, usput ti je pozdravi mi dragog"

Hamdia   Stop it, please. It's bad enough as it is.

Azra   Look, a rainbow. How lovely.

Rudi   That's all we need. (*To* **Gorchin**) You should have left her in the street.

Gorchin   How would you feel if I left you in the street?

Maya (*Taking a photograph*)   This is going to be a great one.

Fata   Must be a sign of some sort.

Muyo (*Looking out to the street*)   Oh, give us a break. I've got things to do.

Sulyo *starts singing again.*

Hamdia   Stop singing, please. Look what's happening!

Scene 4

Song of the Common People

All   We
the common people of Sarajevo
in this hour of darkness
and weakness
and despair
pledge
to heal
and guide
and guarantee respect for observance of rituals
and defend the town against evil spirits.
We will point out places for fruitful hunting
and fishing
increase the wild life
control the weather
ease childbirth
and reveal future events.

They exit. **Sara** *is alone.*

Scene 5

Sara *comes to herself and goes on*
explaining her intentions.

Sara I want to build a city
which would suit us
like the snail's house
suits the snail
free of inner contradictions
to make us richer humans
better humans
human humans.

Either that
or we lose our soul
our heart
and our mind.
(Yes of course,
it sounds pathetic.)

I wish I was
the earth goddess
so that I could plough a circle
and find a lot
and mark the place
and put down foundations
and say
here is a new myth
a new city
with rainbow towers
where the sun always shines
for thee and me
and our children
and the new world.

Scene 6

*Sara meets **Muyo** the taxi driver,*
who is more than that.

*Night. **Sara** approaches a taxi parked in the middle of a street of ruined buildings. **Muyo** is leaning on the car. His back towards her.*

Sara   Hello! Are you a taxi driver? (*Pause.*) Hello!

Muyo   Sure I'm a taxi driver. You can see I'm a taxi driver.

Sara   Are you for hire?

Muyo   Sure I'm for hire. You can see I'm for hire.

Sara   I'm sorry.

Muyo   You're not sorry, you're stupid.

Sara   Can you take me?

Muyo   Where are you going?

Sara   I have no money.

Muyo   You're not going anywhere, then.

Sara   Can't you do it for free?

Muyo *turns his back on her.*

Sara   Why not?

Muyo   Why yes?

Sara   Solidarity?

Muyo   What?

Sara Human solidarity?

Muyo Oh yes?

Sara Yes.

Muyo OK. I'll take you.

Sara I'm trying to find the soul.

Muyo Oh yeah? What soul?

Sara Of the city.

Muyo Oh yeah? Well, good luck.

Sara Drive with the window open. We'll sing. It will hear us.

Muyo I've had people making love on the back seats, suicides, people hurrying to the railway station, people hurrying from the railway station, drunks throwing up down my neck, reputable politicians going to disreputable places, women in the throes of childbirth, married couples who have just decided to get divorced. Now I have you who want to sing to the soul of Sarajevo at midnight.

Sara But you were waiting for me.

Muyo Waiting for you? Of course I was waiting for you.

He puts on a robe and a sufi hat.

Sara Do you always wear this when you drive?

Muyo Recognise me?

Sara Nasreddin Hodja. The Sufi Joker.

Muyo You want a joke? This man said to me: Give me some advice. I said: Think of death. He said: I know about death, give me some advice. I said: If you know about death, you don't need any other advice. (*He brings out a suitcase, opens it and produces yards and yards of the finest silk. It seems endless.*) Once upon a time, as the story goes, I collected all the people of Sarajevo and promised to tell them something important. They were eager to hear. I said: "People, I have something important to tell you. Are you ready to hear it?" "Yes" they shouted at the top of their voices. "Well," I said, "Do you know what it is?" "No" they answered. "Well," I said. "if you don't know what it is, then I can't tell you." A few days later, I gathered them round me again. And I said again I had something important to tell them. "Do you want to hear it?" I asked. "Yes" they shouted. "Do you know what it is?" "Ye-e-e-e-s" they answered as one. "Well," I said, "If you know it, you know it, and there is no need for me to tell you what you know." And I went away. The next time I gathered them together I said, "Do you know what I am going to tell you?" And half of them said "Yes", and half of them said "No". "Well," I said, "let those who know tell those who don't." (*Pause.*) You're not laughing? Well, it's not very funny, is it?

He dances a dervish dance. He takes his robe off.

Sara   Are you a taxi driver again?

Muyo   No. I am Nasreddin Hodja pretending to be a taxi driver. (*He produces a pack of Marlboros.*) Help yourself. Made in the USA. Duty free. I smoke a hundred on a good day. Welcome to Sarajevo, the city of miracles. You cheered me up. I don't know why.

Sara   What you don't know, you can't know. What you know, you can't not know.

Scene 7

Muyo *and* Sulyo *Cabaret*

Sulyo *is standing in the corner with two plastic canisters. He is singing "Moščanice, vodo plemenita" and from time to time blowing into his hands to warm them up. **Sara** comes in.*

Sara What are you doing here?

Sulyo Waiting for water.

Sara Shall I wait with you?

Sulyo Got any cigarettes?

Sara *gives him one.*

Sulyo My name is Sulyo. I am a cleaner. An unskilled worker. I've worked as a dustman and a gravedigger. I've cleaned the cages in the zoo. What do you think the animals in the zoo are eating these days? I've cleaned the parks. This town was clean once. (*He starts singing again.*)

Sara You sing like a blackbird.

Sulyo Thank you. I appreciate you saying that. It really means a lot to me.

Sara I met a funny man a while ago.

Sulyo Muyo?

Sara Do you know him?

Sulyo Do I know Muyo?

Muyo *comes in. He is carrying two water canisters. He stands in line.*

178

Muyo   Hello, we are Muyo and Sulyo.

Sulyo   We are the proverbial Bosnian fools.

Muyo   We are supposed to be terribly stupid. And here is a joke to confirm that. (*He turns to* **Sulyo**.) You should buy a car.

Sulyo   Why?

Muyo   So you can go places.

Sulyo   Like where?

Muyo   Like if you want to go from here to Ilidzha you can get there in half an hour. It's now half past eleven, you could be there by midnight. (*Pause.*)

Sulyo   What would I do in Ilidzha at midnight?

They look to **Sara** *for approval.*

Muyo   And now, the joke about the violet seller who would...

Sulyo   No, no, no. Not that one. How about the one about the Serb, the Croat and the Muslim?

Muyo   You mean the Muslim, the Croat and the Serb?

Sulyo   What's the difference?

Muyo   The Muslim is in the first place.

Sulyo   What's the difference?

Muyo   The difference is war!

They look to **Sara** *for approval.*

Sulyo   Well, then, the joke about the Croat, the Serb and the Muslim.

Muyo   Why the Muslim in the third place, after the Serb?

Sulyo   Well, then the joke about the Serb and the Croat only.

Muyo   Why not the joke about the Serb and Serb and Serb only.

Sulyo   Why do you only say why not?

Muyo   Why not?

They look to **Sara** *for approval.*

Sulyo   Curse the country which doesn't have a Bosnia.

Muyo   Curse Bosnia, which doesn't have a country.

Sulyo   I am a Muslim, but my wife is Croatian. Well, half Croatian, that is, because her father was a Serb, and her mother a Romanian. Well, a Gypsy really, I think, but I never admit it to anybody. But I am a straight Muslim. I am renting a flat from a Jew, I don't like them you know, they don't like me either. My father was a Serb, I hate to admit. His mother was from Skopje, that's Macedonia now, but they are all really Serbs down there, you know. When they are not busy being Bulgarians.

Muyo   I slaughtered you
but only a little,
just a bit,
not completely,
nothing to worry about.
Mr Gandhi, what do you think of Western civilisation?

Sulyo   I think it would be a very good idea.

They look to **Sara** *for approval.*

Sulyo   She's come to look for Sarajevo.

Muyo   I know.

Sulyo   Shall we give her Sarajevo?

Muyo   Why not?

They produce magician hats.

Muyo / Sulyo

> Here are two Sarajevos
> out of a hat
> and three, and four,
> and always more,
> up to a hundred,
> give or take a few.
> But do not believe us,
> it's really not true,
> there are no
> two Sarajevos
> and that is a fact.
> There's only one Sarajevo
> and we can't give you that!

Scene 8

A chant for health and, later, love at first sight

Fata *is sitting in front of a house breastfeeding a baby.* **Sara** *comes in.*

Sara I'm so glad to meet you. I'm Sara.

Fata I'm Fata. What are you doing in the streets? There's madness out there.

Sara I need shelter.

Fata You can stay here with me. I'm a housewife. I take care of the children.

Sara I can help.

Fata Fire can help

Fire... the great transformer... purging and purging... vomiting spew... saliva... bathe in sweat... bathe in steam... bloodletting... burn the polluted object... scorch the polluted thing... incense smoke... rub with ashes and soot... expose to sun... wash... spring water... sweet smells of flowers... rare plants and herbs... bajach kadife... pejgamber chichek... pelin... pazikucha... chukundurk... chelebli perchin... chomolich... anberbuj... karanfil... jagochina... krimez tea... myrrh... perfumes... fragrant oils... incense... milk... ghee... white objects... earth in its natural form... sacred relics... priests... spells... incantations... names of gods... magic amulets and stones... gold... silver... bronze... jade... dust and dry sand... henna... balm... crystal... virgins... the right side as opposed to the left... morning... sunshine... daylight...

whole or perfect objects like circles and wheels... perfect numbers like nine and four... mother's milk from the breast... purging and purging... the great transformer... fire.

Sara *sits down and puts her head in* **Fata**'s *lap.*

Molly Norton as Fata in the American Undermain Theatre
production directed by Naum Panovski

Sara Do you know Muyo and Sulyo?

Fata Do I know Muyo i Sulyo? You can bet your sweet life I know Muyo and Sulyo!

Gorchin *comes in. He looks at* **Sara** *and* **Sara** *looks at him. Love at first sight.* **Fata** *notices that.*

Fata I'd better be going. There's so much to do.

Exit **Fata**.

Gorchin   Thousands of grenades fall on the city every day. It's all in flames. One cannot possibly do one's job properly. (*He gives her an apple.*) An ounce of happiness is paid with the soul here. It's Bosnia, the apple of poison. We are creatures of discontinuity. Individuals who die alone at the end of an amazing adventure we cannot grasp or understand. But we feel the yearning for this lost continuity. And we cannot endure our transitory individuality. And that's why we make love. But that awareness of a ubiquitous, arbitrary death, which descends like a medieval plague, on the just and unjust alike, without warning or reason, is central to our experience of the twentieth century. (*He kisses her.*) I have a model of the Eiffel Tower I made out of matchsticks. You should come and see it some time.

Sara   Is it you?

Gorchin   Who?

Sara   The one I'm looking for.

Gorchin *goes out.*

Scene 9

Sara *is not dismayed by the strange events.*
She goes on talking about her dream.

Sara   I have come here, to the hills
above the city of Sarajevo,
the same hills
from where it was once
mutilated and ravaged
and assassinated.
There are new trees here,
and new birds in the trees,
and new silence,
but the city has since
been chartered and sectored,
and partitioned with walls.
This is where it all
started from.
This is where the Savage God
the City Eater
came in the last century
in the year of
one thousand nine hundred
and ninety two
before he went devouring
other places
on
and on
and on.

And here I am
to look at this place
which was once the pride
and joy of Europe.
I search to find its soul
and its face
and to see whether that soul and that face
will suit the invisible city
of my dreams.

Scene 10

Sara *meets* **Maya** *the journalist,*
who is concerned with beauty.

Park with cut-down trees. **Maya** *approaches* **Sara.**

Maya   I know Muyo, Sulyo, Fata and Gorchin. I am Maya.
Who are you?

Sara   Sara.

Maya   I'm a journalist. I used to write about the prices of
vegetables in the market, what's on at the cinemas, small
ads, who's buying and who's selling what, things like that.
Now I write about life and death. My paper still comes out
every day. And I take photographs. But only of beauty. I can
see my colleagues from the big wide world going mostly for
the blood. Not me. I look for things beautiful. They ask,
"Where do you find beauty in this town?" "Well, look at
the stumps of the trees," I say. "They've all been cut down
for winter. But look at the stumps. They have turned into
gnomes, fairies, funny faces, hairy witches of the tales of
old." And those are the photographs I take.

Sara   I am pleased to meet you.

Maya *puts her camera on a wall. She goes and stands next to*
Sara *and smiles into the camera. The camera clicks. It takes*
an automatic picture.

Maya   So am I.

Scene 11

Amazing things happen in the Strategic Studies Centre.

Rudi/Officer 1, Muyo/Officer 2.

Rudi/Officer 1   Nice job, Officer Two. Now we know what's happening and we can be much more effective.

Muyo/Officer 2   Or less.

Rudi/Officer 1   Precisely, or less effective, depending on the point of view.

Muyo/Officer 2   Or both, I suppose.

Rudi/Officer 1   Or both, he supposes. I like your sense of humour.

Muyo/Officer 2   Given normal weather conditions, only 137,000 will die this winter.

Rudi/Officer 1   Is that official?

Muyo/ Officer 2   It's official.

Rudi/Officer 1 (*Phoning somebody*)   It's official.

Enter **Sulyo/Soldier Blue** *with his Ray-Bans on.*

Sulyo/Soldier Blue   Soldier Blue, sir.

Officers 1 and 2   Speak.

Sulyo/Soldier Blue   They don't want to eat our nonmelt Hershey bars and our nonfat crackers, sir. And they throw the tinned beef to the cats.

Officers 1 and 2   Fuck them.

Sulyo/Soldier Blue Yes, sir. And also Jones, sir.

Rudi/Officer 1 What about him?

Sulyo/Soldier Blue He wants to go home to his Mum. He says he's scared and no grease in his hair or Ray-Bans on his eyes can help him out.

Rudi/Officer 1 Fuck him.

Sulyo/Soldier Blue Yes, sir. And what about the bodies, sir?

Muyo/Officer 2 What bodies?

Sulyo/Soldier Blue The dead, sir.

Rudi/Officer 1 Well, give them a decent funeral.

Sulyo/Soldier Blue Aye, aye, sir.

Officers 1 and 2 Good soldier!

Exit **Sulyo/Soldier Blue**. *Enter* **Sara**. **Rudi/Officer 1** *turns into a diplomat.*

Rudi/Diplomat How did you get here? You're not supposed to be here.

Sara Do you know Muyo, Sulyo, Fata, Maya and Gorchin? Do you know what's happened to them?

Rudi/Diplomat I don't know anybody. I don't know anything.

Sara Something must be done.

Rudi/Diplomat But of course something must be done, it's urgent, we're doing it, there's a meeting in progress, tomorrow, next week, it's on the agenda, high priority, send a fax, give us a buzz on the red phone, don't call us we'll call you, New York, Geneva, London and Bonn, UN channels and the press, what will the international community say, and the voters at election time, we'll talk about it, tête a tête, during reception, tea break and lunch, we know people die, that's what we're here for, gotta fly.

Rudi/Diplomat *goes out.*

Scene 12

UNHCR Nurse *meets* Prince Constant.

Gorchin *on his knees,* **Sara** *standing opposite him.*

Sara/Nurse   What are you thinking about?

Gorchin/Prince Constant *is silent.*

Sara/Nurse   Do you want some soup?

Gorchin/Prince Constant *is silent.*

Sara/Nurse   Is it true they made you put each other's genitals in your mouths?

Gorchin/Prince Constant *is silent.*

Sara/Nurse   Why don't you want some soup?

Gorchin/Prince Constant *is silent.*

Sara/Nurse   Is it true there was nowhere to dispose of your excrement?

Gorchin/Prince Constant *is silent.*

Sara/Nurse   I mean your shit and piss.

Gorchin/Prince Constant *is silent.*

Sara/Nurse   It's very good soup. It's hot. It'll do you good.

She starts to cry. She embraces him.

Scene 13

Sara *and* **Azra** *fly over Sarajevo on a magic carpet.*

Behind the hospital. **Azra** *in white surgical gown, with blood stains. She is smoking nervously. Her surgeon's mask hangs below her mouth.*

Azra   We operate round the clock. I run away from time to time to have a smoke. In the old days I worked for the ambulance service. Entered people's homes round the city. They would offer me cherry preserves with water, which I would accept. And brandy, which I would refuse. I like our people's hospitality. The children would do drawings for me. Which I would put on the wall at home. And they would ring me up to say they'd been good. And that they drink their tea and cough mixture regularly. Hold me tight, please.

Sara *embraces her.*

Azra   Let's hold hands and hide from the wind
Let's hold hands and sigh
And get our tears dry
For now it's winter
Let's huddle together in the dark
and dream of south seas
and prawns
and cocoa.

Azra *kisses* **Sara** *on the mouth. She takes her gown off. Underneath she has beautiful multi-coloured clothes on.*

Azra   I am the daughter of Zehra Midovich, the first Muslim woman who took her veil off. After the war. After which war? The last war. The big war. Is this one small, then? It was a scandal in those days. I'm proud of her. I'm a modern woman really. I used to know the difference between Chanel No.5, Laura Ashley No.1, Lulu Cacharel and Yves Saint Laurent. Now I've forgotten. We forget. Forgetfulness caresses us easily like the sea breeze. The leaves in autumn forget they belonged to the tree. It takes them all winter to remember who they are.

Sara   Do you know Muyo, Sulyo, Fata, Gorchin and Maya?

Azra   Yes, I do. Of course I do.

She produces a magic carpet.

Azra   Let's go.

Sara   Where?

Azra   Over the city.

They get on the magic carpet. They fly over Sarajevo.

Azra   Oh, you bridges
          over the River Milyatska
          Kozia Chyupria
          Chumurya
          Tsareva Chyupria
          Latino Chyupria
          Chechayna Chyupria
          Drvenia
          Chobania
          Skenderia
          Vrbanya
          Oh, you people
          crossing those bridges
          Oh, to take you away

>On this carpet and fly
>To Damascus!
>To Damascus!

They fly. **Sara** *looks down.*

Sara   Look. They've seen us. They're waving.

Sara and **Azra** *wave back.*

Scene 14

The Tower of Sevdah

A tower with a neon rainbow. A large hall. There are a number of exhibits inside – a larger-than-life quince, a shargiya musical instrument, a cigarette holder, tobacco, a coffee cup and coffee pot. In the middle a shadrvan fountain running with water. **Sara** *comes in. Long silence.*

Hamdia/Custodian   Welcome.

Sara   Is this the Tower of Sevdah?

Hamdia/Custodian   Have you been to the other Towers?

Sara   Are there other ones?

Hamdia/Custodian   There must be. Can you hear it?

Sara   I'm sorry?

Hamdia/Custodian   Can you hear it ?

Sara   What?

Hamdia/Custodian   The clock.

Sara   What clock?

Hamdia/Custodian   Listen! (*Pause.*)

Sara   I can't hear anything.

Hamdia/Custodian   Shhhhh!

Sara   What is there to hear?

Hamdia/Custodian   The Kudrat Clock Tower. It takes some time to hear it. It ticks away the meaning.

Sara The meaning? Of what?

Hamdia/Custodian Why have you come here? You feel love and pain. And nostalgia. And melancholy and yearning. And hunger for life.

Sara How do you know?

Hamdia/Custodian It's sevdah.

Sara What does that mean?

Hamdia/Custodian It is heavy and airy and bitter and sweet. You are in love, and you are in love with love, in love with yourself being in love, in love with the world in which love exists, happy and sad that things are as they are, drowning in wine, and sunk in memories and desires. You can't get rid of it. Once you get it, it sticks with you.

Sara This is a strange place.

Hamdia/Custodian Today I will talk about a very ordinary day in the life of you as a grandmother. Do you want to hear?

Sara Me as a grandmother?

Hamdia/Custodian That's how it is. There you are as a grandmother, you see, sitting in your avlia, the cobblestone courtyard of your house. It is girdled with a high wall towards the street. In the middle, a fountain of fresh water called a shadrvan. Up there, a mushebak, a wooden window overlooking the street for the young girls to throw loving glances on the world outside. Roses in the garden. A big apple tree crossed in such a way that it gives 15 different kinds of apples. No roof of any house is higher than the window of the next house, so that everyone can have a view of the city. Behind the house another garden. Big walnut tree. The walnuts make your fingers oily and black. Quinces on the mantelpiece. Try one. (**Sara** *tries it.*) What is it like?

Sara   Bitter.

Hamdia/Custodian   Not close enough.

Sara   Sort of sour sweet. Makes your mouth small.

Hamdia/Custodian   Preserves made of rose leaves. Have some. Salep or julep drink. Boza. Rahatlokum or Turkish delight. You as a grandmother smoke four packs a day.

The Custodian *rolls a cigarette.*

Sara   What is this around me?

Hamdia/Custodian   Lilacs, freshly painted walls, the people brought their coffee pots and coffee cups out of the houses and under the trees, neighbour has called neighbour round, transistor radio on the table, people listen to the sports match report and have thin meze and drink mild rakia.

He gives her the cigarette.

Sara   Thank you.

She puts the cigarette in her mouth, lights it and smokes.

Hamdia/Custodian   Easy.

Sara *starts smoking more slowly.*

Hamdia/Custodian   Easy.

Sara *smokes even more slowly.*

Hamdia/Custodian   That's better.

The Custodian *pours out two small cups of Turkish coffee. They slurp it slowly for a long time.*

Hamdia/Custodian   Now a scene in which nothing much happens. A family in their usual harmonious way. You are a child. Your father is a professor of ethics and he is preparing his lecture for the next day. He is going to talk about the list of atrocities to be found in our folk songs and how that affects each and every one of us. Your younger brother, Aleksandar, is playing with play-do on the floor, and you, his elder sister Mira, are doing your chemistry homework. Mendeleev's Periodic Table.

Sara   My name is not Mira.

Hamdia/Custodian   Your mother has just cooked some chestnuts and is serving them. She is going to call you, the grandmother, to come and have some chestnuts with you, the granddaughter. The rain is falling outside and beating on the windows. The leaves that have fallen on the ground are slippery. It's autumn.

Sara   I don't quite follow you.

Hamdia/Custodian   I apologise if this is the dry insight of a historian. I was one. In reality it's all different. It's all something else.

Sara   But what is reality please? Are we going to survive this?

Hamdia/Custodian   You have been riding on a horse for a long time through the wilderness. And you have been taken over by the yearning to get to this city. And you have come here, to a place difficult to define. Talking about this city is like dancing about architecture. And here are towers with stained glass spiral staircases inlaid with sea shells. They are built according to the laws of the fugue. And these towers make one tower. And this one tower is neither here nor there! Neither in heaven, but then again not really on earth either. A city in mid-air. Wings fluttering in still flight. In this city you cannot decide between four men. But your journey has taken too long. You have become an old woman. And you join the other old women in the market. And your wishes have become memories. Life is very slow here, but death is sudden. Be careful when you go out. Things may have changed terribly.

Sara   Please tell me more. Why is this happening? I have never read more papers in my life, or watched more television or listened more to the news, and I have never understood less. Why so much hatred? Where does this evil come from? What does it mean? What purpose does it serve? (*Pause.*) You don't want to talk about it? (*Pause.*) Well! (*Pause.*) I think it's time for me to go home now. (*Pause.*) Hello! (*Pause.*) I would like to go, please. (*Pause.*) How do I get out of here? Hello!

The Custodian *gazes at her.* **Sara** *goes up to him, and touches him.* **The Custodian** *collapses on one side like a dead statue.* **Sara** *starts looking for a way out in a panic.*

Scene 15

Sara *speaks about the backbone of Sarajevo.*

Sara   Here are a few items
from what once was
Sarajevo.
A skull,
a family album, a rug
two bits of mortar,
a coffee cup.
How did they fit together?
How do they fit together?
What was it like
before it wasn't?
What did it look like
Before it didn't?

But I also have
something else,
something special,
the bone of Sarajevo,
a bone called Luz
or Judenknöchlein,
a bone found just under the
eighteenth vertebra
that never dies.
It cannot be destroyed by fire
or any other element,
nor can it be broken
or bruised
by any other force.

God will use this bone
in the art of resurrection.
When struck with a hammer
the bone will not break
while the anvil upon which it lies
will be shattered.

Scene 16

The tale of the small-time smuggler

Muyo/Small Time Smuggler   I want it to be peace again, so I can go back to my craft of cunning. I'm a small-time smuggler. Foreign currency in small denominations, leather goods from Turkey and jeans from Italy. I'm not a war profiteer and never will be. I'm strictly small-time. Could we go back to the small times please? And watch the match on Sundays like all normal people?

Scene 17

Dubrovnik and Vukovar song

Fata, **Azra** and **Maya**

This is Dubrovnik and
This is Vukovar
Greeting Sarajevo,
Our twin sister,
Our twin town.
We know the story
We've seen it before.
Do not run and hide,
Endure, dear sister,
We're on your side.

Scene 18

The Tale of the Poet

Hamdia/The Poet Shoot, you sniper, you miserable wretch, let's get it over with. I'm a poet. My tombstone will say: Here lieth the one who knew the "silver" soul of Sarajevo. Writing poetry after Sarajevo is barbaric. The rest is silence. All I read now are the poems the astronauts wrote when they came back to earth. "Look at the sky more often," they plead. "Why?" the chickens would ask. Only the eagles need the sky. The chickens never look up. They are busy pecking at breadcrumbs. There is no concept of the sky in a hen house. This spot is where I kissed for the first time. She's gone now. Shame on you! Shame on you!

Scene 19

A performance of the legend of Hasanaginitsa

Storyteller Aga Hasan was badly wounded in a battle and stayed in the soldiers' camp waiting for his wounds to heal. The camp was high in the mountains. His mother and his sister came to visit him. His wife and love, Hasanaginitsa, did not come:

Hasanaginitsa I wanted to go very much but I couldn't. Custom dictates that a wife is not allowed to visit her husband in a soldiers' camp, even if he is the commander-in-chief. So I didn't dare. But God knows I worried and longed for him because we were still deeply in love, after many years of living together. We had four children, and the youngest one was only a baby in the cradle.

Storyteller When Aga Hasan recovered a little, he sent a message to his faithful wife:

Hasanaga Don't wait for me, neither at my home, nor at the homes of my relatives.

Storyteller When Hasanaginitsa received this message from her beloved, she went to the tower of their castle to throw herself off. But her mother-in-law stopped her:

Mother-in-Law Go away and hide for some time with my family. I will calm down the wrath of my son when he comes back. Then you can return to your husband and children.

Storyteller Hasanaginitsa agreed to do as she advised. But when Hasanaga came home:

Hasanaga I don't want to even hear of living together

again with Hasanaginitsa. I am offended by her neglect while I was wounded. She betrayed our love.

Storyteller   The brother of Hasanaginitsa, the Bey Pintorovich, was also offended by the attitude of Hasanaga towards his sister. He was a very rich and influential aristocrat, from a higher class than the one to which Hasanaga belonged:

Bey Pintorovich   You will give a ferman to my sister allowing her to marry again.

Hasanaga   Yes. On condition that she does not take the children away with her.

Storyteller   In those times a divorced woman was always the guilty party and the one who was to blame for not preserving the marriage. Bey Pintorovich did not want to bring this shame on his sister:

Bey Pintorovich   Sister dear, I have arranged for you to marry the Kadia Imotski. He is a judge and an honourable man. Marrying him would make you innocent in the whole affair.

Hasanaginitsa   What about me? Do I have a say in this? Do I have a choice?

Storyteller   When the wedding day came, the guests went to Bey Pintorovich's house to pick up the bride and take her to the groom's place. There were many guests on horses and many horses carrying the bride's wealth to her new home. It was a late spring morning, sunny and bright. Hasanaginitsa rode the darkest horse in the middle. She was covered with a white silk veil embroidered with gold and silver. As they were passing the home of Aga Hasan, she stopped:

Hasanaginitsa   I want to say goodbye to my children.

Storyteller   The guests were astonished by her unexpected request, but they stopped and waited silently. She jumped off the horse and entered her former home. Her steps in her golden wooden sandals echoed on the stone terrace. Her daughters ran to meet her. Hasanaga was sitting in the shade of the old oak. The cradle with their baby was beside him. Hasanaginitsa embraced her daughters, who were shouting for joy. When she looked at Hasanaga, he stood up and turned his back on her. She silently approched the cradle. The daughters went silent. Hasanaginitsa picked up the baby who was quietly asleep. Her tears fell on the baby's little hand:

Hasanaga   Oh, my poor children, this bride used to be your mother.

Storyteller   The horse in the wedding party outside gave a terrible whinny. Hasanaginitsa put the baby back in the cradle. Her heart broke. She fell down and died.

From the original Antwerp 93 production,
directed by Slobodan Unkovski

Scene 20

The Air Song

Fata/Chorus of Clouds

It is we the clouds
Of Sarajevo
Thick and dense and dark
And light and airy and pale.
It is we the fog
And the smog
And the air
And the something
In the air.
It is the fair blue
Of the crisp
Wednesday morning in May
And the foul glue
Of the blue winter night
yesterday.

Scene 21

The Holiday Inn Winter Olympics 1984 love affair

Gorchin/Rocker Winter Olympic World Skating Champion 1984!

Sara/Linn You are my biggest prize.

Gorchin/Rocker Save the last dance for me, Linn, you Norwegian bonnie lass, Olympic magician on skates, you're talking to a rock 'n' roll star in the making.

Sara/Linn I didn't expect there would be a Holiday Inn in Sarajevo.

Gorchin/Rocker It's specially made for us to hide in and make love.

Sara/Linn You've never had so much world in your town before. ABC and NBC and BBC and ITV.

Gorchin/Rocker Have a smoke.

Sara/Linn I'm high enough already.

Gorchin/Rocker Tomorrow when there's war you'll come as a nurse in your suspender belt and black stockings. And give the soldiers a skating show. But I'll be dead and it will be useless.

Sara/Linn I'll kiss you back to life.

Gorchin/Rocker (*Touching her breast*) You're an angel.

Sara/Linn I am. A hibernating one. These (*Pointing to her breasts*) are the remains of my wings.

Gorchin/Rocker (*Singing*) "Sve ove godine, dala bi za

jednu noć, a mene ne bi nikad imala, jer ja moram drugoj
poć."

Sounds of shooting and flashing light.

Sara/Linn   What's that?

Gorchin/Rocker   Fireworks! Don't be scared. Everything's
under control. Everything's under control.

Suddenly a desk at the airport. **Rudi** *is a steward.*

Rudi/Steward   Yes!

Sara/Linn   Two tickets to Bangkok, please.

Rudi/Steward   Holidays far away, ey. 24-hour flight!

Sara/Linn   Sort of.

Rudi/Steward   But the airport is closed.

Sara/Linn   Oh. (*Pause.*) When will it open?

Rudi/Steward *shrugs his shoulders.*

Pause.

Gorchin/Rocker   Is it open now?

Rudi/Steward *nods his head.*

Gorchin/Rocker   Two tickets to Oslo, please.

Rudi/Steward   Holiday weekend, ey? Two-hour flight!

Gorchin/Rocker   Sort of.

Rudi/Steward   But the airport is closed.

Gorchin/Rocker   Oh. (*Pause.*) When will it open?

Rudi/Steward *shrugs his shoulders.*

Pause.

Sara/Linn   Is it open now?

Rudi/Steward *nods his head.*

Sara/Linn   Two tickets to Dubrovnik, please.

Rudi/Steward   A short break away, ey? Half hour flight?

Sara/Linn   Sort of.

Rudi/Steward   But the airport is closed.

Sara/Linn   But you said it was open.

Rudi/Steward   It was open.

Sara/Linn   Oh.

Pause.

Gorchin/Rocker   Is it open now?

Rudi/Steward *nods his head.*

Gorchin/Rocker   Two tickets to Sarajevo, please.

Rudi/Steward   You don't need tickets for Sarajevo. You're in Sarajevo.

Gorchin/Rocker   Oh. Are we?

Rudi/Steward   Yes.

Gorchin/Rocker   Oh. What a relief.

Rudi/Steward   Only, you can't get to it.

Gorchin/Rocker   What do you mean?

Rudi/Steward   You're in Sarajevo, but Sarajevo is not here. It's gone away.

Gorchin/Rocker   Oh.

Sara/Linn   Do you know when it's coming back?

Rudi/Steward (*Shaking his head*)   The airport is closed. The sky is closed. Everything is closed.

Scene 22

The Tale of the Cello Player

Azra/The Cello Player I was with the Sarajevo Philharmonic when all this started. I was working on Bach's solo partitas for cello. You know, the ones Pablo Casals did so well in 1938. I'm pregnant. I didn't ask for this baby, but decided to have it. I don't know the father. There were many of them. Some of them were my neighbours. It sounds unbelievable. But then what is believable? You give me one believable thing and I will turn into a dumb fish and dive low into the dark depths of the purple seas. Never to return. Never. Not here.

Scene 23

The Tale of Ivo Andrich

Hamdia/Ivo Andrich. *Hat on his head, long coat. Hands in his pockets.*

Hamdia/Ivo Andrich An ordinary enemy you kill from a distance. In cold blood. But your brother, you kill looking into his eyes. Passionately. You two are one. The only way you can free yourself from him is to carve yourself out of him with a knife. (*Pause.*) My name is Andrich, I won the Nobel Prize for Literature. They called me a mandarin. Above it all. And now, I am below it all. Motherfuckers. What else can I say?

Scene 24

Song of the Migrant Birds

Maya/Migrant Birds Chorus

> I am a stork
> Or a migrant bird
> Known to fly south
> When the weather gets rough.
> Now it's winter
> And we should really go
> But we are staying
> In Sarajevo
> With all other birds
> And creatures of feather,
> Sparrows and pigeons
> Magpies and ducks,
> As they have no other place they can go.
> We think it's unfair
> To leave them so
>
> We'll stay and sing
> With double our might.
>
> So here we are
> Brother helps brother
> I hope it's a lesson
> of some kind or other.

We
the birds of Sarajevo
pray
for abundance of peace
and full vessels of charity
and rich treasures of mercy
and we pray
that the real
will unveil itself
and the world will start again.

From the original Antwerp 93 production directed by
Slobodan Unkovski

Scene 25

The Santa Claus Press Release

Rudi/Santa Claus   No comment. Are you accusing me of something? No? Very well, then, 'cos, you see, I don't feel guilty. I tried my best. It was difficult. I'm not saying it was impossible, nothing is impossible, but it was very, very difficult. I couldn't put all of my other operations at stake. They're not the only children in the world, you know. It's not as if I didn't try. I feel for those children as much as you do. If not more! Yes, if not more! I tried, it didn't work. There you are! I'm sorry. What else can I say. Let them go without toys for one Christmas. Next year I'll bring them double. All right? Say hello from me to them. And Merry Christmas! Nothing else to say. No comment.

Scene 26

The Song of the Roofs

Sulyo/The Chorus Of Roofs

> We
> the roofs of Sarajevo
> Sing
> We the mosques, the spires and the domes,
> We the red tiles
> We the flat tarmac of the apartment buildings
> We the chimneys
> Of the poor people's homes
> And the rich,
> We the thunder rods
> The crosses on the churches
> And the aerials
> Sing.
>
> We the roofs of Sarajevo
> Sing
> And pray
> For gentle rain
> For new wool snow
> For pigeons and sparrows
> For cats and moon
> And sleepwalkers.
> We sing and pray
> That they should come back
> That they should come back
> To us
> Again.

Scene 27

A Street Incident in a United Europe with Mystical Consequences

A street in a United Europe. Perhaps in Rostock. **Rudi/Skinhead** *meets* **Sara/Refugee**.

Rudi/Skinhead   Hello fucking there! I smell the blood of a fucking refugee polluting our streets! You fucking stick out a mile, you know. Fuck. You know who my idol is? The Laser Man, guy in Sweden, he's got fucking guts. Heard of him? You fucking must have! Famous for dealing with the likes of you. Around Ringvägen he spreads terror and fear. You carry your fucking slime and disease wherever you go, but I'm not gonna take it! There's this fucking church where refugees take shelter! Yeah? Well, it'll go up in fucking flames soon. Why? Ask me. I should know. Ha, ha. Nod, nod, wink, wink. How shall I fucking hurt you now? Ey? I give you a choice, because, I fucking like you, you know!

Sara/Refugee *looks at him.*

Rudi/Skinhead   What is it?

Sara/Refugee *looks at him.*

Rudi/Skinhead   What're you doing?

Sara/Refugee *looks at him.*

Rudi/Skinhead   What're you fucking looking at me like that for?

Sara/Refugee   Look! Your hair's gone all white.

A strange transformation takes place. The **Skinhead** *collapses on his knees in front of the* **Refugee**. *She puts her hand on his head. Pause. He goes out on his knees.*

Scene 28

The Tram Song

Muyo/Tram

> I am a Tram
> made and born in England
> but a naturalised
> Sarajevan now.
> Here are a few good reasons
> Why I want my freedom back.
> First I want to take the children
> to kindergarten and school,
> then to take the students
> to the uni and on dates,
> then mothers and fathers
> to work and the market place,
> pensioners to the parks,
> sportsmen to their matches,
> and also last
> but by no means least
> I am rather proud
> and I simply want
> to be free
> and moving again.

Scene 29

The Assassination in 1914

Summer of 1914. Ladies and gentlemen in Central European costumes sit in cafés and sip brandy and coffee. **Gorchin/ Gavrilo Princip** *and* **Rudi/Major Tankosich** *are sitting in two coffee houses one next to the other.*

Gorchin/Gavrilo Princip   My friend, Major Tankosich, of the anarchist Black Hand organisation. He's helping me with my target practice.

Rudi/Major Tankosich   My friend Gavrilo Princip, the future assassin of the ruler of the Austro-Hungarian Empire.

Gorchin/Gavrilo Princip   He is sitting in the Vienna Coffee House.

Rudi/Major Tankosich   And he in the Istanbul Coffee House.

Gorchin/Gavrilo Princip   He is having some Sachertorte and Mozartkuglen and cappuccino.

Rudi/Major Tankosich   And he is having tufahiya and sherbet and strong tobacco and Turkish coffee.

Gorchin/Gavrilo Princip   That building is in the Viennese Baroque style.

Rudi/Major Tankosich   And that one's a typical example of Middle Eastern kerpich, meaning mud and brick. This is the navel of Europe.

Gorchin/Gavrilo Princip   The seam.

Rudi/Major Tankosich   And the navel is the most fragile part of the body.

Gorchin/Gavrilo Princip   And the seam is where things come apart and crack.

Rudi/Major Tankosich   Such an obvious place.

Gorchin/Gavrilo Princip   Such an obvious target.

Both *(Together holding a pistol and playing a children's game)*
Eni meni seni
seni chokolada
bur bur
limunada.

(Singing)
Europe is a whore,
Europe is a bitch,
Let's pull the trigger,
Let's press the switch.

She gives with one hand
and takes away with two
well, if that's how it is,
let's see what we can do!

Let's do some damage
and blow off the crown
make Prince Ferdinand
come tumbling down.

They shoot.

Scene 30

The Song of the Waters

Maya/Chorus of Waters

> I am the water in the shadrvan
> Gurgling
> And speaking
> To you.
> I am the spray in the fountain
> The spring
> The source
> And the mouth
> The eye crying
> And the tongue licking
> And the vein
> Gushing.
> Please don't say
> It can't happen here
> It can't happen here
> can't happen
> can't happen
> can't happen here
> You say that
> and it can happen
> and it will.

Scene 31

The Tale of the Window Woman

Azra/The Woman At The Window, *nicely dressed and made up, her hair well combed, is watering the flowers in her window box.*

Azra/The Woman At The Window   I water the flowers every day and speak to them. They like to be spoken to. And I pretend that nothing is happening. And I clear the rubbish the grenades leave. And go on with my life. Everything would be normal if only I had glass in the windows and if half the wall wasn't missing. Which is not a pretty sight on the seventh floor of an apartment building. (*Waving at somebody*) My neighbours are crossing a minefield. They look as if they're dancing. An old man carries a canister of water in one hand and an umbrella in the other. (*She waves.*) He disappears into the distance. But we shall overcome. Love will overcome. It always has. It always will.

From the original Antwerp 93 production
directed by Slobodan Unkovski

Scene 32

The Cook's Tale

Sulyo/The Cook   To make a good Bosnian Pot you take quarter of a kilo of beef, quarter of a kilo of pork, garlic, onions, kale, potatoes, beans, tomatoes, green peppers, carrots, parsley, salt, pepper, white wine and water. You put the meat in the earthenware pot and place the vegetables on top. You mix in the garlic and the onion, pour in the water and the wine, and finally season with salt and pepper. You cover the pot with parchment paper that you've made little holes in with a needle. You cook it in the oven for two to three hours... (*He starts crying.*) I'm sorry. I can't go on.

Scene 33

The Tale of Josip Broz Tito

Hamdia/Josip Broz Tito *comes in dressed in a general's uniform.*

Hamdia/Tito   There are only two things I would like to add to this. Firstly, people who have such a generation of young people as we have in Yugoslavia should have no fear for their future. And secondly, safeguard brotherhood and unity as preciously as your eyes.

Scene 34

The Tale of the Asylum Caretaker's Wife

*A heap of clothes left by a relief operation. The **Wife** takes clothes and measures them against her husband's body. He's reading a newspaper.*

Asylum Caretaker's Wife   The first three days after he came back everything was all right. But now he tells such strange tales and reads old newspapers. All the doctors ran away and left him there with the patients. 40 mad women and no medicines. What could he do? He's only the caretaker. They nearly ripped him apart. Oh well. I'm not complaining. Here they've been very nice to us. We were in a hotel first. Beautiful room, with tiles in the bathroom. And what a bathroom! I've never been in a hotel like that. Couldn't afford it! Now we're in a tent, but it's OK. We've got a view of the sea. And, oh, what sunsets! And the smell of fir trees. It's like a holiday. Or could be. If they were here with us. Our children. And if he was better. Sometimes I'm so afraid. Though I shouldn't be. We used to be afraid in the good old days. Not anymore. Now we're numb. Something is flickering in the distance. Is it a train approaching, or leaving, or both?

Sulyo/Caretaker (*Singing*)
>Bila je tako ljepa
>uvijek se sećam nje
>bila je tako ljepa
>kao tog jutra dan
>divna je ona bila

kada sam ostao sam
više se nismo sreli
jer nju je odnio dan.

Scene 35

An Article from the Oslobodjenje newspaper

Maya (*Reading*)   "We could have done something if we had really wanted." "If we had known then what we know now, we might have done something." "It is the great excuse of the 20th century, and perhaps it is even the great excuse of all human history. But we did know, and we still did nothing. If they write a book about us one day, it should be called *The Triumph of the Lack of Will*'. (*She stops reading.*) It's still not good enough. I've been writing this for months. It's never good enough. And how can it be? I'm shooting at a moving target. An open wound. Perhaps I should show some common human decency. And shut up.

Scene 36

The Song of the Two Skyscrapers Momo and Uzeir

Muyo And Sulyo/Skyscrapers

> We are two skyscrapers
> the pride of the city –
> Momo and Uzeir
> are our nicknames.
> We had elevators
> and sophisticated gadgets
> like all skyscrapers
> in the big wide world.
> We belonged to a city
> which is a city no more.
> What is a city?
> Let's look at it this way –
> the city is a place
> where you can have
> tea and toast
> in the morning –
> think about it –
> a city is a place
> with shops
> where you can buy
> the tea,
> have a home to take it to
> and means to take it to in –
> bus, taxi or underground –
> where you have electricity or gas
> to boil some water on,

and where you have water
in the first place
coming through a tap
and miles and miles of pipes,
and if you want to drink the tea
in a warm room
the heating should be on,
there should be people working
to get it on and send it to you
through miles and miles of pipes.
And to get the toast
is up to the bakeries
and the bakers working there
in sleeveless shirts all night.

You need all that
in a city
if you want to have
tea and toast in the morning.

One little thing missing
and there's no tea
and no toast
and no city.

Scene 37

The Tale of the Angry Wife

Maya/The Wife   Get out of here. I don't want to see you again. For years it didn't matter who I was or what I was or who my parents were, and now it's all that matters. I didn't know I had a nation until all this started. And now it's your nation against mine. I married you, not the past, not your glorious ancestors, not the dead. I can't take this any longer. This is what I call irrationality and aggression and you try to make me see it as new rationality and meaning. Thank you very much. You go out and join the boys and fight it out, for your tribe, for your motherland, for your rosy future on the horizon. History calls! Blood and soil! Your motherland gains a son and your children lose a father. Oh well, it's a small price to pay. I'm taking my children, our children, out of here. Goodbye. Have a good war and fuck yourself! (*Pause.*) These were the last words I said to him. I never saw him again. And now it's too late. And I'm so sorry.

Scene 38

The Four Priestesses look for the centre of the city

Azra/Imam This must be the dead centre of the city.

Maya/Catholic Priest Perhaps slightly more to the right?

Fata/Orthodox Priest Or the left?

Sara/Rabbi Or down here, maybe.

Azra/Imam We must be close.

Maya/Catholic Priest We have measured.

Fata/Orthodox Priest And measured again.

Sara/Rabbi And again and again.

Azra/Imam We must be certain.

Maya/Catholic Priest Or the prayer won't work.

Fata/Orthodox Priest Couldn't work.

Sara/Rabbi And time is short and we are in a hurry.

Azra/Imam This must be it. This is the place.

Maya/Catholic Priest The pillar of the city.

Fata/Orthodox Priest The place where it all starts from and comes back to.

Sara/Rabbi Here we must place our support.

Azra/Imam Of the Kuran and Tasawuf.

Maya/Catholic Priest The Bible.

Fata/Orthodox Priest And the Apocrypha.

Sara/Rabbi   The Torah and the Talmud.

Azra/Imam   This is the rose of the four winds.

Maya/Catholic Priest   The door of four doors.

Fata/Orthodox: The arch of four spires.

Sara/Rabbi   The still and shifting point.

Azra/Imam   If this tumbles...

Maya/Catholic Priest   Everything tumbles.

Fata/Orthodox Priest   If this fails...

Sara/Rabbi   Everything fails.

All   Let those come
That want to come
And let those go
That want to go
With no harm to me
Or mine.

The priestesses pray in different languages.

(English)   Peace be to this house
And to all who dwell in it!

(Slovenian)   Mir, mir, tej hishi
in vsem ki v njej zivijo!

(Hebrew)   Shalom al kol habait
Ve al kol joshvav!

(Macedonian)   Mir, mir na ovaa kucha
i na site koi zhiveat vo nea!

(Swedish)   Vare Fred i detta Hus
Ock till All som vistas dari!

236

(Serbo-Croat) Mir, mir ovoj kuchi
i svima koji u njoj zhive!

(Spanish) Que la paz sea en esta casa
Y con los que aqui moran!

(Arabic) Salaam 'Ala Hatha Al Bayt
Wa 'Ala Kol Men Yaskon Fih!

Scene 39

The Tower of Names

Sara Professor Hamdia?

Hamdia *nods his head.*

Sara I have read your books on the history of the city.

Hamdia Do you want to hear the names?

Sara What names?

Hamdia Here are the names:

Dunja, Midhat, Damir, Ismeta, Bojan, Bahra, Dushka, Mujesira, Slobodan,

Edin, Abdulah, Fuad, Emina, Goran, Miroslav, Ivo, Hrvoje, Jasna,

Vasvija, Sena, Nihad, Vladimir, Srdjan.

Amra, Alma, Dzenana, Mirela, Nezira, Fadila, Nenad, Mirsad, Mirza, Amir, Jelena, Iris, Dzenita, Marina, Vesna, Sanja, Ankica, Muhamed, Ibro, Zlatko, Ivan, Tarik, Zdravko, Slavko.

Here are the surnames:

Hadzibegich, Mujezinovich, Diklich, Hadzijusufbegich, Fejzagich, Finci,

Pashich, Markovich, Lovrenovich, Marjanovich, Osti, Sulejmanovich,

Mirnich, Mandich, Agovich, Atijas, Popovski, Pervan, Petrovich, Veber, Lukich, Ferhatovich, Oljacha, Pardo,

Bomostar, Sarajlich, Lajtner, Vagner, Fisher, Blum, Shlosberg, Valdeg, Kubi, Andrlon, Agoshton, Adjanjela, Olenjuk.

Here are the nicknames:

Bucko, Bega, Zlaja, Faco, Caco, Kampo, Glava, Hare, Dino, Dzeni, Jaca, Bimbo, Avdo, Duca, Daca, Jaca, Mica, Cica, Deki, Zoki, Kiki, Miki, Pasha, Sasha, Fuko, Zuko, Miro, Chiro, Zinka, Minka, Pike, Biba, Hiba,

Bera, Cera, Futa, Guta, Cigo, Shvabo, Ogi, Koki, Zdena, Gigi, Boki, Sena, Zena, Kena, Deja, Fisko, Gugi, Pape, Nechko, Tvigi, Zirka, Bilja, Bichoka, Hase,

Kemo, Koka, Izo, Hame, Kana, Bibi, Neka, Fazla, Dzidzi...

Sara   Are these the names of the living or the dead?

Hamdia   Or the unborn?

Sara   Do you have Muyo, Sulyo, Fata, Maya, Azra and Gorchin on the list?

Hamdia   Muyo, Sulyo, Fata, Maya, Azra, Gorchin. Now I have them. And what is your name?

Sara   Sara.

Hamdia   And Sara. Now I have you too.

Scene 40

Song of the Common People

All We
the common people of Sarajevo
in this hour of darkness
and weakness
and despair
pledge
to heal
and guide
and guarantee respect for observance of rituals
and defend the town against evil spirits.
We will point out places for fruitful hunting
and fishing
increase the wild life
control the weather
ease childbirth
and reveal future events.

Scene 41

Back to the shelter. Finale with a rainbow.

As in Scene 3. The shelling is still going on.

Rudi   She's dead.

Gorchin   She's beautiful.

Azra   She's not dead, she's unconscious.

Fata   God knows where her mother is.

Maya (*Reading a newspaper*)   Look at this. I wrote this.

Muyo (*Looking into the street*)   Come on then, stop it. I've got work to do.

Sulyo (*Singing*)   Mošćanice, vodo plemenita,
                        usput ti je pozdravi mi dragog

Hamdia   Stop it, please. It's bad enough as it is.

Pause. **Gorchin** *is holding* **Sara**'s *head. She opens her eyes and comes round.* **Gorchin** *looks at her in surprise.*

Gorchin   We thought you were dead.

Sara   Was I?

Gorchin   I mean, that you had died.

Sara   Had I?

Gorchin   Well, you hadn't. You're still around.

Sara   Am I?

Gorchin   You're funny. Who are you?

Sara   Sara.

Gorchin   Sara who?

Sara   Just Sara.

Gorchin   What do you do?

Sara   I fly.

Gorchin   Fly? How come you fly?

Sara *is silent.*

Gorchin   Do you have wings?

Sara *is silent.*

Gorchin   How come you have wings? Where are they? Are they invisible?

Sara *is silent.*

Gorchin   You mean, you have wings like an angel?

Sara *nods.*

Gorchin   Like a soul?

Sara *nods.*

Gorchin   Don't tell me you're a goddess or something.

Sara *is silent. She looks at him.*

Gorchin   If you're a goddess, how come you're sick?

Sara *looks at him.*

Gorchin   Why do you let all this happen?

Sara *looks at him.*

Gorchin   You certainly wouldn't hide here in the shelter with us.

Sara *looks at him. All of a sudden a huge rainbow begins* *to grow out of her. A small miracle happens in the bleak Sarajevo wonderland. Everybody looks at it. They look at her in amazement. Has she died or risen from the ashes like a phoenix?*

CURTAIN

Additional Scene 1

This scene is based on texts from the Sarajevo chronicles written by Mula Mustafa Basheskia - Sefki in the 18th century.

Karadjoz Theatre
Hamdia And now scenes from life in Sarajevo from the 12th century, according to the Arabic calendar, or the 18th century, according to the Christian one. As performed and dreamt by the Sarajevo Karadjoz Puppet Theatre of Shadows directed by me, Mula Mustafa BasheskiaSefki in 1772. During the performance "twice a meteor could be seen flying through the sky, which was very brilliant".

The woman without hands
They brought a woman to Sarajevo from the provinces who from birth had had no hands but used her legs to weave and do other things. She was taken to Istanbul to be exhibited there.

Earthquakes
For three nights between aksham (evening) and yatsia (bedtime, two hours after sunset) at the same time and repeatedly, there were earthquakes. After that, all through the year every day and every night thumps could be heard from under the ground, similar to thumps in a barrel or drum.

Camels with ammunition
One thousand camels came to Sarajevo and brought ammunition. Then seven hundred camels came to Bosnia carrying gunpowder and bullets. A decree came from the

Sultan to have the arms taken away from the people, that the Judge should see they were sold and the money given to the owners of the arms.

The Plague

The plague came to Sarajevo, first at Vratnik. Then it appeared at Hrid, Chekalusa, Banski Briyeg, then it spread in the Sunbul mahala, Pasya mahala, then in Kosevo, Berkusa and Souk Bunar. So, the plague at the beginning hit the outskirts of town and the poor people. That is why the well-to-do citizens believed it would not strike them. This disease ravaged the town for full three years and in the city of Sarajevo itself killed 15,000 people. The prayer for the plague to stop is the following: "O God, you who are the treasury of all goodness, keep us away from all we fear."

The first man to die was Tsabrich or Kabrikogli.

20 days later his brother Suleiman Tsabrich, the kettle maker, also died of the plague. Let it be known!

> Then died: the old saddler
> the father of AliBasha Skender
> the son of the baker
> Mula Osman, the brother of the muftia
> Mula Avdia, the dervish, died of the plague in Belgrade
> Rehin's brother, died in Skopje of the plague
> That well-known fat man, serdar Ahmet, died in Edrene
> Zimia Atsim, the milkman
> Kisho, the policeman
> Graho, the blacksmith
> Devetaban, the porter

Old Durak
Ibrahim, the gardener, Jashar's brother
Salih, the carpenter
Bulbul, the barber
The town crier
The lantern man
The tobacco man
Tuzlo, the apprentice
The medresa acolyte
The poor man, who was always borrowing money
The Arnaut, the bricklayer
Dugo or Dugi, the muezzin
Salih, the stone thrower
Focho, the blind man
That demented Alia, our neighbour
Ahmed efendia Hodzo. God have mercy upon him
Mula Jahya Obralia, the librarian
Masho, the builder of the grand seraglio.

The following also died in different ways:
Halats, the caretaker, killed
The Alibasha, the tax collector, with the moustaches,
also killed
The son of Black Omer, drowned on Bendbasha
The shop owner, from Pasya Mahala, died from
smoking opium
Hadzia Mlatso, died on the way to Mecca
One man was strangled, God only knows why.

The Children
All children in Sarajevo caught a cold.

The Crops
The fruit trees in Sarajevo didn't bear any fruit. The leaves on the trees dried up. There appeared lots of maggots, which God made food for the birds. Wounds appeared on the ears of the dogs, which the flies attacked to lick the blood.

The Ostrich and Rams
The Calligrapher and Egyptian merchant Hasan Efendia brought into Sarajevo an ostrich and two strange rams. He made lots of money from the people who came to see them.

The Flood
A great flood came and destroyed a mill in the Kasap Charsia. And a few shops in the Kazandziluk. All of the market was under water. The water reached up to half the height of the beds. It caused great damage and loss. Lots of dogs drowned, and also two people, one of whom died immediately and the other one at a later stage.

Winter
The winter was so cold that there is no man who remembers such a one. The waters froze, and there were a few layers of ice. Words cannot describe this. All through the winter the children were sledging and at least they were happy. In the cellars the pickles and cabbages froze, so there you are. Lots of birds died because of the cold, too.

Dreams
Enemies go behind the rabbis and carry the corpse of a Jew. A barber shaves the judge with an axe. The tax collector invites people to a feast in his house. They come but there

is no food there, nothing, just a few breadcrumbs. Many skinned horses gallop out and fall down.

A Vision
In the Oman Sea there is a crooked island which you can see from afar but which no one has ever reached. On the island there is a tree that can give cool shade to 100,000 people. And it gives fruit that makes a man young, makes his face smooth and his white beard black again.

Prayer
May winter be winter and summer summer, may friends be many, and enemies few.

The Veiled Girl
There appeared a woman with a mace, and she was wild and no one could ask her anything because she would run after them. She wore her veil and no one knew who she was.

The Town Crier
I announce that the Jews and the Christians must not wear yellow slippers any more, but only red. I announce that the announcement for not wearing yellow slippers of earlier this year is not valid anymore.

The Gun Powder Man
The teferich of the bootmakers was very well attended and there were thousands of people who wanted to see what was happening. There was a man who let off fireworks. He knew how to do all kinds of things with gunpowder and fire. And made lots of money.

Additonal Scene 2

These are the original texts of a few Bosnian folk songs.

The Tower of Song
Songs heard and unheard, real and imaginary, coming from one and many sources, in one and many voices, multiplying, resounding, echoing and dying away.

Kad ja podjoh, na Bembasu
na Bembasu na vodu
ja povedoh bijelo janje
bijelo janje sa sobom.

When I went to Bembasa,
to Bembasa to get some water,
I took the white lamb,
the white lamb along with me.

Ah meraka u veceri rane
sastalo se drustvo aksamlija

Ah, what joy in the early evening
for a group of merry men
to gather

bez meraka nema zivovanja
bez Fadile nema milovanja.

without joy there's no life,
without Fadila there's no love.

Kolika je Jahorina planina
sivi sivi soko je preleteti
ne moze
devojka je pregazila bez konja.

How high is Mount Yahorina!
A grey falcon cannot fly over it.

Yet the girl crossed over it
without a horse

S one strane Plive
On gajtan trava raste
po njoj pasu ovce
cuvalo ih momce
momce tuzno place
jos tuznije jeci
svaka tudja zemlja
tuga je golema.

On the other side of the Pliva
thick grass grows,
sheep graze.
A boy looks after them.
He sadly weeps,
he sadly shrieks.
What deep anguish it is
not to be on your own land.

Blow, oh, Wind, just for a
while
From the Neretva side,
From the Neretva side.

And blow away the Mostar
fog,
the Mostar fog, the Mostar
fog.
Then I will see my dear Dara,
My dear Dara.

And ask her whether
she lets boys kiss her
she lets boys kiss her.

What girl would I be if I
Didn't let boys kiss me
Didn't let boys kiss me?

Put putuje Latif Aga
sa jaranom Sulejmanom
moj jarane Sulejmane
jel ti zao Banjaluke
banjaluckih teferica
kraj Vrbasa aksamluka.
Jes mi zao Banja Luke

Banjaluckih teferica
kraj Vrbasa aksamluka.

Latif Aga is journeying on
with his friend Suleiman.
My friend Suleiman,
Aren't you sorry
to leave Banja Luka,
the Banja Luka parties,
the merry gatherings by
the Vrbas?
I am sorry to leave Banja Luka,
the Banja Luka parties, the merry
gatherings by the Vrbas.

Muyo kuje, konja po mjesecu
Muyo kuje, a majka ga kune,
ne kuju se konji po mjesecu,
vec po danu i zarkome suncu.

Muyo is shoeing his horse
in the moonlight,
Muyo is shoeing
and his mother is cursing:
Don't shoe horses
in the moonlight
but in daylight under the
hot sun.

Nema te vise Alija, sevdalija
nema te vise sa nama
da pijes i pjevas
i staro drustvo razveseljavas.

Alia, you sevdah soul,
You are no longer with us,
You are no longer with us,
To drink and sing
and make merry your old friends.

ODYSSEUS
(A PLAY FOR THE THEATRE)

by Goran Stefanovski (2012)
Translated from the Croatian by Patricia Marsh-Stefanovska

Poster for the Ulysses Theatre production on Mali Brijun, Croatia,
2012, directed by Aleksandar Popovski

(The 'islands' depicted are actually the six former
Yugoslav republics.)

253

Characters

(with possible duplication of roles)

Odysseus

Athene

Penelope (Mother, Siren)

Telemachus

Maid (Helen, Siren, Nausicaa, Circe)

Calypso (Siren, Hecuba, Dog)

Zeus (Menelaus, First Soldier)

Poseidon (Nestor, Second Soldier)

Bard (Tiresias)

Cyclops (Suitor, Refugee, Astyanax)

Other Suitors

Fragments from Robert Fagles', William Cowper's, Alexander Pope's and E.V.Rieu's translations of Homer's *Odyssey* and from Philip Vellacott's translation of Euripides' *Trojan Women* are used in the play.

The play was commissioned by the Ulysses Theatre of Zagreb and first performed on 20th July, 2012.

Prologue

Enter the **Bard** *with a group of actors.*

Bard (*Singing*)
> Home is where
> I spend the night,
> Home is where
> I feel all right.
>
> I can never go back home
> For now I've lost my way,
> I can never leave my home
> No, never go away.
>
> Home is where
> they know my name,
> Home is where
> I lay my claim.
>
> I can never go back home
> For now I've lost my way,
> I can never leave my home
> No, never go away.
>
> Home is where
> My love is strong,
> Home is where
> My pain is long.
>
> I can never go back home
> For now I've lost my way,
> I can never leave my home

No, never go away.
The actors disperse. Pause.

Bard   Sing to me of Odysseus, Muse, the man of twists and turns[4], the cunning destroyer of the sacred city of Troy. (*Pause.*) No, wait a minute. Start again. Sing to me, Muse, *a version of the story* of Odysseus, the man of twists and turns . . . (*Pause.*) Once there was a great civilisation, whose capital was called Troy. It so happened that Troy was attacked by various factions who smelt blood. The mighty invisible forces of the gods helped the league of local human interests. The war lasted ten long years. The alliance was victorious. Troy was razed to the ground and no longer exists. Everyone agrees it was the most brutal war in history. Blood flooded the earth and screams the sky, as is the way with wars. The cunning of the Greeks put an end to it, entering Troy in a wooden horse and slaughtering its remaining defenders. Twenty years have passed since the beginning of the war – a short time in history, but a long time for us ordinary mortals. The world has changed. In the place of great kings, whose word was respected, there are now petty tribal chiefs of dubious honour. The war veterans have taken over the old states. Now they squander Trojan capital. They live in arrogance and debauchery. The gods who conspired to make all this happen have withdrawn, leaving the world in chaos. Of the surviving victors of Troy only one hasn't returned home. The gods have sentenced him to endless exile and eternal yearning. The gods have sentenced him to nostalgia.

---

4   Fagles, Book 1, 1

Scene 1: Assembly of the Gods

Olympus. **Athene** *and* **Zeus**.

Athene   Father Zeus, King of Kings! My heart aches whenever I remember brave Odysseus, the cleverest of all men. There he is, he's been suffering for years, far away from his loved ones, forgotten on the island of the nymph Calypso. His heart is torn apart by the desire to see his native Ithaca just one more time.

Zeus   My child, he was sentenced to life.

Athene   Why are you so angry with him, Father?

Zeus   You know very well. He thought he was greater than us, the gods. After victory at Troy he had the cheek to raise his head towards the sky and shout: "I won without your help, gods! My power is equal to yours, if not stronger!" Do you really think, daughter, that we should have overlooked that? How could Poseidon have ignored those words from a mortal? You know yourself how vain Poseidon is.

Athene   Odysseus has served seven years.

Zeus   The case is closed. Done and dusted.

Athene   You've destroyed his house. His son's lost and insecure. His wife's worn down and almost ready to give in to one of that rabble of merciless suitors. Isn't that enough punishment for him? Odysseus always sacrificed to you on the field of Troy.

Zeus   And what's it to you?

Athene   There aren't any heroes left down there. Just thugs and swindlers. Odysseus is the nearest thing to a hero. He should be supported.

Zeus Why?

Athene Because without heroes there're no gods. Without them, there's no us. And when there's no us, the sky's empty, and then there's nothing. Please, Dad, release godlike Odysseus!

Zeus "Godlike"? You're not in love, are you?

Athene Let's send the nymph news of your decision to have him return!

Zeus So you are. You're in love.

Athene So much, Dad, that I can't even breathe.

Zeus This is a bit sudden, isn't it?

Athene Ten years I panted under the walls of Troy with him in battle. I smelt his armpits while he slept.

Zeus I thought you were all mind, but now I see you're body, too. With all these gods, giants and titans who want you, you've decided to fall in love with a mortal! It's not on. Human love is like a hole in water. If the others hear about it, you'll be the laughing stock of Olympus. Does he know?

Athene He hasn't got a clue. For him I'm just a friend, counsellor, helper.

Zeus So why don't you just take him?

Athene Is that what you think love is? That's rape. I want him to fall in love with me himself.

Zeus Well, good luck to you, then.

Athene Thank you, my good, great father! I'll go straight to Ithaca. His son must be encouraged to go and look for his father! He must set out immediately!

Athene *flies off like the wind and comes down on the threshold of Odysseus's palace.*

Scene 2: Telemachus Prepares for a Journey

Penelope *and* **Telemachus**. **Telemachus** *is looking at the fire.* **Penelope** *is sitting beside him, her head on his chest.*

Penelope   Your father'll come back and everything'll be as it used to be. I saw him again last night proudly walking through those doors. He was wearing a helmet, and carrying a shield and a spear. But when I ran to put my arms around him – nothing there.

Telemachus (*Revealing his right arm, on which the name Odysseus is tattooed*)   What was he like?

Penelope   You already know. I've told you so many times.

Telemachus   Tell me again.

Penelope   He had strong hands. He mastered many a beast with them. His voice was deep and dark. Resolute, manly. Everyone adored him and followed in his footsteps wherever he went. Our house was always echoing to sounds of joy and merry-making. And he loved joking and laughing. And he loved me. He loved me in silk gowns and without them. He knew the soul of the winds and how to tame them. He made a bed of olive wood the like of which no mortal had ever seen. We shared secrets which were ours alone, signs which no one else knew.

Enter a **Suitor**. *He puts a gift down before* **Penelope**. *Enter the* **Maid**, *the* **Bard** *and* other **Suitors**.

Suitor   I'm losing patience. I've brought a gift, because that's the done thing, but I'm feeling less and less like giving you anything. It's high time, Penelope, that you gave *me* something! Or one of us, if I'm not to your taste. Time's working against you, Queen. Have you had a look in the mirror lately? Your face isn't much to look at anymore. Hide that wrinkled neck of yours, cover those rough hands. You've become dull, washed out. How else can I put it and make it sound less hurtful? You're old. But I'd marry you anyway because the kingdom can't be without a leader any longer. Somebody's got to sit on that too long empty throne. So, here I am, I'm putting myself forward.

Telemachus   Get out of this house! Out, all of you!

Suitor   Whose is that little voice I hear? Is it a boy's or a girl's? You don't give orders round here! The king's heir can only take power when the nobles of the previous king recognise his right to succeed. And, as you should have realised by now, we don't recognise anything! Go and suck your thumb somewhere else, because if you stay here someone might rip it off and throw it to the dogs!

Penelope   Please, don't quarrel. Let's get some wine and meat, and have dinner in peace. Melantho, come, serve us! Bard, sing something. (*The* **Bard** *starts singing.*) Sing something else.

Bard   This one was requested. I sing by request.

Penelope   And I'm requesting another song!

Bard   One about Odysseus, the hero you loved?

Suitor   Anything but that! You can't sing about someone who's not here. There are other heroes now and they're here. Sing about us and for us! (*The* **Suitors** *applaud.*) Friends, isn't it time we razed this palace to the ground?

Penelope   Don't! Please, give me a little more time! I promise I'll choose one of you as the new king! I just have to finish Odysseus's father's shroud so the wool doesn't go to waste.

Suitor   Finish it then! And after that I expect you to wash my feet and kiss them! Understand?

The **Maid** *throws herself on the ground and kisses his feet.* **Telemachus** *pulls her up.*

Suitor   The shroud, the famous shroud! She weaves it by day and unpicks it by night! She keeps making promises, and for years the country has no king! Anarchy, chaos, nobody afraid of anything. You can't tell the difference between good men and murderers. Our fathers are dead, obeying Odysseus's commands at Troy. Now it's only right we should get power in return. (*To* **Telemachus**) It's a simple matter: your father's dead and you can't marry your own mother. Or perhaps you'd like to?

Telemachus   It's easy for you to shout now when he's not here. If he were, you wouldn't be able to get away fast enough, not a peep out of you! Pigs.

Suitor   But he's not here. And one of the pigs'll be king. Of all, you included.

The **Maid** *brings food and wine. The* **Suitors** *go out to music. Enter* **Athene** *in disguise. She approaches* **Telemachus**.

Telemachus   Who are you, stranger?

Athene   I'm Mentes, King of the Taphians. Friend to Odysseus.

Telemachus   That's becoming a rare thing around here.

Welcome. I don't know if you've heard, but my father's bones are rotting away somewhere, or have been swept away by the waves of the sea.

Athene And you believe that? The son of such a hero falling for the lowest kind of gossip? Have you looked for him anywhere so you can say for sure he's gone? Have you sailed the seas, roamed through cities? No, you haven't. And why haven't you? You're young and strong – don't give credit to their lies. I'm no prophet, but I tell you: Odysseus is alive and he won't be away much longer, even if they shackle him in irons!

Telemachus So where is this father of mine, then, who I've never seen? Does he exist at all?

Nataša Matjašec Rošker as Athene and Branko Jordan as Telemachus in the Ulysses Theatre production on Mali Brijun

Athene You must set out immediately! Prepare the best ship with twenty oarsmen and head for Pylos, go to Sparta. Don't stop till you find him.

Telemachus   How can I leave my mother to these vultures who are eating us out of house and home?

Athene   I'll protect her and Odysseus's palace for thirty days. But I can't do any more than that. You'll have to come back with Odysseus by then and liberate the kingdom together.

Telemachus   Stranger, let me reward you for this.

Athene   Don't delay any longer. Do as I told you.

Athene *flies off like a bird.* **Telemachus** *looks after her in amazement. He begins to make preparations.*

Penelope   You're talking to yourself. You're going out of your mind, my poor boy.

Telemachus   I'm going to find my father.

Penelope   Where?

Telemachus   Pylos, Sparta, the ends of the earth if need be, till I find him.

Penelope   Pylos and Sparta are far away, my only son.

Telemachus   Fear not, mother, it's the will of the gods.

Exit **Penelope**. *Enter the* **Maid**.

Maid   Beautiful evening. The moon's full.

Telemachus   Has my mother sent you to initiate me into the secrets of manhood?

The **Maid** *says nothing. She and* **Telemachus** *make love.*

Scene 3: Stories about the Father

Enter the **Bard.**

Bard   I sing to you, Muse, the next instalment of this story, tale and legend. Young Telemachus set off into the big wide world. The first people he came across were the famous general Nestor, Commander Menelaus and his beautiful wife, Helen of Troy.

Exit. Enter **Helen***, heavily made-up, the insane general* **Nestor** *in uniform with war medals, and the commander* **Menelaus***. Enter* **Telemachus***. He goes up to them.*

Helen   Oh, you do look like Odysseus! Tall and upright, those regular features, blue eyes.

Menelaus   Rubbish. Odysseus wasn't in the least bit tall. On the contrary. He was titchy and hunchbacked with a crooked nose.

Nestor   His eyes weren't blue. They were red and staring. Like a wolf's.

Telemachus   You knew my father? Is he still alive?

Menelaus   Well, I hope he isn't! That fraud! That piece of shit who took the credit for victory over Troy. My name has been wiped from history! Just Odysseus this, Odysseus that! And who started that war? I did. Me, Menelaus!!!

Helen   Didn't I have anything to do with it?

Menelaus   And you, my love, of course, you too. (*They kiss.*) This lady set Europe against Asia! Credit where credit's due! She never found it hard to sleep with whoever she had to or didn't have to. But Paris kidnapping her – that was my idea! We had to make up a cause for war. Agamemnon, Palamedes and I formed the alliance and set off for Troy. All right, it's true I didn't really plan for her to stay in bed with Paris for ten years. I decided I'd never ever forgive her and I'd cut off her head. But when I laid eyes on her again, my old love worked its magic. Here, take a look at her yourself, and you'll understand.

Telemachus *looks at* **Helen**.

Helen Once he came to ask for my hand, that father of yours. Empty-handed. Of course I refused him. And then he married that duck you call your mother. Never had any taste, you see.

Nestor Enough of that deserter! When Menelaus, Agamemnon and Palamedes went to call him to war, he pretended to be crazy to shirk his responsibilities. He harnessed a donkey and an ox to the plough and sowed the soil with salt.

Menelaus He acted as if he didn't recognise us. And I said to myself, so you're crazy, are you, coward, let's see just how crazy you are. You were just a baby, so I threw you in front of the plough, to crush you if he was really mad. (*He laughs.*) He remembered us straightaway and got his wits back!

Helen Then he set out to seduce women wherever he could. Without any consideration or moderation. Vulgar, really.

Nestor And then there was Philoctetes. Out of pure jealousy he threw the most renowned archer of our time onto a desert island and left him there to croak from hunger. And he slaughtered all the Trojans one by one, although we'd agreed to spare the ones who didn't offer any resistance. He butchered women, children, old men.

Menelaus And, my friends, what he did to Palamedes!

Telemachus But didn't Odysseus build the Trojan horse? And wasn't that the turning-point in winning the war?

Nestor There you are, there's your war propaganda. It turns out that those who've never seen Troy even in a picture book know all about it, while we, who left our youth there, we don't know anything.

Menelaus The Trojan horse was my idea. Odysseus had nothing to do with it.

Helen But he certainly had something to do with raping the Trojan women. And he left you as soon as you were born. Your father was a mole. An informer. Our man in Troy. He wormed his way into the city itself as a beggar and deceived everyone. I was the only one who recognised him. I massaged him with oil and he told me everything. He killed a lot of Trojans and went back to the Greeks with all the information.

Menelaus Did he try it on with you? Of course he did. Did you let him? Of course you did.

Helen Not in front of the children.

Menelaus What children? He's old enough to try it on with you himself.

Helen And, goodness me, to have his way as well. He's so sweet, he's blushing. (**Telemachus** *turns to leave.*) Where are you going now?

Telemachus To find my father. Suitors have taken over Ithaca, my mother and our home.

Nestor Listen, if you need weapons you're in the right place. We'll make a good deal. Bows which bend themselves, swords and knives of all sizes, spears, shields, clubs. Or this new product. The T10 mace. T for Troy. 10 for ten years of war. And we can negotiate an army. Day hire. Two units'll sort out the suitors in an afternoon. Transport, food and incidental expenses included. Listen to me, I know. (*Showing his medals*) Services to the nation, labour award, national hero, army general, liberator. (*Something falls out of the sky onto his head.*) Eagle droppings! That's a good sign! (*To* **Telemachus**) The gods are with you, dear boy. You can't breathe for the gods. They ramp up taxes, take commission and there's nothing left for us honest businessmen.

He takes out some powder. They all take a sniff.

Telemachus What kind of world have I been thrown into?

Helen What's wrong with the world?

Telemachus A couple of feathers, to fly.

Exit **Telemachus**.

Scene 4: Calypso Releases Odysseus

The island of Ogygia. **Odysseus** *is sitting on the beach. His eyes are closed. He is dozing. There are wine and salted fish on a table in front of him. He suddenly cries out and opens his eyes. As if he's been wakened from some kind of nightmare.*

Ozren Grabarić as Odysseus in the Ulysses Theatre production on the Croatian island of Mali Brijun

Odysseus   (*Looking at a tooth which has fallen out*) This tooth tore off bread and meat under the walls of Troy, cracked walnuts and hazelnuts, bit the nipples of lovers, caressed Penelope's tongue, helped me whisper and shout. And now it's decided it doesn't need me anymore and it's abandoned me. (*He puts it back in his mouth. It falls out into his hand again.*) Should I swallow it? It's mine, I'm not letting go of it. Or should I throw it to the fish in the sea? Or sow it in the earth as seed for some monstrous plant? Or throw it in the air for a bird flying past to grab and take to Olympus so the gods can see what flimsy stuff they made us of? Disgraceful. How can I laugh now with a hole in my teeth? How can I speak without making that whistling noise? How can I chew? What kind of hero is toothless? Not to mention the constant heartburn. And the creaking knees.

Enter **Athene**, *invisible.*

Athene   Poor Odysseus!

Odysseus   Athene. You're here.

Athene   When you see me and when you don't.

Odysseus   Goddess, you've been keeping me here like a dog on a chain for years. For years I've been dreaming of revenge and trying to find peace. My soul has been stretched across the four corners of the Earth. I beg you on my knees and bang my head on the ground. Either kill me or let me go home. Does Ithaca still exist? Is anything left of my homeland?

Athene   Ithaca exists. But it's never been worse there. You can go home. Zeus has released you.

Odysseus *slashes through trees and plants with a sword. Enter* **Calypso** *from the other end.* **Athene** *goes up to her, disguised as Hermes.*

Calypso   What are you doing here, messenger? You don't come often.

Athene   I bring bad news. Zeus commands you to despatch Odysseus from here post-haste.

Calypso   Come again?

Athene   You heard me. He came here to do hard labour – not to have a good time. This is prison, not a holiday home. He was supposed to be banging rocks, not *you*! The prison warden fell in love with the prisoner!

Calypso   You gods are so callous. You're envious if a goddess loves someone in public and takes him for a husband.

Athene   It was male gods who punished you. They can go with mortal women but you're not allowed mortal men.

Calypso   Someone else thought this up.

Athene   Who?

Calypso (*Very softly*)   Athene.

Athene   Why d'you suspect her?

Calypso   Because she's jealous. A shrivelled virgin. Stupid cow. If she's female at all.

Athene   I've got to go. Don't worry. I won't tell Athene.

Calypso   No. Do. Please tell her everything I said. Word for word.

Exit **Athene**. **Calypso** *goes to* **Odysseus**.

Calypso   Lunch.

Odysseus   Not hungry.

Calypso I'm just saying it's on the table. What's up? What's happened?

They look at each other. Pause.

Odysseus Calypso. The one who hides things.

Calypso I've never been able to hide anything from you.

Odysseus You've hidden me away from the whole world. For many years, as well.

Calypso But I haven't managed to make you forget Ithaca. The gods know how hard I've tried. Stay here with me. You'll be immortal and forever young.

Odysseus Calypso, I don't want your eternal youth, I want my old age. I'm going home.

Calypso What d'you mean, home? What's home? This is your home.

Odysseus My home is Ithaca! That's where rivers of milk and honey flow. The grapes come three times a year and the corn five times. The sun shines from three sides and the moon from four. There's hardly any sickness, old age or death. Peace and eternal love rule. And everyone sings: "Let others be wherever they like, just so long as we're here, at home."

Calypso Go then. You're free, old man. I'm serious. Go! I'm fed up with you. You've been screwing me here for seven years every night till dawn. Then you go and sit on the beach and drown in self-pity, wanking over Penelope. Go, and have a nice trip. (*Pause.*) What're you waiting for? Me to change my mind?

Odysseus I'm waiting for a fair wind. (*Pause.*) Aren't we going to say goodbye?

Calypso *undoes her dress and stands naked.* **Calypso** *and* **Odysseus** *kiss.* **Athene** *looks on invisible from the sidelines.*

Odysseus You'll kill me with love.

Calypso Better to die of love than hired assassins. You've got no idea what awaits you on your journey.

Odysseus Who d'you work for?

Calypso You should go if you can't tell friends from enemies.

Odysseus I'm an eel of a man. Even my shadow can't follow me.

Calypso If you think you're still as good as you used to be, you're wrong. You're not.

Scene 5: A Quarrel on the High Seas

Enter the **Bard.**

Bard   I sing, Muse, of further permutations and variations on a theme.

Exit.

Odysseus *is sailing a boat. Night. He is looking at the sky and stars. Enter* **Poseidon**.

Poseidon   Where d'you think you're going?

Odysseus   Home.

Poseidon   Have you asked anyone? Who gave you permission? What d'you mean, home?

Odysseus   Home is where everyone's always known me and I've always known everyone. The place where everything is *mine*. The sun which comes up at dawn and the shadows which fall at twilight. I sit at my table a happy man, and the guests listen to me talking and ask me where I've been and how I became famous. The tables are heaped with bread and meats, and, drawing wine from a mixing-bowl, the servant makes his rounds and keeps the winecups flowing[5]. People coming together, singing songs. I embrace my wife, Penelope. And feel proud of my son, who's growing up to be my worthy heir.

Poseidon   Ooh, you gave me goosebumps. Nothing's the same there anymore. Everything's upside down.

Odysseus   I'm going to make it right again.

---

5   Fagles, Book 9, 8-10

Poseidon Everything that was sacred is now silly.

Odysseus I'm going to take revenge on the reptiles who think they've taken my place, the rats who lead the dance in my house. They don't even mention my name anymore, as if I never existed. They've buried me and erased me. And, as time goes by, *I*'ve started behaving as if I don't exist. I miss myself. But that's enough of that. I won't allow it anymore. It's mine! I'm going to reclaim what's mine!

Poseidon What the eye don't see, the heart don't grieve over! Why d'you think you're better than them?

Odysseus I don't. I know it in my heart. I feel it in my blood! (*Looking at the sky*) I'm coming, home, you poison, you bone in my throat, you thorn in my soul! I greet you, sister stars! And you, mother, cosmic winds!

Poseidon You're not going anywhere. You're just drifting.

Odysseus Why have you so taken against me?

Poseidon You know all our codes. How could we have let a mortal like you make up our codes, manage our accounting and HR policy? Negotiate in our name. You got a taste for it. You gained power. You thought you were one of us. The man who knew too much. You want to betray us. Go there and look important, as if you know everything, tell them how it is and why it all happened.

Odysseus I wouldn't dare do that.

Poseidon And why should I worry about whether you will or won't? Instead of just nicely getting rid of you.

Poseidon *raises his hand to kill* **Odysseus**. *Enter* **Athene**.

Athene No. My father promised me he'd stay alive.

Poseidon   If you want a toy, Daddy can buy you a hamster. Or a dog.

Poseidon *whips up a storm.*

Odysseus   Oh, ye gods! Where do I stand? Am I in favour or out? Punish me or spare me, but at least come to some agreement! Alas, unhappy me! My Athene, my shadow, my sadness, my only true comrade. I kiss your honeyed lips.

Athene   What colour lipstick do you like?

Odysseus   Sorry?

Athene   I could put some on.

Odysseus   It doesn't suit you. Forget that now and give me a hand!

Athene *gives* **Odysseus** *a veil which covered her breasts.* **Odysseus** *looks away.*

Athene   Gird yourself with this immortal veil. Swim with all your might!

Odysseus *struggles with the storm. The boat falls apart.* **Odysseus** *swims. He reaches land. He falls into mud and loses consciousness. Pause. Enter the* **Bard**.

Bard   I sing to you, Muse, the continuation of this fable, with further convolutions. Animals wander, people wander, entire nations wander, gods wander and history wanders. We're suspicious of wanderers. As we are of refugees. Why aren't they at home? What was it that ousted them and exiled them? If home is Eden, why did they go east of Eden? Why did they rebel? Wandering can be physical or metaphysical, deliberate or forced, it can be adventurous or bewildering, pleasure or pain, a game or an identity crisis, it can be fun or fatal. On the one hand, we envy wanderers their freedom, on the other we pity them for that same freedom.

Scene 6: Nausicaa

Enter **Nausicaa** *with a bundle of clothes to wash. She doesn't see* **Odysseus** *who is sleeping behind some bushes. She soaks her washing and tramples it with her feet. She puts it out to dry in the sun.* **Odysseus** *cries out suddenly and opens his eyes. As if he's been wakened from some kind of nightmare. He stands up naked and muddy behind a bush.*

Nausicaa   Oh my!

Odysseus   Who're you? Where am I?

Nausicaa   Oh my, oh my!

Odysseus *breaks off a branch and covers himself with it.*

Odysseus   Don't be frightened, girl.

Nausicaa   I'm Nausicaa. This is the land of the Phaeacians. I'm washing clothes. I'm going to be married soon. I have to wear the prettiest dress because that's how you get a good name among the people. I won't be a virgin for much longer.

Odysseus   I have never laid eyes on anyone such as you, neither man nor woman. I marvel at you, my lady: rapt, enthralled, too struck with awe to grasp you by the knees[6].

Nausicaa   Stranger, now you have come to our lands you shall want for nothing.

Odysseus   Maiden, stand apart, that I may cleanse my shoulders from the briny surf[7].

Nausicaa (*Turning her back*)   This man must have been sent by the gods of Olympus. Oh, if only destiny intended

---

6   Fagles, Book 6, 175-6; 184-5
7   Cowper, Book 6, 272-3 (adapted)

such a husband for me. (*To* **Odysseus**) How did you swim here and save yourself from the terrible sea?

Odysseus   I don't know myself.

Nausicaa (*Sidling up to him*)   Oh my. Oh my, oh my! (*She tries to kiss him.*) Why don't you want to?

Odysseus   I can't just do it like that.

Nausicaa   Like what? It's my first time.

Odysseus   I'd like to, but I'm afraid.

Nausicaa   You don't like me.

Odysseus   I'm old.

Nausicaa   You're not old. What d'you mean, old? I really like it that you're old.

Odysseus   I don't know who you are. Who's behind you?

Nausicaa   I'm on my own.

Odysseus   Nobody's on their own.

Nausicaa   I hate you. I'll kill myself. I'll tell my Dad you raped me. He's the king.

Odysseus   Help me. The whole world's after me. I must get home to Ithaca.

Nausicaa   Kiss me.

Odysseus   Who are you? Who d'you work for? Did Poseidon send you after me? I wasn't born yesterday. Those tears aren't real. Admit everything.

They kiss. Pause.

Nausicaa   You see I was a virgin.

Odysseus   I've become a beast.

Nausicaa   Oh my, yes.

Odysseus   My wine has turned to vinegar.

Nausicaa   Quiet. I'll never forget you. Just so long as nobody sees me. I couldn't stand the gossip. People here don't like strangers.

Odysseus   So what about me? Where shall I go?

Nausicaa   Go back into the sea, where you came from. I love you.

Scene 7: Telemachus, the Bard and the Refugee

An inn. The **Bard***, who is now blind, is playing and singing to the* **Refugee***, who is drunk. Enter* **Telemachus***.*

Telemachus Good evening.

Bard Welcome, stranger, to this great casino.

Telemachus Casino?

Bard Phaeacia is now one big casino. Caviar, sparkling wine, flashy suits, plenty of bling, make-up, glamour, vanity fair.

The **Bard** *sings. The tone is ironic and facetious.*

Bard (*Singing*)
> Who's that man?
> Who's that eel man?
> Who's that eel man, faster than his shadow?
> Who's that, faster than his shadow and more cunning than Fate?
> Who's that, more cunning than Fate, bright as the sun and fickle as the moon?
> Who's that, bright as the sun and fickle as the moon, who storms the heavens?
> Who's that who storms the heavens, lover of nymphs and goddesses?
> Who's that lover of nymphs and goddesses, the mortal who outwitted the gods?
> Who's that mortal who outwitted the gods, jumped over time and cheated death?
> It's him,

It's him, hey,
It's him, hey, Odysseus!

The **Refugee** *laughs.* **Telemachus** *takes the* **Bard** *aside.*

Telemachus   I know you from before. You used to sing at our house on Ithaca. You're weren't blind then.

Bard   Sometimes I am, sometimes I'm not. Depending on where I'm performing.

Telemachus   You sing that song as if you're mocking him. What, if anything, d'you know about Odysseus?

Bard   I travel around. From island to island. You hear one thing here, another there. People say all sorts of things.

Telemachus   What do people know? Odysseus was a hero, not a crook!

Bard   I sing what the audience likes. Once there was a fashion for songs about how the Trojan veterans were heroes. Now it's the opposite. Now it's democracy. Freedom. Earlier it was just the gods and the muses who sang, and now everyone tweets away. Universal din and competition. Calypso's a goddess for some, for others a high-class whore. It's all spin. I've got a repertoire of templates, phrases, rhythms, tempos, hexameters, a pack of characters. Action, schemes, wars, floods, adventures on land, sea and air, family feuds, births, marriages and funerals.

Telemachus   Sing differently or I'll break your neck!

Bard   How shall I sing?

Telemachus   Seriously. Movingly. Odysseus had strong hands. He mastered many a beast with them. His voice was deep and dark. Resolute, manly. Everyone adored him

282

and followed in his footsteps wherever he went. He knew the soul of the winds and how to tame them. I'm his son.

Refugee Whose son are you?

Telemachus Odysseus's.

Refugee Odysseus's? D'you want me to tell you a story about Odysseus? D'you know where the city of Ismara is? I'm from Ismara. We had a nice peaceful life there. That is until one day at the break of dawn your father turned up with six ships and three hundred soldiers. They set fire to our houses, raped our mothers and sisters, slaughtered our brothers and fathers. Just a few of us escaped and now we roam from place to place. Here, have a look what Odysseus did to me. (*He pulls out his trousers so Telemachus can see inside.*) There, that was your father. (*Pause.*) Sing, bard!

Telemachus *vomits.*

Bard Who's that mortal who jumped over time and cheated death, swallowed his own head and was born again from himself?

> It's him,
> It's him, hey,
> It's him, hey, Odysseus!

Scene 8: The Army

Odysseus *is travelling, searching for his home. He passes* **Telemachus** *who is travelling and searching for his father.*

Bard People wander in search of their identity, the story of who they are and what they are. They invent various tricks while they're doing that. They present being lost as being found. They think up new maps and pretend they're exactly where they should be. They look for an alibi for their actions, think up excuses for their mistakes, try to give sense to their lives at any cost. So it comes about that adventuring is presented as principled travel, selfishness as aspiration towards higher goals, robbery as a fight for freedom, attack as self-defence, genocide as a sacred quest.

Enter **Odysseus**. *Enter* **First Soldier** *and* **Second Soldier**, *covered in blood.*

First Soldier Odysseus! Worthy commander!

Second Soldier Master, leader, what're you doing here?

Odysseus My soldiers. What're *you* doing here?

First Soldier Just a bit of looting.

Odysseus Who else is here?

Second Soldier There're more than a hundred of us.

Odysseus Didn't you go home after Troy?

First Soldier We did, but then we left again. Some of us, our neighbours had taken our land, some our wives, some went mad, and some of us found it boring without a war on.

Second Soldier Some of us wondered why we'd bothered

to come back at all. Only fools go back to sweat away ploughing the soil and shearing the sheep.

First Soldier   It's boring respecting the law. Some of us said: our Odysseus did the clever thing not coming back at all.

Second Soldier   So we got together again and set off. There's always work for a good army.

The soldiers eat lotus.

First Soldier   Have some. Lotus fruit.

Second Soldier   Makes you forget.

First Soldier   We all followed your example, Master. I never did care much for tilling the soil and running a household. I only really liked ships, oars, battles, sharp spears and death-dealing arrows. What others found terrible and repulsive, I was rather fond of.

Second Soldier   And this is where the winds have blown us to. And we've taken the city and massacred the people. Just like you taught us.

First Soldier   Blood flowing down the streets. Houses burning, smoke and weeping to high heaven. And me with five of them in front of me. I ordered them to strip and squat, one above the other. And then one by one, from bottom to top, from top to bottom. Some old man appeared from somewhere and tried to protect them, so he got my sword in his balls.

Second Soldier   Happy days.

First Soldier   And it was pure chance that we came here.

Second Soldier   The wind blew us out here.

First Soldier Fate!

Second Soldier Free will and choice don't exist.

First Soldier Let the currents take you.

Second Soldier You don't know the circumstances.

First Soldier You don't know the motive.

Second Soldier You can't know the consequences.

First Soldier What you see, that's it.

Second Soldier There's nothing else.

First Soldier The important thing is to survive.

Second Soldier At any price.

First Soldier One man's loss . . .

Second Soldier Is another man's gain.

First Soldier May it always be the other guy's loss . . .

Second Soldier And our gain!

Odysseus (*Going for them*) Who d'you work for? I'll rip your heads off, you rabble, sorry excuse for soldiers!

First Soldier We're not soldiers anymore. We were soldiers at Troy!

Odysseus So what are you now?

Second Soldier We don't know anymore. We've forgotten.

The First Soldier *and* **Second Soldier** *laugh hysterically.*

Odysseus From now on you're under my command again! My word is final! We're going back to our old homeland, to build a new world!

Scene 9 : Penelope and the Maid

Penelope *is asleep. Enter* **Athene**. *She goes up to her.*

Athene   What does he see in you that he doesn't see in me? What do you have that I don't? Your marriage bed is still here where it was. The bed posts of thick green olivewood, inlaid with gold, silver and ivory, with purple straps of stretched oxhide. Some deity has disturbed your sleep for it seemed as if Odysseus was lying beside you and your heart rejoiced and thought it was no dream but reality. Do you dream of him as I do? Dreams are pure absurdity. Two are the portals through which those fleeting visions come: of horn is one, the other of ivory. Pure illusion are those that reach us through the finely wrought ivory, never to come true, but dreams that enter through the portal of polished horn foretell real events, sure to come to pass. You'll be famous because you waited for him. But who will ever know that I waited for him too?

Penelope *wakes up.* **Athene** *disappears. Enter the* **Maid**.

Maid   I've brought you figs, honey and sweet wine.

Penelope   Thank you. I'm most interested in the wine.

The **Maid** *pours some wine for* **Penelope** *and for herself.*

Maid   Your health.

Penelope   And yours.

Maid (*Giving Penelope a little box*)   From last night.

Penelope (*Opening the box and taking out gold jewellery*) Who were you with?

Maid   Antinous.

Penelope Again.

Maid He asked me to.

Penelope And? On your face?

Maid On my body. On my neck. He said: "Eh, if I could only do the same thing to your mistress."

Penelope Right, to work.

Maid Yes, Mistress. They expect me to whisper your messages in their ear.

Penelope "Dear . . . " – here put in the appropriate name. "Last night I went to bed with you in my thoughts."

Maid Hot.

Penelope Hot and wet. Add something along those lines.

Maid You must put the price up. There's great demand. We can't meet it. There are only so many of us maids.

Penelope Oh, if that was all I had to think about . . . I bear the whole kingdom on my shoulders. I carry out domestic and foreign policy, diplomacy, put up smoke screens, discharge black ink like squid. I take heed that the right hand doesn't know what the left is doing. I carefully organise confusion. I sustain a situation so that it is unsustainable. Controlled chaos. I take care of fishermen, peasants, shepherds, swineherds. Of you slaves. That Odysseus might deign to come back and do a bit himself.

Maid Did you love him a lot?

Penelope I was a girl. He was already thirty. Arranged marriage. Love? Yes. And no. And maybe. I didn't have time to decide before he went off to war.

Maid   How can you stand all this?

Penelope   I'm the daughter of a Naiad, a water goddess. My mother gave me just one piece of advice: "Act like water!" And Odysseus gave me another: "When everyone thinks you're here, you be there." You can't escape your fate, but make it hard for it to follow you. Wriggle out of it.

Scene 10: The Cyclops

(*A cave. The one-eyed* **Cyclops** *is finishing his dinner. He's eaten a few soldiers.* **Odysseus** *is watching him.*)

Cyclops   That's eight of your soldiers I've eaten.

Odysseus   Nine.

Cyclops   You'll make a nice round ten.

Odysseus   With whom do I have the pleasure . . . ?

Cyclops   I'm the cyclops Polyphemus.

Odysseus   And I'm . . .

Cyclops (*Interrupting him*)   You're No One! You're dinner. (*Pause.*) What do you think of me at first sight? Am I repulsive? Silence – that means I am. My brothers and I make weapons. Not the kind of toys you have. These are weapons for the gods. Thunderbolts for Zeus. When a volcano erupts, that's us letting off steam from our furnaces. I'm a grumpy old sod, I hate myself in the morning and the whole world in the afternoon. I say *Yes* when everyone else says *No* and *Well, I'm going to* when everyone else says *Don't*. I'm the master of spite, the eternal nay-sayer, cutting off my nose to spite my face. I've got one eye and I see everything from only one point of view. I'm a brainfucker, I drive people insane. Anyway, let's just devour you now.

Odysseus   Wait a minute. We were having such a nice chat.

Cyclops   What's there to wait for?

Odysseus   I look at you and think what a pity it is.

Cyclops   What's a pity?

Odysseus   The fact that you're genetically a cyclops, but you don't try to avoid the clichés and the stereotypes. You have your own life and your cyclopean habits, of course, but why shouldn't you be able to be, say, a poet as well?

Cyclops   What's that?

Odysseus   Someone who expresses their feelings. Have you ever tried to do that? Has love ever touched your heart? Silence – that means it has. Who was she?

Cyclops   Her name was Galatea. But she didn't fancy me. She found some stupid Sicilian, a mortal. I killed him with a rock.

Odysseus   Unrequited love. What a theme! And all you asked for was a little human warmth. Why is love impossible in the political world?

Cyclops   My Dad Poseidon'd kill me if I started writing poetry.

Odysseus   Well, write and then eat what you've written, so he doesn't see. And in the end if you're not a lyric poet by vocation, you can always write about manly epic themes. You can be a war poet. Your task would be to use poetry to stir things up, arouse passions, call up the ghosts of the past. There's no war without its poet.

Cyclops   How do you write?

Odysseus   Oh, my dear sir, what an infinitely complex topic that is! First we need a pen. Allow me to sharpen that olive twig. (*Taking the twig and beginning to sharpen it*) Next we need a little inspiration. You ask how to begin? What to write about? Well, the best thing is to start from yourself. This cave of yours, for instance, is not just a cave, it's your

291

home as well. It's a house. A little house. Little house, little cave. My little house, my little cave, my little freedom.

Cyclops   My little bedroom.

Odysseus   That's it. Brilliant!

Cyclops   My little threshold, my little roof, my little chimney.

Odysseus   Excellent. You're a born poet.

Cyclops   I dig my little garden.

Odysseus   You see, you can do it!

Cyclops   I plant my little fruits, look after my little chickens and little goats. My little milk, my little cheese. My little field, my little grass. My little sun and my little moon in my little sky. My little willy, my little thumb and my little finger.

Odysseus   My little chest and my little heart. That is, *your* little chest and your little heart.

Cyclops   My little chest and my little heart.

Odysseus   On which is engraved: My little house, my little cave, and so on. You see. Then it'll all go round in a circle and repeat itself. Well done! Your first poem and you hit the jackpot!

Cyclops   Is that all?

Odysseus   That's just a working version, it's not ready yet. (*He stabs the* **Cyclops** *in the eye with the pen. The* **Cyclops** *cries out, bleeding.*) It all begins with poetry and ends in blood!

Cyclops   My eye! My eye! (*He tries to catch* **Odysseus**.)

Odysseus   Cyclops, you monster! If any man should ask who blinded you, say Odysseus, raider of cities, *he* gouged out your eye, he who makes his home in Ithaca[8]. (*Exit.*)

Cyclops   Listen and take this to heart. Of all the creatures that breathe and creep about on Mother Earth there is none so helpless as man[9].

---

8   Fagles, Book 9, 560-2 (adapted)
9   Rieu, Book 18, 129-131

Scene 11: Circe

*Enter the **Bard**.*

Bard   Outraged at the treatment of his son, Poseidon thought up a new scheme. The Lestrygonians, savage cannibals, stacked the sailors up on spikes like fish, preparing a horrific feast for themselves. The ships sank, all except Odysseus's, which somehow managed to escape. Five hundred and fifty men lost their lives in that place. They fought for ten years at Troy to finish up as food for cannibals. One of the survivors tells Odysseus: "Poseidon is after you, but he kills us." And Odysseus replies:

Odysseus   A great misfortune has befallen me. I no longer know which way is west, which east, nor where the sun sets, nor where it rises. Here I am, Poseidon! Drag me to the bottom of the ocean and bury me a hundred feet deep in the mud. And let me find peace.

Bard   Fate threw Odysseus onto the island of Aeaea, where the enchantress Circe lived.

*Island of Aeaea. Enter **Circe** the Witch, singing. She looks like the madam of an S&M salon. Enter **Odysseus**.*

Odysseus   Who are you?

Circe   I'm Circe. And you're a pig. (*She blows in his face.* **Odysseus** *goes weak and falls to his knees.*) Now you're my willing slave. (*Exerting himself to the extreme,* **Odysseus** *draws his sword.*) Who are you? Why haven't you succumbed to my magic breath? You must be Odysseus whom the prophecy told me of. Sheathe your sword and come to my bed so we can be reconciled in love and make friends. (**Circe** *helps*

Odysseus *up*.) Come, eat and drink wine, and you'll feel strength in your breast again. (*She pours wine for him into a golden cup*.)

Odysseus   A weariness has taken over my limbs, sapping my soul away.

Circe kisses him.

Circe   Tell me. How you kill.

Odysseus   I shoot an arrow, straight at the nose, penetrating white teeth, cutting through the tongue to the root. The copper tip flies through the lower jaw and the man collapses. Then I thrust a spear into his chest. And his blood spurts out on all sides.

Circe   That's it. Talk to me. Don't stop.

They kiss.

Odysseus   Winter's passed, Circe, and spring's come. I'm not well. My sight's going. Everything's blurred. I've lost my sense of time. How long have you kept me here?

Circe   You're alert and bristling like a lone wolf. You're attracted to danger like a child to a rattle.

Odysseus   The war haunts me.

Circe   It doesn't haunt you, but you haunt it. You miss it. You don't know what to do with yourself when you're not warmongering.

Odysseus   I'm a hero, a star, a superman. I want fame and applause. Achilles died in the arena before the eyes of the world. What about me? Who's watching me? No one. Except you.

Circe   Isn't that enough? I'm your death. Your first true love. Penelope's nothing. She's a housewife.

Odysseus   Penelope is my one true love. She takes care of my house and my son. And prays every day for my soul's salvation with the whole nation. They all stand to attention three times a day and look towards the sea with tears in their eyes, waiting to see my ship's mast on the horizon.

Circe   They all think you're dead. And nobody even mentions your name any more.

Odysseus   Who d'you work for?

Circe   For myself. I'll drink your brain through a straw. I'll tear your cock off with my teeth.

They kiss.

Odysseus   Summer's here. I want to go home, sorceress! What spells have you put on me? My mind's like a flock of birds scattering. My heart's pounding. I have no will of my own. Tell me, is there a way back? Show me the way out of this magic circle!

Circe   You want to find a way. There isn't one.

Odysseus   There must be.

Circe   The only way is no way. How much are you willing to pay to find a way?

Odysseus   What's the price?

Circe   The price is your life. You have to die to be born again. Go against your very self. Swallow your own head, go through your own entrails, and reinvent yourself.

Odysseus   What does that mean?

Circe   You must descend into Hades and ask Tiresias the Theban, the blind prophet.

Odysseus   Well, I've come to hate my life. How can I get there?

Circe   Raise the mast, unfurl a white sail, and the north wind will take you to the ends of the Ocean, to the mouth of the Acheron, which flows from the Styx.

Scene 12: Hades

The ends of the deep Ocean. A land veiled in fog and clouds.
Enter **Tiresias**. *Enter* **Odysseus**.

Odysseus   Tiresias!

Tiresias   Wretched man, you'll die twice for entering Hades alive. You long to return to your home but Poseidon won't make it easy for you. To be honest, I've got no idea how you can get home. In my time I prophesied according to the laws of probability. You have a look at the case, make some sensible points, job done. Now it's all gone to the dogs. Now the uncertainty principle rules. But who knows what that's good for? (*Pause.*) Say hello to Athene for me. I saw her naked while she was bathing. She blinded me, but, hand on heart, she gave me second sight. Which has also more or less gone now.

Exit **Tiresias**. *Enter* **Hecuba**.

Odysseus   Hecuba!

Hecuba   You slaughtered me.

Odysseus   I had no choice.

Hecuba   You slit my throat just so you wouldn't look like a coward in front of your soldiers. The whole world can go hang just so long as your name isn't soiled, your heroism denied.

Odysseus   What could I do?

Hecuba   I mourn for my dead world, my burning town, my sons, my husband, gone, all gone! What pride of race, what strength once swelled our royal sails! Now shrunk to nothing, sunk in mean oblivion! Dust mingled with smoke spreads wings to the sky,

I can see nothing, the world is blotted out! Earth and her name are nothing;

all has vanished, and Troy is nothing[10]!

Exit **Hecuba**. *Enter* **Astyanax**.

Odysseus Astyanax?

Astyanax Why did you throw me from the walls?

Odysseus You're Hector's son, Prince of Troy.

Astyanax Why did you throw me from the walls?

Odysseus We couldn't allow you to live as the heir to Troy.

Astyanax Why did you throw me from the walls?

Odysseus It was war.

Astyanax Why did you throw me from the walls?

Exit **Astyanax**. *Enter* **Odysseus's mother**.

Mother Oh my son – what brings you down to the world of death and darkness? You are still alive[11]!

Odysseus Oh, Mother, misfortune has brought me to Hades.

Mother Not yet returned to Ithaca[12]?

---

10 Vellacott, Penguin Classics, 1974, p.93 & p.133
11 Fagles, Book 11, 177-8
12 ibid. 184

Odysseus   I have never once set foot on native ground[13]. What form of death overcame you[14]?

Mother   I simply died. No sickness conquered me. No, it was my longing for *you*, my shining Odysseus, that tore away my life that had been sweet[15].

Odysseus   Mother!

Mother   I know, son. You yearn to kill yourself, to end the tension, the constant vigilance, suspicion, the weariness of the body, the exhaustion of the soul. You've been coming back from the war for ten years now. A new generation has grown up who don't remember the war and only know peace. You'll soon have no one to talk to about the war. Everything calls you towards the past, to your old glory. You'd like to surrender to that temptation.

Odysseus *tries to embrace her*.

Odysseus   Let me embrace you.

Mother   You can't. There are terrible waters between us which no one may cross. My dear son, this is just the way of mortals when we die. Sinews no longer bind the flesh and bones together – the fire in all its fury burns the body down to ashes[16]. You see that Hades is no kind of solution. Rather hasten back swiftly to the light!

Exit **Odysseus**.

---

13   ibid. 188-9
14   ibid. 204
15   ibid. 230-232
16   ibid. 249-251

Scene 13: The Sirens

The ship is sailing by the island of the **Sirens**. *They sit with piles of skeletons and rotting corpses around them.*

Sirens

> Oh stay, O pride of Greece! Odysseus, stay!
> Oh cease thy course, and listen to our lay!
> We know whate'er the kings of mighty name
> Achieved at Ilion in the field of fame;
> Whate'er beneath the sun's bright journey lies.
> Oh stay, and learn new wisdom from the wise[17]!

Odysseus *puts wax in his ears. The* **Sirens** *sing.* **Odysseus** *takes the wax out of his ears to hear their song. He listens. He weeps. He puts the wax back in his ears. He takes it out again and listens to the Sirens' song. He weeps and wails. He throws himself in the sea.*

---

17 Pope, Book 12 (adapted)

Scene 14: Quarrel Among The Gods

Zeus, Athene *and* **Poseidon.**

Poseidon   But, Zeus, nobody will respect me any more. We worked together on making the Greeks suffer on their journey home. And you, Athene, suddenly start helping Odysseus. Why? How come you changed sides like that? I'd understand if you were in love. But you just look at him from the sidelines like an old maid.

Athene   What d'you know about love?

Poseidon   Oooh!

Zeus   Aaah!

Athene   You've shagged everyone and everything and you've shagged far and wide. Disguised as swans, bulls, snakes, faithful husbands of faithful wives. Disguised as fire and air. You've raped your own mother. You've shagged half the universe. Begotten a horde of children. But you know nothing of love.

Poseidon   Sweet little Athene.

Athene   Is that what you called me when I was a child? When you came to take care of me?

Poseidon   What? What's that?

Athene   What did you do to me then?

Poseidon   What're you talking about?

Athene   I have some hazy memories, Uncle Poseidon!

Zeus   Family love has a magic power. Let's look for a moment now into the cold abyss of the truth.

Poseidon *grabs* **Odysseus**, *who is drowning in the sea.*

Poseidon   Why d'you think you're better than me? And if you are, have you ever asked yourself why? Who made you like that? Me. I did. One afternoon, when I had nothing better to do and I happened to come across your Mama. She immediately married the first man who walked by after that. All right then, you're free. Go back to Ithaca and flail around like a scarecrow in the wind. Go and try to work out who's who there, who's what, and who's with whom. And who on earth *you* are.

Scene 15: Ithaca

Odysseus *is asleep on the beach. Enter* **Athene**. *She looks at him. She kisses his armpit.*

Athene I spent many happy years as the goddess of wisdom. I was quite content and confident. But one day I met my evil fate and my ruin. I was walking with Hera and Aphrodite when we ran into the goddess Eris. I knew nothing good would come of it. That Eris is the goddess of envy and discord. She threw a golden apple at us and said: "This apple is for the most beautiful among you." How could I have fallen for that? Taken over by vanity, blinded by jealousy? Why did it suddenly matter to me to be beautiful? We couldn't decide who the apple belonged to. And who did we choose to be the jury? Handsome young Paris. Hera offered him a kingdom as a bribe, but he refused because he wasn't interested. And what did I offer him? Listen, I ask you – strategic superiority in military matters. Who was I offering this to? A young man who thinks only with his cock. Aphrodite cleverly offered him Helen. And that's how she got the apple, Paris got Helen, and we all got the Trojan War. I realised I was stupid in matters of the heart, that I didn't feel anything. Everyone talked about coming, and I didn't know what it meant. I desperately wanted to find out. And from you, first among men, who I had always loved. It's not enough for me to be a wise and clever virgin. I want you to see me as a woman. I want to have you for a husband. I've followed your loves and infidelities for years. (*Whispering*) I dream of being in your arms. And of new grass springing from the sacred ground beneath us. Dewy lotus, saffron and fragrant hyacinth shooting up from it. Us covered by a golden cloud with sparkling drops of dew. (*Pause.*) Odysseus, you've reached home on Ithaca. Ithaca, Odysseus.

Odysseus *suddenly cries out and opens his eyes. As if he's been wakened from some kind of nightmare.*

Odysseus   Goddess, tell me, am I really in my homeland?

Athene   Unbeliever. Here it is – Ithaca!

Athene *clears the mist.* **Odysseus** *falls on his knees. He kisses the earth.*

Odysseus   Ithaca, my dear land, I never dreamed I would see you again . . . Now rejoice in my loving prayers[18]. (*Pause. He looks around.*) This doesn't look like Ithaca to me.

Athene   You don't look like Odysseus either.

Odysseus   Where's that Ithaca of mine?

Athene   Gone with that Odysseus.

Odysseus   I thought . . . it'd be the same.

Athene   You're not the same either.

Odysseus   What about Penelope? Is she the same?

Athene   You mean faithful? Let's have a look at your side of the story. You had three children with Circe – Telegonos, Agrios and Latinos. With Calypso you had Nausithous and Nausinous. And one child each with Callidice, Euippe and Thoas.

Odysseus   Nobody knows that. Nobody saw that.

Athene   Except me.

---

18   Fagles, Book13, 406-7 (adapted)

Odysseus Let's keep it that way. What about Penelope? What's her story?

Athene Nobody saw that either. (*Pause.*) Except me.

Pause. They look at each other.

Odysseus I'm nervous. My knees are shaking. Give me courage.

Athene I'll be on your side.

Odysseus First I've got to kill the suitors. How am I going to do that? And Penelope? Will I be able to, you know, when I see her again?

Athene There's nothing I can do about that.

Odysseus What kind of goddess are you?

Athene Let me make it so no one'll be able to recognise you! I'll turn you into a doddering old beggar!

Odysseus You always want to have your own way. Where's my freedom in all this?

Athene What d'you know about freedom? You're mortal.

Odysseus What d'you know about freedom? You're immortal.

Athene *touches* **Odysseus** *with her staff. He is turned into a beggar.*

Scene 16: The Dog

Odysseus *goes up to the* **Dog**.

Odysseus You're still alive. My faithful dog. Guarding my threshold. How many times did we go hunting together? D'you know who's come?

Dog My master Odysseus.

Odysseus It's me.

Dog I can hardly see you. Hardly hear you. I waited for you.

Odysseus How are you?

Dog You can see for yourself.

Odysseus You've often been in my thoughts.

Dog And you in mine.

Odysseus It's been twenty years. They told me you were with the shepherds. That you fearlessly protected the flock from wolves.

Dog The shepherds loved us, shared their life with us, we ate and slept together. I was the chief dog. Others chased the wolves and tired them, and then I was the one who ripped their throats out at the end. They put the best food aside for me and the best place by the fire. I was famous. But years went by, I grew old, I lost my sight and sense of smell, I started to limp. And the day came when the shepherds decided we must part. They left me my last meal and moved the flock on. I watched them go, but there was no help for it, life goes on. I was left alone. And then the wolves appeared. They remembered me well, had known me for years. They surrounded me and I was helpless. I waited for them to kill me. That would have meant my salvation and a heroic death. But no. They had other ideas. They left me alive. And started to screw me. One by one, all of them. Several times.

Odysseus Oh, heavens!

Dog An old dog, sport for the wolves. There. That's what I wanted to tell you. Now leave me to die.

Odysseus No.

Dog Yes.

Jasna Ðuričić as The Dog in the Ulysses Theatre production

Scene 17 : Father And Son

Telemachus *and* **Odysseus.**

Odysseus   Is this where the swineherd Eumaeus lives?

Telemachus   Eumaeus is dead.

Odysseus   We were friends long ago. I've come from far away to ask for shelter.

Telemachus   Strangers, travellers and beggars are sent by Zeus.

Odysseus   How many suitors does Penelope have?

Telemachus   First there are fifty-two choice young men from Dulichium, and six servants with them. From Cephalonia there are twenty-four, twenty from Zakynthos, and from Ithaca twelve.

Odysseus   I met Odysseus on Crete.

Telemachus   Any tramp passing through Ithaca comes and pretends to my mistress that he's seen Odysseus.

Odysseus   He'll come home. His ship's already put to sea to bring him back to his dear homeland. What would you do if Odysseus suddenly appeared here right now?

Telemachus   I'd hold him to my breast and weep.

Odysseus   And he'd weep.

Telemachus   Then we'd both weep.

Odysseus   I'm Odysseus.

Telemachus   He'll never come.

Odysseus   I'm your father.

Telemachus I really wanted to find you, but as time went by I became more and more ashamed of you.

Odysseus How are you? What's it like for you here?

Telemachus Ithaca's a windblown place. There's nothing here. Actually, it's not that there's nothing here. Here there *is* nothing!

Odysseus I didn't want to go to war. You were a baby. I'd bought you a dog. I was happy. I wanted to watch you grow up, be a father to you. But they came for me, mobilisation. I sacrificed myself for you. Everybody in the war swore by a god, but I swore by my son Telemachus.

Telemachus I know you gave me life, but I don't feel anything for you. Mother tried to praise you, say how good and famous you were in the past. But the more she praised you, the more ashamed I was of your name. I wanted to ask her where you'd been when my first tooth came through. But that wouldn't have changed anything.

Odysseus I'm a veteran. I've been there.

Telemachus Where is there?

Odysseus There is Troy.

Telemachus What is this Troy? For years it's been a bloated corpse dragged around by hyenas.

Odysseus Troy is my whole life!

Telemachus Everyone says that when they get old. They were all at Troy, they were all heroes. Ah, if you'd seen me then! Ah, how it was in my time!

Odysseus But I was there! Ten years I lived with death, slept with it, ate with it.

Telemachus   Are you sure you've been anywhere at all? Where's this island of Ogygia? It's not on any maps. How come you're the only one left alive?

Odysseus *hits* **Telemachus**.

Telemachus   We bow down before you, great commander, destroyer of cities, you who made rape and looting into an honourable profession, our father! We bow down before your image. We're in exile here at home. Not every house is a home. Grant us a new world, law and order. Show us where we are, where we come from and where we're going.

Odysseus   You're not my son!

Telemachus   Daddy came home from the war a psychopath.

Odysseus *raises his hand.*

Telemachus   You touch me again and I'll kill you!

Exit **Odysseus**. **Telemachus** *tries to scratch the tattooed name of his father off his arm with his nails.*

Scene 18: Husband And Wife

Penelope's chamber. **Odysseus** *and* **Penelope**.

Odysseus   Madam, you sent for me.

Penelope   Stranger, who are you, where are you from and who are your parents?

Odysseus   Lady, your fame reaches the heavens. Ask me something else, just not about my origins and homeland. I saw Odysseus on Crete and showed him hospitality.

Penelope   Come, tell me what sort of clothing he wore[19].

Odysseus   A tunic bright as the sun, as thin as dry garlic skin.

Penelope   I gave him that garment from the storeroom. I folded it neatly, fastened the golden brooch to adorn my husband[20].

Odysseus   He's close, close at hand[21].

Penelope   Stranger, this house no longer has a master. Tomorrow will cut me off from Odysseus's house[22]. I mean to announce a contest, a trial for my suitors. The winner is the man I follow, yes, forsaking this house[23].

Pause. They look at each other.

Odysseus   You recognised me.

Penelope   Yes.

---

19 Fagles, Book 19, 251
20 ibid. 293-4
21 ibid. 346
22 ibid. 643
23 ibid. 651

Odysseus   When?

Penelope   As soon as I saw you.

Odysseus   Why didn't you tell me?

Penelope   I was embarrassed.

Odysseus   You were embarrassed?

Penelope   Why all the acting?

Odysseus   Athene disguised me.

Penelope   Why?

Odysseus   How should I know?

Penelope   Didn't you ask her?

Odysseus   You go and ask her.

Penelope   No need to get angry.

Odysseus   Is that all you've got to say to me? That the costume's not very good?

Penelope   I've been waiting for this moment for twenty years.

Odysseus   What about me?

Penelope   I didn't expect you to turn up as a fake beggar.

Odysseus   Do you want me to come back in again? Stage the meeting again?

Penelope   This is unpleasant.

Odysseus   You've taken the words right out of my mouth.

Pause.

Odysseus   Why don't you hug me?

Penelope   And you me?

Pause.

Odysseus   Come on. What're you waiting for?

Penelope   You come on.

They stand and don't move. **Odysseus** *glares at* **Penelope**. *Pause.*

Odysseus   What's the matter now?

Penelope   I'm looking at you.

Odysseus   Why? (*Pause.*) You're looking at me as if I were a stranger! You don't recognise me anymore! Did you wait for me? Home is where they wait for you. Where's this I've come to? D'you know who I am? D'you know my name? D'you want me to tell you my name?

Penelope *quickly turns and makes for the exit.*

Odysseus   Come back here! D'you hear me? Cheeky bitch! Did you take Antinous of Dulichium as your lover?

Penelope   I beg your pardon?

Odysseus   I'm just asking.

Penelope   Yes, I did.

Odysseus   And is it true you made love with all one hundred and eight suitors? And that you had a son, Pan, with them? The ugliest of creatures, lover of Bacchantes and Maenads. Is it the truth?

Penelope   Yes, it is. (*Pause.*) So? What do you want now? What do you want? You want me to swear I was faithful? Beg mercy from you? Why should my chastity be taken for granted? Have you ever asked yourself what twenty years of chastity means? And what you've done to deserve them?

314

If you're really free, why do you keep comparing yourself with us? You measure your victories against our defeats, your freedom against our slavery, your merry madness against our boring normality. You want to keep changing, and us to stay the same and immobile, like an anchor, like the North Star in the heavens, as a measure of your distance from us. We're not your point of arrival, but the transit station for your departures. Ithaca is a place to avoid! Ah, your painful return to your homeland and your wife! How many other people's homelands have you destroyed, how many other men's wives have you fucked? Your son's caught your disease. He'll get married, too, and go off to some bloody Troy of his own, leave his wife and children and come back to them a stranger. Your mother died of loneliness. And me? Every day I long to get the hell out of here. What do you think, the fishermen and peasants have nothing better to do than sit and sigh and worship you? "Ah, where's our free Odysseus now?" They have their own work and worries, trying to make ends meet. They're not even aware of your exploits, nor do they give a damn about them. You've managed to escape from everything, including yourself. There, that's the price of your freedom! So do the sums. How many Ithacas for one man's freedom?

Scene 19: Deus Ex Machina

Athene *suddenly appears.*

Odysseus   Is this really happening to me or I just think it is?

Athene   It comes down to the same thing. I've worked hard to get you home. Put an end to your yearning. Bring you to your wife, son and people, spend enough time with them to get bored, really fed up, disillusioned, and then long to set out again. And finally realise that it's actually me you've always wanted. I wanted to live with you. Make you immortal. I made an agreement with the gods. They all signed. Even Poseidon. "Athene is permitted to marry Odysseus and live with him forever and make him immortal".

Odysseus   And?

Athene   I was over the moon with happiness. And then I discovered a secret annex to the agreement. Which says that Odysseus can be immortal, but not forever young. They want you to turn into a decrepit old man who throws up, pisses and shits in his pants. And for me to spend the rest of time with a corpse in my bed of love.

Odysseus   So you have fate too. You don't have the last word.

Athene   Fuck life and the gods. It's terrible how people get old. It's not slow or gradual. It happens all of a sudden, one afternoon, overnight, from Tuesday to Wednesday. I can't watch you get old. Does that make me stupid?

Odysseus   No, you're not.

Athene I've spent eternity like a strict school mistress. I've educated the universe. Given morals, warnings, doled out slaps. But love, love I haven't known. May I kiss you? (**Athene** *kisses* **Odysseus** *on the forehead. Pause.*) Do you love me just a bit? You were my Ithaca. Ithaca is where you set out from but can't go back to. It's time to part.

Odysseus Are you toying with me?

Athene I pictured it differently. But even I can be wrong.

Odysseus Who do you work for? Pallas Athene, I'll kill you! I'll kill you all! Odysseus has come for his own! Odysseus is back! Odysseus has come home!

Enter the **Suitor**.

Suitor Save us, dear gods! Master Odysseus, I can explain everything. It's not at all what you think. We thought you were dead.

Odysseus Did you think I'd never return from Troy, you dogs? Is that what you thought?!

Enter **Zeus, Poseidon** *and the* **Bard**.

Athene Listen to me, people of Ithaca. It's your fault all this has happened. Now you're going to stop killing each other with hatred, you're going to be reconciled with love. Zeus will make you forget your distress altogether and love each other as before.

Zeus Ladies and gentlemen, comrades, friends. My dear people, that is, dear mortals. Respected colleague gods. So the hour has come . . . Allow me to say a few words on the occasion of . . . regarding . . . It's a great honour and special pleasure that the task has fallen to me to declare peace. What is peace? Peace is thus . . . not war. Peace is youth, making jokes and making merry. It's peaceful cooperation between mortals and gods in all fields for a better life for future generations. And therefore long live peace! There, that's all I have to say. More or less. Thank you. (*Applause.* **Zeus** *addresses the* **Bard**.) Come now, sing of this, may it be heard by mortals far and wide. Tell them everything.

Bard   Everything?

Zeus   The whole story.

Bard   There isn't a whole story.

Zeus   What d'you mean, there isn't?

Bard   There're just parts. Versions.

Zeus   Mind how you tell it, then.

Bard   You mind how I tell it, then.

Zeus   I beg your pardon?

Bard   It's not easy for us bards. It all needs summarising. Make it consistent in places, sound nicer in others, add something here, cut something there. Telling stories is waging war by other means.

Pause. **Odysseus** *looks around him.*

Odysseus   Now I see what you're playing at. War and hatred cut short. Brushed under the carpet. Replaced by peace and unity. And that lasts a few years. Then peace and unity are cut short. And war and hatred again. Well done. How come you don't get fed up with it all? You've ruined Ithaca! You've destroyed my homeland! No trace left of empire or great rulers. Only a handful of upstarts left who call themselves kings, each in his own dark hole. You've spat on the vows that were made. You've put up

318

monuments to foreign gods. You've burnt the flags, banned the songs, changed the locks on the doors. What kind of people are you? I thought you'd wait for me, but you haven't even waited for yourselves. You've turned my home into a wasteland. You've plucked the heart out of Ithaca's breast and put a stone in its place. For ten years the gods wouldn't let me have my revenge. D'you know what revenge looks like when it's been brewing for ten tears? Like this!

Odysseus *frenziedly swings his sword around in thin air for a long time. They all look at him. Pause.* **Odysseus** *stabs the sword into the ground, out of breath. Pause.*

Odysseus   Help me to take out the dead. Bring sulphur to clean the chamber. Home is where it hurts! (*Long pause*) Let's move on!

The group of actors start singing.

All   Home is where
I spend the night,
Home is where
I feel all right.

I can never go back home
For now I've lost my way,
I can never leave my home
No, never go away.

Home is where
they know my name,
Home is where
I lay my claim.

319

I can never go back home
For now I've lost my way,
I can never leave my home
No, never go away.

Home is where
My love is strong,
Home is where
My pain is long.

I can never go back home
For now I've lost my way,
I can never leave my home
No, never go away.

They exit singing into the darkness. Their shadows find it hard to follow them too.

CURTAIN

FIGURAE VENERIS HISTORIAE

by Goran Stefanovski (A Play for the Theatre) (2014)

Poster for the first production of *Figurae Veneris Historiae* at the
Slovenian National Theatre in Ljubljana, 2014,
directed by Aleksandar Popovski

Characters[24]

Baroness

Baron

Young Lady, their daughter

Ploughman

Land Woman

Student

Handyman

Widow

Maid

Convict

Magnus

---

24 Language Editor's Note: The original English text of the play was not edited – it was the basis for the Slovenian translation. (The play was commissioned by the Slovenian National Theatre and was to be performed in Slovenian.) For the publication of the play in English I have changed the names of some of the characters to better convey in British English the essence of what Stefanovski intended for each role. Thus I have used Young Lady instead of Damsel, the original name of the role, as 'damsel' is only used in the modern language to refer, usually ironically, to a "damsel in distress". The original Farmer role has changed, as we learn in the play that he is not the owner of a farm but a ploughman. The Farmer Woman, his wife, is a woman who works on the land, so I have coined the term Land Woman, reflecting the Land Girls who were commandeered to work on the land during the world wars when the male farm labourers had been called up.

ACT 1

1. Prologue

The curtain is down. Enter ten characters, in modern dress.

Magnus Do you sometimes feel like you're hypnotised? Like you have no control of yourself? Like you're under a spell, a curse bending your will, messing you up, making you do things you don't want to do? Like you're in the head of someone insane? (*Pause.*) Why do we let this happen? How is it that we allow ourselves to be such easy prey? Could it be that we really want to be hypnotised, that we're actually asking for it? Let me demonstrate. I will say two words and you observe what happens in your mouth: sour lemon. Sour lemon. Can you feel your mouth contract, as if sucking on a real lemon, just at the very mention of the word? Well, if it's that easy to manipulate us, then it's no surprise we follow blindly. Then it's small wonder they use us as cannon fodder. (*Pause.*) I learnt a little about these things. I wrote a book called "Sittengeschichte des Weltkrieges", The Sexual History of the World War. It was published in Berlin in 1931. It was a study of war as sexual hypnosis, pornographic trance, mass orgy. (*He looks at the characters around him.*) Millions were raped. Some in their bodies, some in their minds, some in both. I was one of them. My name is Magnus Hirschfeld. I was a doctor of sexology. I invented the term. They called me The Einstein of Sex. (*Pause. He addresses the characters around him.*) Why are we here?

All (*As if suddenly waking up, repeating one after the other*)

We're here... because we're here... because we're here... because we're here...

Magnus Listen! (*Pause. There is no sound.*) Can you hear it? The silence! (*Pause.*) The silence behind. (*Pause.*) Behind the noise. Behind the pressure in the ears. Behind the humdrum, the explosions and the din. Behind the clamour, the racket and the uproar. (*Pause.*) It's the silence – of love.

Magnus *makes a gesture. The curtain goes up. He disappears. The year is 1914.*

2. War At Last!

Enter **Baroness**. *Enter* **Magnus** *behind her. During her speech he seems to be shadowing her. She is not aware of his presence.*

Baroness   For as long as I can remember, I've had a war raging in me. Passions tearing me apart. Sometimes small, sometimes big. Armies in endless battle. I'm a conflict of day and night, sun and moon, male and female. One minute I'm in love, the next I don't care. First I attack, then I retreat. And then both at the same time. One day I build, the next I pull down what I've built.

Exit **Magnus**.

Sudden Changes
Summer. **Baron** *and* **Baroness** *at home. The* **Baroness** *is trying on a huge floral hat.*

Baron   At last! At last! War at last!

Baroness   What do you think of this one?

Baron   Who cares? We're going to a war demonstration.

Baroness   One should always look one's best. Shall I bring a hamper?

Baron   This is not a picnic.

Baroness   Everyone will be hungry, with all the shouting.

Baron   Bring some wine.

Baroness   For how many?

Baron   Ten! A hundred! Let wine flow free!

Baroness   One would think you ran a charity, not a bank.

Baron   War is good for banking. There's no business like war business.

Baroness   Now that it's started maybe we will love each other more.

Baron   We will. Oh yes, we will!

Baroness   I can't wait.

Enter **Young Lady**, *wearing bridal white.*

Young Lady   I'm getting married.

Baroness   Who to?

Young Lady   To an unknown soldier.

Baroness   Who is that?

Young Lady   No one knows.

Baron   That's the point.

Young Lady   I will give myself freely to a man going to war.

Baroness   Why?

Young Lady   Out of patriotism.

Baroness   Have you discussed this with your father?

Baron   You'll bring shame upon the family.

Young Lady   I'm acting on gut instinct. It's stronger than me.

Baroness   I'm going to shoot myself.

Young Lady   Half the town is rushing to get married. "For tomorrow they're going away".

Baron   It'll all be over by Christmas.

Young Lady   Then I'll get divorced.

Baroness   Maybe he'll get shot.

Baron   What if he comes back a cripple?

Young Lady   Fate consists of too many imponderables.

Baron   I told you not to let her read so much.

Baroness   I've been hiding her books.

Young Lady   Except for the Bible. I ruined my eyes on the juicy bits.

Baron   You must show me where they are.

Young Lady   It's the family Bible. They're all underlined.

Baron   You're aware that class imposes certain obligations.

Young Lady   And those are: Do what I please. No restraints. No apologies, no excuses.

Baroness (*To* **Baron**)   You were reckless, too, when you stole me away from my family.

Baron   That was different.

Baroness   This is also different. I married beneath me.

Enter **Maid**. *She takes off her apron.*

Maid   I've come to say goodbye. I'm leaving.

Young Lady   This sudden acceleration of everything.

Maid   Of history. I've found work. In a munitions factory.

Young Lady   So this is a new chapter.

Maid   Seven million soldiers are under arms. The weapons are all new. No one knows how to use them. There hasn't been a war in Europe for over 40 years. Don't bother to learn the geography, it'll all change soon.

Young Lady How exciting!

Maid I'll never forget you.

They kiss. The **Maid** *throws her apron at the* **Baron**. *She goes out.*

Give Me Your Pigs
A farm in the countryside. **Handyman** *is talking to* **Ploughman** *and* **Land Woman**. *They carry spades.*

Handyman (*Kissing the hand of the* **Land Woman**) Allow me to engage you in a short but substantial conversation.

Ploughman What d'you want?

Handyman You're a ploughman. And you're a hard-working woman. Mother of many.

Land Woman Three.

Handyman May they live long and prosperous lives. May we dance at their weddings.

Ploughman Who are you?

Handyman I'm a handyman. I come from town. Do you ever visit town?

Ploughman Last Christmas I took suckling pigs to the Baron's mansion.

Handyman I recently repaired their plumbing. How would you like to have a mansion of your own?

Ploughman What're you talking about?

Handyman   War's been declared. The order will be overturned. The last will be first. Mansions are useless in a war. Pigs are the thing. You've got pigs. You can buy a mansion with those pigs.

Ploughman   You said mansions were useless.

Handyman   After the war they become useful again.

Land Woman   What's in it for you?

Handyman   I'm the middle man. Pigs over here, mansion over there, me in the middle.

Burning The Flag
A street in town. **Student** *carrying a flag.*

Student   I object! I refuse to go to war. I'm deaf to the cries of my ancestors. I will not fight for my motherland and fatherland, for the King and his army and the secret police. I will not sacrifice myself for the baby in the cradle and the infirm old people. I have no patriotism, it is the passion of the stupid! I am an artist! I belong to no one! I stand on the edge of nothing!

He sets fire to the flag.

I've been released
At an address in town.

Widow   You!

Convict   I'm out.

Widow   I thought you got forty years.

Convict   I've been released to join the army.

Widow   Nowadays I just pray for an ordinary life.

Convict   You're wearing black.

Widow   I'm a widow.

Convict   But I'm alive.

Widow   We're divorced. It's too late for everything.

Convict   Not if you still love me.

Widow   There's no place for love in the political world.

Convict   Is there someone else? I want to hear it from you. After the war we can get married again.

Widow   Don't open up old wounds.

Convict   We'll have children.

Widow   I'm still a virgin. And we lived together for two years.

Convict   Not even two. And then he came between us.

Widow   It was a momentary lapse of reason. You murdered him so brutally.

Convict   It was a momentary lapse of reason. I did it for you.

Widow   I'm going to church. I will pray for us.

Convict   I'm going to war. I will kill again, but this time they will give me a medal. Wait for me.

Widow   Will this heart be strong enough?

Oh La La, Love
At the **Baron**'s *mansion.* **Student** *and* **Young Lady**.

Student   You sent for me.

330

Young Lady You've been called up.

Student We're leaving tomorrow.

Young Lady You still stutter.

Student Only when I get excited.

Young Lady You told me once that you loved me with three kinds of love.

Student Agape, Philia and Eros.

Young Lady Tell me again.

Student I love you with Agape, unconditional, spiritual love – that is, with all your faults and shortcomings, not that you have any. I also love you with Philia, mental love. And as for Eros, the physical love, I wouldn't dare dream of that one.

Young Lady Oh please do! (*She kisses him.*) We're getting married. You'll be boarding a train and I'll cry on the platform. It'll be embarrassing. The train doesn't move and we've already said our goodbyes many times over. Then you disappear and I drown in my own tears.

Enter the **Baroness**.

Baroness You must be the unknown soldier.

Student I'm a conscientious objector.

Baroness Are you coming on the picnic?

Student I went and protested. I told them that war is legalised mass murder, that it leads to cruelty and sadism.

Baroness What did they say?

Student   They said that it also offers infinite erotic possibilities.

Mass Hysteria
All *come together for war demonstrations.*

Convict   Here I was, wild and intoxicated, hysterical and delirious, screaming: Peace is no longer tolerable! The barbarian in me came to the fore. My repressed darkness was now legalised. Here was a chance to taste extremes. Here was the freedom to eradicate the world around me. Everything was allowed, even taking human life. This was seductive and addictive and I hoped it would lead to some final catharsis. And if it destroyed me, so be it!

He pricks up his ears as if he is trying to hear something inaudible. Pause.

3: Drill

Intro

Enter **Ploughman**. **Magnus** *silently helps him dress in a soldier's uniform. He combs his hair.* **Ploughman** *is not aware of his presence.*

Ploughman   I was at the same time a private, a sergeant and a captain. It was I who was making the whole hierarchy possible. I was a sadist to those below me and a masochist for those above. I kneaded myself and those around me into human material, into a machine!

Bayonet Sequence
Field exercise.

Convict   Listen here. I'm your sergeant. Team spirit, personal sacrifice, dedication to the cause. Fuck. You know all that! We all stand for Muscular Christianity! To enforce what's good and true, to fight the good fight. Today we're going to practise the bayonet drill sequence, in other words stabbing the enemy. Those bags are enemy soldiers. Attack!

Ploughman   Die, pig! *(He charges and stabs the bag many times.)*

Pause. The **Convict** *looks at the* **Student**.

Convict   You!

Student   I can't.

Convict   You can't?

Student   I won't.

Convict   For *can't* you go to hospital, for *won't* you go to jail!

Student   Oh, well!

Convict   They'll kill you! They'll kill him, too! (*To the* **Ploughman**) Do you want to die because of this piece of shit?

Ploughman   No, sir!

Convict   Well then, strangle him.

Ploughman   You mean now? Here? Bare-handed?

Convict   You want gloves? Strangle him!

The **Ploughman** *starts strangling the* **Student***. The* **Student** *turns blue.*

Ploughman   Say when, sir!

Convict   You slimy worm! I'll shove you back in your mother's cunt. And I'll fuck her so hard that you fall out of her arse. I'll drill you until you get down on your knees and plead to go to the front and die there.

Knitting Session
Café in town. **Baroness** *and* **Widow** *are drinking coffee together.*

Baroness   We're in the papers today.

Widow (*Reading*)   "Truly, a change has come over the womenfolk of this town. Under the auspices of the Baroness, they are all knitting now, even those who have never knitted before. Why knit at home when you can do it in a church social group?"

Baroness Give my compliments to your ladies.

Iva Babić as the Widow and Polona Juh as the Baroness in The
Slovenian National Theatre production, 2014

She examines the knitted items.

Widow Gloves, wristlets, jumpers. Fingerless mitts to
allow trigger access. Our boys need socks. We knit our bit.

Baroness Must it all be this dull colour?

Widow Grey and khaki yarn. That's regulation. We could
always add your name stitched in red.

Baroness That would be a lovely touch.

Widow Soldiers marching with your name woven into
the fabric.

Baroness How intimate. What are these?

Widow Stump socks.

Baroness Mmmm.

Widow For amputated limbs.

Baroness *giggles, covering her mouth.* **Widow** *looks at her.*

Collaboration Pact
Army office. The **Handyman** *and the* **Baron**

Handyman Thank you for finding time to see me.

Baron Why aren't you on the front line?

Handyman I have a certificate. "Applied to join the Army. Unfit. Poor physique."

Baron What's wrong with you?

Handyman Too short. Short-sighted. Flat-footed. I have bad teeth.

Baron What can I do for you?

Handyman Times are hard. Everything is rationed. Cigarettes, chocolate, coffee and butter. There's high demand.

Baron Yes.

Handyman Many would pay a good price.

Baron Some call that a black market.

Handyman There's no black or white market. There's a single market.

Baron Who are you?

Handyman I'm nobody, sir.

Baron What do you want?

Handyman You have a big say in requisitioning and centralised buying.

Baron   You should be court-martialled.

Handyman   I'm ready to face the consequences.

Baron   I call that dedication.

Handyman   All in the line of duty, sir. There are millions of soldiers on the front line. They have their manly needs. Provision should be made in an organised fashion.

Baron   Bring me the sums tomorrow morning.

Handyman   Bright and early, sir. Much obliged.

Burying Children
Graveyard. **Land Woman** *and Gravedigger* (**Magnus**).

Land Woman   An old woman told me they could be cured if I put snails in a muslin bag and rubbed it anti-clockwise around their tummies. It helped a bit. But they still died. Within a week of each other. I have no one to lose now.

Gravedigger   You're young. You'll have more.

Land Woman   Will I?

Gravedigger   Yes. (*Pause.*) Shall I?

Land Woman *nods.* **Gravedigger** *starts digging.*

Land Woman   Twinkle, twinkle, little star, how I wonder what you are. Up above the clouds so high, like a diamond in the sky, twinkle, twinkle, little star, how I wonder what you are.

Gravedigger   Amen.

Gravedigger turns into **Magnus**. *He pricks up his ears as if he is trying to hear something inaudible. Pause.*

4: Propaganda

Grenade Story
Home. **Maid** *wearing uniform of worker in munitions factory. Her father (***Magnus***) is a mutilated man in pyjamas. She feeds him.*

Maid   I have a new job now. Look (*Showing him her uniform*). I make grenades. We fill shells. Some of them come up to my waist. It's new scientific murder. I work all day and then I come home to feed you. It's overcrowded with you and mum and nine kids. You were a blacksmith. Huge fists, great corns and calluses. Sometimes you'd get out the leather belt. It was good for us. You made us what we are. Was there something else you would do to me, Father? If I remember rightly. Do I remember rightly? (*Pause.*) Have you had enough? What else can I give you? One of these? (*She takes out a grenade.*) Do you know what some women do with these? When they're lonely in the night? 'Cos all the boys have gone to the front. And the only men left behind are fathers not fit for service. (*She puts the grenade in his mouth.*)

The father turns into **Magnus**. *He pricks up his ears as if he is trying to hear something inaudible. Pause. Enter* **Land Woman**. **Magnus** *listens to her speech. She is not aware of his presence.*

Land Woman   I spread lies and I believed the lies I heard. I was always right and high-minded and God was always and only on my side. The enemy were all blood-sucking sub-humans. I helped fictitious evil become factual truth.

I discovered an effective way to destroy myself – which was to deny and obliterate my understanding of my own history.

Motorcycle Messenger

At the farm. **Land Woman**. *Enter* **Young Lady** *wearing a motorcycle helmet, goggles and uniform.*

Young Lady (*Giving her an envelope*)   A letter for you.

Land Woman   I could hear you for miles, coming over the fields.

Young Lady   People turn and gape at me.

Land Woman (*Opening the envelope*)   A ration book.

Young Lady   Could I have some water to wash the goggles?

Land Woman   All it's good for these days. They say the well's poisoned. The enemy put plague germs in there. A neighbour told me. She was told by someone who'd heard from someone who knew.

Young Lady   Degenerates.

Land Woman   I drink rainwater now. My husband was called up. He was a ploughman. He'd get up at four in the morning and go on until dark. And then see to the horses. He did all the little things, fastening the windows at night, locking the door, chopping wood. We had pigs. Eggs, milk. But the authorities took it all. Now I have this (*Waving the ration book*).

Young Lady   The thing is, we're fighting a just war. And they're fighting an unjust war. That's why victory will be ours. It's simple really. I can do semaphore. (*She does a few letters of semaphore.*) I can also do whistling, heliograph and lamps.

Land Woman   Do you know they use our nuns as bell clappers? They take a nun and tie her against the clapper of the church bell.

Young Lady   Would the bell ring? Wouldn't the nun muffle the sound?

Land Woman   It would ring, but not very well. It'd kill the nun, though.

Young Lady   How long would it take for the nun to die?

Land Woman   It depends whether she's young or old. Thin or fat.

Young Lady   What a way to go.

Land Woman   They never clean up after their dogs. They just eat the shit off the street.

Young Lady   We never knew any of this before.

Land Woman   It was hidden from us.

Young Lady   We must bury them all.

Land Woman   And piss on their graves.

5: Trenches

Enter **Baron**. **Magnus** *enters behind him. He shadows his speech, as if whispering words in his ear.* **Baron** *is not aware of his presence.*

Baron   Everyone has their wars and I've had mine. But it so happened that my small war was enveloped by the Great War. The Mother of All Wars, the Global War, The War of the Nations, the War to Put an End to All Wars. World War One. I followed its development, like a photograph, in the dark room of my soul. My capitalist greed exploded! My great empires went for each other's throats. I'd been piling up armaments for decades. My bourgeois morality fell apart. I descended into a spiritual cave. My base urges were unleashed and I turned into a – beast!

Exit **Baron**. *Exit* **Magnus**.

The Medal

The trenches. **Ploughman** *and* **Student**. **Student** *is examining the top of the trench.*

Student   When you crawl in the dirt, you see a scuttling beetle here, a little flower there. And you think to yourself: What a world of wonders! Then you see a close-up of barbed wire and you say: What a world of miracles! What's this white stuff in the air, floating like a flurry of snow?

Ploughman   It's pukh. From the poplar trees. It lasts for two weeks a year.

Student   So mysterious. It looks like sperm. Nature is multiplying. Out in the open. Shamelessly.

Baron *comes in. He is smoking a pipe.* **Ploughman** *jumps to attention.* **Baron** *gives him a sign to stand at ease.*

Baron   Congratulations, private.

Ploughman   Thank you, sir.

Baron   We're proud of you. So, how was it?

Ploughman   What, sir?

Baron   How did you do it?

Ploughman   What, sir?

Baron   Modesty, eh? I like that in a hero.

Ploughman   I'm not a hero, sir.

Baron   Well, this medal says you are. Wear it with pride.

He pins a medal on the **Ploughman**'s *chest.*

Ploughman   Thank you, sir. (*He looks at the medal.*)

Baron   How's life in the trenches?

Ploughman   I won't complain. It's just the lice, sir. They're everywhere. For every one I pop with my nails, ten more appear. And the rats are big. They ate the cat we used to hunt them with.

Baron   Still, I can see you find time to shine your buttons. (*Looking at the* **Student**) He should be doing the shining for you. What's the matter with him?

Ploughman   He's sad sir.

Baron   Sad, eh? Poor soul!

Ploughman   He killed an enemy soldier. And he came back with his ear in his mouth.

Baron Aha. So he's the man with the ear. (**Baron** *takes the medal off the* **Ploughman**'s *chest and pins it on the* **Student**'s *chest.*) Well done, private! (*Pause.* **Student** *looks at the medal.*) Well then, what are you in your real life?

Student In my real life I was a student. And in this here non-real life I act as a soldier. I wear this costume. And I don't even know my fucking lines. And often I think I'm not here. Even now as I'm speaking, I'm up there, high above, looking at me talking to you.

Baron What are you on about?

Student You wouldn't know, would you?

Student *takes off the medal. He holds it with two fingers. He hangs it on a pipe. He takes the ear out of his pocket and puts it in the pipe.* **Baron** *looks at it. He holds it with two fingers. Tense pause.* **Baron** *throws the ear away.*

Baron Is that an ear?

Student It was.

Baron Are you mad?

Student Yes, I am!

Baron What's the matter with you?

Student I'm mad!

Ploughman *comes between them.*

Ploughman It's a joke, sir. (*He starts singing.*)

> They shagged her up, they shagged her down,
> They shagged her all around the town,
> They shagged her in, they shagged her out,
> They shagged her up her water-spout.

343

Now seven months later all was well,
Eight months later she began to swell,
Nine months later she gave a grunt,
And a little fat bastard popped out her cunt.
The fat little bastard he grew and grew,
He fucked the cat and the donkey too,
The fat little bastard he went to hell,
He fucked the devil and his wife as well.

A Beautiful Corpse

Battlefield. **Convict** *lies next to a corpse* (**Magnus**). *His face is muddy and bloody. He looks at the corpse. He pokes it with his hand. Pause. He smells it. He puts his head down on it. Pause.*

Convict   Before you go into the brothel, rub some vaseline on it. Then have an injection to prevent gonorrhea. Afterwards, don't forget to disinfect it again. A pipette with three drops of twenty per cent protargol. (*Pause.*) Don't you just love this wholly masculine way of life. Uncomplicated by women! (*He sticks a knife in the corpse.*) Making a wound on a body is like opening new lips on my beloved. (*He embraces the corpse. Pause.*)

> There was an old miner named Dave,
> who kept a dead whore in his cave.
> You have to admit, he hadn't much wit,
> But look at the money he saved!

6. Nurses

Morning Hygiene
A field hospital.

Baroness   Let me wash your face.

She starts washing his face.

Ploughman   Is that vinegar?

Baroness   Yes.

Ploughman   Why vinegar?

Baroness   Water can be dirty. It contains bacteria.

Ploughman   Vinegar smells.

Baroness   But it's healthy.

Ploughman   I don't want to sound ungrateful, but the other ladies have already washed me.

Baroness   What other ladies? Today? What day is it today? (*Taking out her diary*) Tuesday. How many came to see you?

Ploughman   Three.

Baroness   On a Tuesday? There must be some mistake. What else did they do?

Ploughman   One of them had a picture taken with me.

Baroness   We are all trying our best. Tea?

Baroness *pours some tea for the* **Ploughman**. *He takes the cup and saucer. She pours some tea for herself. She sits on the right-hand side of the bed. Pause. Silence. She puts her left hand under the sheets and touches the* **Ploughman**. *He opens his eyes* *wide. She touches him further in slow motion. He gets excited, but is careful not to spill his tea. The* **Baroness** *looks straight ahead. The* **Ploughman** *crosses his eyes. The* **Baroness** *takes her hand out and wipes it on a handkerchief. Pause.*

Baroness   More tea?

Strangers in the Night
Enter **Handyman**. *Enter* **Magnus**. **Handyman** *is not aware of* **Magnus**'*s presence.* **Handyman** *vomits. Magnus holds his forehead and helps him throw up.*

Handyman   Anywhere I went, anything I did, the need for sex dogged me. I couldn't stand still, I had no time for thought or reflection. My lethargy and my restlessness became twins. Sex was urgent and it couldn't wait. Love could wait. Love had time and patience. And it would appear one fine day, in the future, hand in hand with peace.

Night. At the munitions factory. **Maid** *is making love to the* **Handyman**. *She pushes him aside.*

Handyman   What is it?

Maid   It's not working. I thought I'd feel something. I felt nothing.

Handyman   Aren't I good enough for you?

Maid   I'm not good enough for you. I want to feel.

Handyman   Why did you choose me?

Maid   Any stranger is as good as any other.

Handyman   I could have the clap.

Maid   I could have the clap too.

Handyman   We both could have the clap.

Maid   The rotten fruit of war.

Handyman   Who was the person who had it first? Who did they get it off?

Maid   God gave it to them. That was the original sin.

Widow *comes in with a torch.*

Widow   What's going on in here?

Handyman   Good grief!

Widow   Are you one of the dizzy girls? The khaki fever pleasure seekers who do it in public parks and back alleys?

Maid   What business is that of yours?

Widow   It's my business to save them from themselves. (*To the* **Handyman**) And against vultures like you!

Maid   How dare you? This is my husband. On a three-day leave from the front.

Widow   This is a restricted military area.

Maid   I work in the factory.

Widow   Let me see your pass.

Maid   Let me see yours. (*They show each other their permits.*) So you're one of the White Feather volunteers. The Sin Police. We're proud of you. (*She kisses the* **Widow**.) Goodbye and good night!

Pause. **Widow** *looks at her. Then she gives the* **Maid** *a kiss.*

Widow   'Till we meet again!

Widow *leaves. Pause.*

Maid   She put her tongue in my mouth.

Handyman   I have to go back.

Maid   Where?

Handyman   The hospital. I sneaked out for a walk. Can't you see my pyjamas?

Maid   What's the matter with you?

Handyman   You don't want to know.

7. Brothels

Tender Touch
Brothel. **Land Woman** *is half naked. Enter* **Student**.

Student   I have two army loaves of bread.

Land Woman   Ten minutes. (*Pause.*) Get your pants down.

Student   Can we talk?

Land Woman   I haven't got all day, you know.

Student   I mean only talk.

Land Woman   You don't want to fuck?

Student   No.

Land Woman   Talk.

The **Student** *is staring at her. Pause.*

Student   The eternal feminine. I dreamt of your skin. Your lips on mine. There's a long queue outside. How many have you had today?

Land Woman   I'm serving a battalion for a week. After three weeks I'll go back to my ordinary life. With considerable pride in my achievements.

Student   Brothels destroy the sense of morality we're fighting for! Can you count for me?

Land Woman   What?

Student   Just count for me, please.

He gently takes her hand. He kisses it.

Land Woman   One, two, three, four, five.. (*She keeps on counting.*)

Student   I spit on humanity. Society should be destroyed and remade again. Returned to point zero. There should be a new language. Which is independent of reason and logic and causality. Abstraction is not an aesthetic principle. It's a moral necessity. (**Land Woman** *goes on counting. He puts his head in her lap. She pats his hair.*) Sixty thousand died in the last battle. How long will it take to count them all?

Land Woman *keeps counting. She takes out her breast and puts the nipple in his mouth.* **Student** *closes his eyes.*

The Rape of Europe
A restaurant. **Handyman** *puts some veronal powder into a glass of champagne. Enter* **Young Lady**. *He gives her the glass. They drink.*

Handyman   I want to be like the gods. I want to have everything, rape everyone. Like Zeus.

Young Lady   Even he wasn't almighty. Some women wouldn't let him. So he had to put on disguises.

Handyman   Like what?

Young Lady   For Leda he turned into a swan. For Europa he disguised himself as a bull. He carried her on his back over the sea.

Handyman   Did he do her during the journey?

Young Lady   How do you mean?

Handyman   Did he screw her in the water or when he got to land?

Young Lady   I'm drowsy.

Handyman   Now you know what Zeus really used. Veronal powder. He spiked the drinks of his women.

Young Lady (*Realising what has happened*)   Oh no.

Handyman   Oh yes!

Young Lady   You ugly pervert.

Handyman   Take it easy. There's nothing to it. It's only sex and violence.

8. At Hirschfeld's

Group Therapy
The curtain is down. Enter **Magnus** *in front of the curtain, wearing slippers and a casual silk robe. Enter* **All Characters**, *wearing contemporary clothes. They sit around* **Magnus**. **Magnus** *makes a sign.*

All (*One after the other*)   We're here... because we're here... because we're here...

They all prick up their ears as if trying to hear something inaudible. Pause.

Magnus   I remember that day vividly. In the evening I went to the opera with some friends. Strauss, "Die Fledermaus", end of the second act. The cream of society are living it up at a masked ball in a civilised summer villa. Husbands don't know that their wives are in disguise. Lovers entertain each other with practical jokes. The champagne flows, everyone flirts with everyone else. Then the big aria came, "Brüderlein und Schwesterlein". "Brother mine and sister mine, we're together forever. First a kiss, and then my dear, Du, Du, for evermore." Suddenly somebody ran onto the stage and shouted: Ladies and Gentleman, war has been declared. The audience started laughing, thinking it was part of the show. The day was the 28th of July 1914. A Tuesday.

Magnus *starts singing. First they listen huddled together, like a big family. Then they join in.*

> Love lies
> Under the Here
> And There

And Nowhere
Under the When
And Then
And Ever and Never
Under the Who and Why
And Yes and No
And But and How
Under the What
And Shame and War
And One and All
Lies Love

Act 2

9. Civilian Babylon

Spend, Spend, Spend!
Summer. Apartment in the Ritz Hotel. **Handyman** *is shuffling cards. Enter* **Widow**, *wearing male clothes.*

Widow   I can't find you a hyena.

Handyman   What do you mean?

Widow   I can't find you a hyena.

Handyman   What am I paying you for?

Widow   I found you a tiger cub and two snakes. I found you a peacock.

Handyman   It couldn't fly.

Widow   Peacocks can't fly. You threw it off the top of the Ritz. Now you want a hyena. Who's ever heard of a pet hyena?

Handyman   I'll be the first to have one!

Widow   Hyenas stink.

Handyman   They're sweet.

Widow   You're a debauched lunatic.

Handyman   Who gives you money for cocaine and morphine?

Widow   How low I've stooped to depend on the charity of a pimp!

Handyman The army would collapse without my services.

Widow If the war stopped tomorrow you would be penniless.

Handyman So I'll spend it all today. The diamonds, the vintage furniture, the Persian carpets! There's no tomorrow!

Widow You haven't slept for days. Don't go gambling. You'll lose badly.

Handyman Find me some young cunt to keep me awake.

Widow If they were any younger they'd be children.

Handyman They're never young enough. Cherries on my pie. (*He snorts cocaine.*) I'll buy a Zeppelin and fly off with a bunch of virgins, over the front line, while there's a battle raging below. (*He snorts again.*) War rules, peace sucks! We're going deep. We're hunting for whales.

Handyman *exits. Pause.* **Widow** *snorts cocaine. Enter* **Baroness**, *wearing black dress, black gloves and a veil.*

Widow My Lady, it's all arranged. This is the key to your apartment.

Baroness Who do I have this time?

Widow An athletic gentleman to your exact specifications. Your full satisfaction is guaranteed.

Baroness The usual?

Widow Yes. He'll be hypnotised. You can do anything with him and to him. He won't remember anything.

Baroness Good.

Widow You do look fetching in black.

Baroness   I know. The "widow look" has proved to be a big turn on this season. I like your uniform. What are you today? An elevator operator? A telegraph boy?

Soup Kitchen Romance
A street in town. Soup kitchen.

Young Lady   It's you!

Student   It's you!

Young Lady   What are you doing here?

Student   I've deserted. Gone AWOL. Absent without leave.

Young Lady   Good for you.

Student   You eat in the soup kitchen?

Young Lady   I had some dandelion sandwiches.

Student   I had the cow heel stew.

Young Lady   For a long time I thought I was responsible for it all. That all of this started because of me.

Student   You were wrong. The war started because of me.

Young Lady   Don't say that word. It's evil. It shouldn't be named. (*Pause.*) I'm homeless. I mix with artists and students, revolutionaries in exile, passing tourists, faith healers, spies and other questionable characters.

Student   I'm a poet, an anarchist and a pacifist. And a performer. (*He takes out a portable "Punch and Judy" stage.*) Ladies and Gentlemen, pray, how you do? If you all happy, me all happy too. Stop and hear my merry little play; If me make you laugh, me need not make you pay. (*He suddenly produces little puppets on the top of his fingers.*) Come closer

356

to see the greatest orgy on earth! The crazy French, the mad Germans, the idiotic Austrians, the perfidious British and the offended Serbs! They have all come out to measure their cocks. Aaaaaaand there they go! *(The **Student** holds his hands tightly together, the fingers fighting each other.)*

The **Young Lady** *laughs. Pause.*

Young Lady   Where are you staying?

Student   The park.

Young Lady   I sleep in the graveyard. You can come with me. It's quiet.

Student   You're so beautiful.

Young Lady   They put me to sleep. I woke up with my vagina slashed. They're after me.

Student   Who is?

Young Lady   Spies. The agents of darkness.

Student   I'll protect you.

Young Lady   Can you kiss me without kissing? Can you touch me without touching?

They kiss without kissing and they touch without touching.

Exit **Young Lady**.

Enter **Magnus**. *He shadows the* **Student** *who is not aware of his presence.*

Student   Death herself was courting me. And who was I to say No? We were dancing cheek to cheek. She was breathing down my neck. She was not a corpse, or a skeleton or an old hag. Not at all. She was a devouring fair maiden. Lusty for young life, always at it, advancing in short, sharp, spasms. No one escaped her assaults. No one. Not one.

The Black Widow Dance

*Room in the Ritz Hotel. Client (**Magnus**) comes in. **Baroness** goes up to him. She forcefully embraces him in a tango position and swirls around the room. She pushes him into an armchair. She fixes her eyes upon him and starts taking off one of her long black gloves. Pause.*

Baroness   What's wrong?

Client   I'm afraid there's been a misunderstanding.

Baroness   Don't you find me attractive?

Client   I asked to see a man. I was sent to the wrong room.

Baroness   Are you hypnotised?

Client   No. But I won't remember any of this.

Baroness   I'm not a nympho.

Client   I've already forgotten it all.

Baroness   Get out!

Client *quickly gets out.* **Client** *turns into* **Magnus**. *He pricks up his ears as if trying to hear something inaudible. Pause.*

10. Front Line

Enter **Maid**. *Enter* **Magnus** *behind her. He shadows her speech, as if he was her prompter. She is not aware of his presence.*

Maid I put my body and my soul into a meat mincer. And they came out at the other end – in pieces. I had no concept of the future and no desire to have one. And all the time I could hear the Muses. They were singing lewd songs. It's not true that in war the Muses are silent. They are obscene!

Life in the Trenches
The trenches. **Ploughman** *is sitting down on a wooden box, preparing tea on a primus. Enter* **Maid** *in soldier's uniform, with a rifle in her hand.*

Ploughman Who are you?

Maid I'm a soldier, attacking the enemy!

Ploughman There'll be some tea in a minute.

Maid Where is everyone?

Ploughman The men are asleep, playing cards. Sit down and put your feet up.

Maid Don't tell me what to do! No man tells me what to do!

Ploughman You don't just attack like that. This is the reserve trench. Arc de Triomphe no 3. You attack from the firing trench. Over there, five hundred yards. Past the Eiffel Tower.

Maid Take me there.

Ploughman Who's in a hurry to get killed? There are people out there. (**Maid** *looks through the periscope.*) They respect us, we respect them. Those who were trigger-happy are all dead. The rest of us are now living in peaceful co-existence.

Maid *offers him a cigarette.*

Ploughman   I roll my own.

Maid (*Lighting up a cigarette*)   Do you think I'm a man or a woman?

Ploughman   Makes no difference to me. My wife used to be my right hand, now my right hand is my wife.

Maid   They wouldn't let me enlist. So I made my own way here. I joined the Ghost Battalion. Deserters from all armies. We creep out at night to pillage corpses and gather food.

Ploughman   You can't touch me. I have my talismans. My lucky coin, a button, a dried flower, a hair cutting, a pebble from home, two medals – St Christopher and St George.

Maid (*Sniffing*)   What's going on? Are you taking a crap? Have you been taking a crap all this time?

Ploughman   I started long before you came.

Maid   Shit! (*Looking away*) What's that green vapour?

Ploughman   Gas?

Maid   Chlorine!

They quickly put their gas masks on. Pause. They look at each other. They slowly get closer. They start kissing with their gas masks on.

Submission

The officers' quarters. Enter **Widow**. **Baron** *sitting behind the desk.*

Baron Welcome to the front line. A long journey?

Widow I'm honoured you sent a car specially for me.

Baron (*Pouring two drinks*) Your fame precedes you. The fibre of the home front. The moral rectitude. How do you do it?

Widow I was brought up that way. A proper girl should be virginal and have no sexuality. Unless she has been awakened by bad influences. Pornographic reading or pathological temperament.

Baron There's a lot of moral disorder in the army.

Widow Have you been bad?

Baron In my hours of darkness I've wanted to go down on my knees. Pray for someone to draw the line for me. Correct me when I'm wrong.

Widow Have you sinned?

Baron I have.

He gives her a box. **Widow** *opens the box. She takes out a pair of shiny leather boots with high heels.*

Widow Oh, you naughty boy. Put them on for me, then.

Baron *goes down on his knees, takes off the* **Widow**'s *shoes and puts the boots on her. She stamps a foot on his hand.*

Baron Oh, yes.

Widow What do you say?

Baron Yes, please!

Widow When you touch filth, you become filth.

She presses her foot down hard.

Providence
The farm. **Land Woman** *and wounded man* (**Magnus**) *who is completely bandaged and with a bandaged head.*

Land Woman Who are you? Where do you come from? Are you one of us? Are you one of them? Where are you going? Are you in pain? Do you understand me? Can you hear me? Can you speak? Are you hungry? Do you have a family? I had a family. What is your name? You are safe here. I will take care of you.

The **Land Woman** *puts her hand on his crotch. Pause. The wounded man turns into* **Magnus**. *He pricks up his ears as if he's trying to hear something inaudible. He starts wailing without making any sound.*

11. Eunuchs

Raging at the Sky

The trenches. Suddenly a Zeppelin appears in the sky. **Convict** *looks at it and starts following it.*

Convict   Father, have you come for me? Here I am! (*Looking at it*) Shoot me with your arrows, strike me with your hand, crush me with your anger. (*He starts taking off his clothes.*) Look at me! I'm sick. You've covered me with sores of puss. I'm twisted and bent. No friends or neighbours will come near me. (*He is now naked.*) My holy wounds have opened up on the body of all mankind.

Enter **Baron**. *He has shaving soap on his face. He looks at the* **Convict**.

Baron   Could you repeat that for the soldiers on Sunday afternoon? For some fun and recreation. (*Pause.*) Throw in a song or two. That always goes down well. (*Pause. He looks at the Zeppelin.*) It looks like a cock, doesn't it, the Zeppelin?

Electro Convulsive Therapy

A military hospital. **Student** *tied to a chair. Enter* **Dr Kaufman** (**Magnus**).

Dr Kaufman   So the deserter has come back to us. What's wrong with you?

Student   I have typhus, malaria, dysentery, gangrene, gingivitis, trench foot…

Dr Kaufman   You also have a sense of humour.

Student   Tic convulsif. Shaking palsy.

Dr Kaufman You're a malingerer. And I'm here to weed out malingerers. This will heal you in one single session.

Dr Kaufman *attaches wires to* **Student***'s head.*

Student I can see their silhouettes at sunset. Christ and Buddha, Aeschylus and Shakespeare, Little Red Riding Hood, and Hansel and Gretel. Hand in hand, going towards an open grave.

Dr Kaufman This will hurt a little. Just enough for you to beg me to send you back to the front so that you never have to face me again. Anything to say before I turn it on?

Student Kiss me goodnight, Sergeant Major!

Dr Kaufman *turns the electricity on. Pause.* **Dr Kaufman** *turns into* **Magnus***. He pricks up his ears as if he is trying to hear something inaudible. Pause.*

12. Spies

Street Speech
Maid *is giving a speech.* **Land Woman** *is listening.*

Maid   Capitalist morality is brothel morality. Woman is the property of man. He pays for sex by giving her sustenance. This must change! No more husbands who beat and abandon their wives! The new woman will never again be treated as inferior! She will be a full-time worker, wife and mother! And a communist citizen!

Land Woman   What is a communist?

Maid   A woman who is an equal participant in society.

Land Woman   What is society?

Enter **Baroness**.

Maid   Bourgeois marriage locks couples together and keeps them away from other people. The sexual act is not shameful and sinful. Communist morality allows contacts with a range of persons of both sexes.

Baroness   Of the same sex?

Maid   Sex should not be judged as moral or immoral. It is a function of the body, like hunger and thirst. We are at the start of a new era. *(Taking out condoms)* These are not vulcanised rubber any longer. This is new material, thin, but strong and cheap! Liquid latex!

Baroness   Do you work for the company?

Enter **Widow**.

Maid   I work for you! Free contraception and abortion for every woman! Your body belongs to you!

Widow   Are you a communist spy?

Maid   There are only two ways out of this war. One is to go mad and the other is to become a communist.

Widow   Well, I've made my choice. I've gone mad.

Espionage

Young Lady   I met all kinds of colourful people and they all met colourful me. Amongst them were female spies, the "light cavalry", with their amatory adventures. We all have our extravagances, aberrations and erotic fantasies. If you were an important player, spying centres would want to know about them.

*A brothel. Bounty hunter (**Magnus**) and **Young Lady**.*

Bounty Hunter   This is the end of your road.

Young Lady   How so?

Bounty Hunter   Your name is Bella Donna.

Young Lady   Maybe.

Bounty Hunter   You are paid by the Germans and used by the Americans to transmit documentary evidence of the great Alsace hoax.

Young Lady   That's preposterous!

Bounty Hunter   You fell into disfavour. You were flirting more than you were spying. You haven't supplied any worthwhile information for some time.

Young Lady   I beg to disagree on that point.

Tina Vrbnjak as the Young Lady and Janez Škof as Magnus
Hirschfeld in the Slovenian National Theatre production, 2014

Bounty Hunter   Madame Bella Donna, you are not who
you are. Your name is "Turkish Delight". You come from the
Balkans. You have been known under the names of Countess
de Louziers, Elinor Hawkins and Gina Raffalowittsch.

Young Lady   Mme Mezi.

Bounty Hunter   Mme Hesketh, Mme Davidowittsch and
Dame de Belleville.

Young Lady   Come to the point.

Bounty Hunter   The point, my dear lady, is that you are
under arrest.

Young Lady   Says who?

Bounty Hunter   Say I, a bounty hunter. I don't do it for
the money. It's my hobby.

Young Lady   Not so fast, Monsieur le Marquis.

Bounty Hunter Marquis? Me?

Young Lady You've blushed cherry red.

Bounty Hunter I'm cool as a cucumber.

Young Lady Come, come. As one professional to another. In your false teeth you hide four yards of thin paper with coded messages. Your left eye is a glass one behind which you store microfilm.

Bounty Hunter It takes more than this to blow my cover.

Young Lady I can give you more. I happen to know a thing or two about your passions. I'll put on a white dress. And get a rooster. And then I'll stick a knife in it and let it bleed all over you.

Bounty Hunter You really are the queen of erotic blackmail.

Young Lady And then the police will break in to find you bloody and naked.

Bounty Hunter You're cruel.

Young Lady Cruel but fair.

Bounty Hunter *turns into* **Magnus**. *He pricks up his ears as if he is trying to hear something inaudible. Pause. He sings a song without making any sounds. Pause.*

13. Armistice!

Intro

Enter **Widow**. *Enter* **Magnus**. *She is not aware of his presence. He shadows her. He holds her hand and takes her for a dance.*

Widow   And then the war ended. And I felt caught like a cockroach in the light. In the war every activity was directed towards a definite end. Life had meaning. But peace didn't seem to lead to anything. It was an anti-climax. I had worked myself up into an unnatural pitch of excitement and daring. And then I collapsed. I felt soiled and spent. It was time for despair.

Coming Home

The **Baron***'s mansion.* **Baroness** *wearing a floral hat. Enter* **Baron** *in a soldier's overcoat, on a crutch.*

Baroness   I've been waiting for you.

Baron   You are still as beautiful as the first time I met you. I should have brought you flowers.

Baroness   What matters is that you are back home.

Baron   I was an ace pilot. I shot down five planes.

Baroness   I've been good. As good as I can be. What happened to you?

Baron   Don't ask.

Baroness   Sorry.

Baron   I can't tell you.

Baroness   Why not?

Baron   I'm not allowed to talk about it.

Baroness   Not even to your wife?

Baron   Especially not to my nearest and dearest.

Baroness   So it's that bad.

Baron   It is.

Baroness   Syphillis?

Baron   How did you guess?

Baroness   Just a hunch. Why the crutch?

Baron   To deflect attention.

Pause. He suddenly swings the crutch at her, barely missing her. She looks at him in horror.

Baron   Don't pity me.

Talismans

*A street. On the corner stands the **Handyman**. He is wearing shabby clothes and is dirty and dishevelled. Enter **Convict**, wearing a white suit, which is too small for him, and a white hat. He walks five steps forward and one back.*

Handyman   Can I interest you in some opium? (*He opens his coat, showing a range of opium pipes.*) A game of poker?

Convict   Not today.

Handyman   Nice suit.

Convict   It's my lucky suit. It belonged to a fallen comrade of mine.

Handyman   Why do you make a few steps forward and then one back?

Convict It's a routine. It saved my life in the war. As did this. (*He takes out a crystal stone.*) Don't touch it.

The **Widow** *appears from the corner. She looks like a man. Dark rings around her eyes.*

Widow You don't touch an amulet. It's an amplifier of the universal life force. It controls feelings. Leads one to achieve one's destiny.

Convict Have we met before?

Widow I don't think so.

Convict You look like someone I knew.

Widow You look like someone who might be interested in the project.

Convict The project?

Handyman The war is finished. Everything's collapsed. Now it's time to invest. In fun and entertainment.

Widow One thing people can't do without.

Handyman Prime business opportunity. Would you happen to have a disposable sum of five thousand? (**Convict** *walks out.* **Handyman** *shouts after him.*) Three thousand?

Pause.

Widow I think he was my husband.

Handyman You think?

Widow Hard to be sure of anything these days.

Who's been sleeping here?
The farm. **Land Woman** *and* **Ploughman**.

371

Land Woman   I thought I'd never see you again. You never wrote.

Ploughman   I did.

Land Woman   Once. "We're having a bit of rain at present". Couldn't you think of anything else to say? Did you get my letters?

Ploughman   Yes.

Land Woman   I thought you were dead. (*Pause.*)

Ploughman   I was. (*Pause.*) I walked through the fields. Nobody's worked the land for years.

Land Woman   It is now *after* the war. We never thought this day would come. (*Pause.*) I'm not alone anymore. He's gone out to sell some wood. We've been together for nearly a year. He sleeps in your bed. He wears your clothes. (*Pause.*) He's black. (*Pause.*) I'm pregnant. (*Pause.*) You can stay if you want. (*Pause.*) We can all live together. (*Pause.*) Think it over.

14: Psychodrama

Calling The Dead

Enter the ten characters. **Baron** *is on crutches,* **Baroness** *is wearing spiritualist headgear,* **Young Lady** *is paranoid and wearing dark glasses.* **Widow** *is stoned.* **Handyman** *is trying to find someone to do a three matchbox gambling trick on.* **Ploughman** *is wearing wellies.* **Land Woman** *has come with a pram and a balloon on it. The* **Maid** *is wearing We-Can-Do-It overalls.* **Student** *is wearing a bizarre swimming costume.* **Convict** *is in a white suit. A spiritualist séance begins. They all sit around a table. On the table are an open Bible, a bowl and two candles.*

Baroness   Ghosts are harmless. There is nothing to fear. Put your hands flat on the table. The little fingers of each hand touching the next person. When a candle flame burns blue, a spirit is present. I need a volunteer for a drop of blood. (**Handyman** *puts out his hand.* **Baroness** *takes a drop of blood from his finger.*) It draws the spirits. It opens the portal to the other world. Keep silent. (*The séance starts. Pause.*) Can you hear it?

Baron   What?

Baroness   I can hear a voice.

Baron   What voice?

Baroness   His voice!

Convict   What does he say?

Baroness   Quiet! (*Pause.*) He says he's been trying to reach us.

Widow   Tell him we've been trying to reach him.

Baroness (*Talking to the spirit*)   *We* have been trying to reach *you*.

Pause.

Convict   What does he say?

Widow   Is he saying anything?

Baroness   I can't hear him with all of you shouting!

Baron   *You* are shouting!

Baroness (*Talking to the spirit*)   No, no, no, *you* are dead and *we've* been trying to reach you!

Handyman   And I thought *I* was high.

Maid   I hate superstition!

Student   It's all in the game.

Baroness (*Talking to the spirit*)   You're wrong! We are alive and *you* are dead!

Widow   This isn't going well.

Baron   Let's get out of here!

Baroness   I thank the spirits. Tomorrow in the light of day we will ring a bell throughout the house to clear the area of all entities.

They all look at each other. **Baroness** *quickly closes the Bible and extinguishes the candles. Pause. Silence. Enter* **Magnus**. *They are not aware of his entrance. They look hypnotised, as if under a spell.*

Magnus   We are celestial bodies, like the planets. We all emit a unique hum, resonances, an ocean of harmony.

Musica humana universalis. But we hardly hear it, we're so busy doing other things. And love just sits there, silent and abandoned, drowned in the noise of shrieks and explosions. But we are strongest where we hurt. We will pan the bloodshed of war to search for the gold dust of love. Listen! (*Pause. There is no sound.*) Can you hear it? The silence! (*Pause.*) The silence behind. (*Pause.*) Behind the noise. Behind the pressure in the ears. Behind the humdrum, the explosions and the din. Behind the clamour, the racket and the uproar. (*Pause.*) It's the silence – of love.

Pause. Silence. **Magnus** *makes a little sign. They all disperse. He pricks up his ears as if he is trying to hear something inaudible. Pause.*

Magnus   My name is Magnus Hirschfeld. I was founder and director of the Institute for Sexology, Institut für Sexualwissenschaft, in Berlin. In our study of war morals we aimed for scientific objectivity, with no prejudice on behalf of any warring groups. We were situated in an elegant three-storey mansion, in the central district of Tiergarten. I had my own living quarters there as well as my medical practice. We had Departments of Psychotherapy, Somatic Sexual Medicine, Forensic Sexology, Gynaecology and Marriage Counselling. Archives, a library and a hall for public lectures.

The ten characters are back around the séance table, as at the beginning of the scene. Silence. **Magnus** *makes a little sign. They suddenly become aware of his presence, as if a spell of hypnosis has just been lifted from their eyes.*

Convict   Magnus?

Widow   Doctor Hirschfeld!

Baron   Doctor Magnus Hirschfeld?

Baroness   Is it you?

Ploughman   How long have you been here?

Land Woman   Did you hear us calling?

Maid   Are you dead?

Student   What's it like on the other side?

Young Lady   I feel as if I've been hypnotised.

Widow   Have you put a spell on us?

Handyman   What happened to you?

Magnus   In 1933 I was on a lecture tour of the US. On 6th May the Deutsche Studentenschaft made an organised attack on the Institute of Sex Research in Berlin. The contents of the library and archives were carted out in broad daylight and burned in the Opernplatz. Around 20,000 books and journals, and 5,000 images were destroyed. Also seized were the Institute's extensive lists of names and addresses. In the midst of the burning, Joseph Goebbels gave a political speech to a crowd of around 40,000 people. The leaders of the students also proclaimed their own Feuersprüche, "fire decrees", against the un-German spirit. I stayed in exile in France. I tried to set up another institute there, but I failed. I died in Nice in 1935. That was the end of my story.

Handyman   There is no end in sight to ours.

Widow   We can never rest.

Convict   Old wounds have opened up again.

Land Woman   It's all being repeated.

Baron   A new war is approaching, and we haven't recovered from the old one yet.

Student   Are we going to be fucked again?

Maid   Are we going to be cannon fodder again?

Ploughman   We won't survive it this time.

Student   All this beautiful suffering!

Magnus   You think you called me? I called you to call me. I have unfinished business, too. What am I doing here? Am I a doctor or a quack? Am I a scientist or a circus ventriloquist? Telling stories and playing mind games. Is this a way to heal you? You treat me as if I was your bloody father or brother or uncle or lover. I am a homosexual. And a Jew. Am I only licking my own wounds by pretending to heal yours? Who am I? Will the real Magnus Hirschfeld stand up!

He makes a little sign.

15. On the Front Line

The curtain is down. In front of the curtain, enter the ten characters, in modern dress. Enter **Magnus**. *He makes a gesture.*

All *(One after the other)*   We're here... because we're here... because we're here... because we're here...

Suddenly there is a magic transformation. Idyllic dawn. Endless fields. They are in front of an old burnt tank.

Magnus   Here we are again.

Maid   Where?

Magnus   On the old front lines. The no man's land. We've come back to the scene of the crime, like thieves in the night. We've returned to the minefields, to let it all explode in our faces again. We get up where we fall. This is where I live. In the tank. The cannon. Where there is cannon fodder there are also cannon spirits.

Young Lady   Don't leave us.

Magnus   It was my job to get you ready

Widow   For what?

Magnus   For what is to come.

Baron   Are we ready yet?

Magnus   As ready as you'll ever be. Pull yourself together. Get a grip. Keep calm and carry on. Give us that old song.

All   Love lies
Under the Here
And There
And Nowhere
Under the When
And Then
And Ever and Never
Under the Who and Why
And Yes and No
And But and How
Under the What
And Shame and War
And One and All
Lies Love

Magnus   If you asked me, I would say that wars happen when love goes wrong. It's like wine turning into vinegar. How come love is constantly annihilated and yet always survives? Against all the odds! How come? Answer me that. We hurt, we wander blindly. History has abused us, many times and in various positions. Figurae Veneris Historiae. Don't let it do it again.

Pause. They all prick up their ears as if trying to hear something inaudible. Silence.

Student   Such a hush.

Maid   Dead air.

Young Lady   Must be an angel flying over.

Magnus   During this silence, the last delicate strings of my heart will snap.

He disappears.

Pause.

They remain with their ears pricked up, as if trying to hear something inaudible.

Silence.

CURTAIN

A Note on the Translator

Goran and Pat in Pula, Croatia, 2007

Patricia Marsh-Stefanovska (Pat Marsh) is Goran Stefanovski's widow. They were together for 44 years, 18 of them living in Skopje, then the Republic of Macedonia, and 26 in Canterbury, UK.

Pat is a linguist with an MA in General Linguistics from the University of Manchester. She went to take up the post of British Council lector in English at the University of Skopje in 1974. She met Goran after a month there and they were married in 1976. As a native speaker of English, Pat was much in demand as a translation editor from the beginning of her life in the Republic. After she had become a competent speaker of Macedonian, she began to make her own translations of all kinds of texts, especially Goran's plays. Her translations of *Hi-Fi* and *The False Bottom* were published by BkMk Press, Kansas City, Missouri, USA, in 1985 and the same year *Flying on the Spot* was published in the theatre magazine *Scena,* English issue 8, Novi Sad, pp.170-188. *Selected Plays by Goran Stefanovski,* volume 99 of the 130 books of Macedonian literature in English, are Pat's translations of *Wild Flesh*, *Flying on the Spot* and *The False Bottom* published by NUB, Skopje in 2011.

From 1998 Goran began to write most of his plays in English, and Pat took on the role of language editor.